MACMILLAN

PROFILES IN POWER
General Editor: Keith Robbins

ELIZABETH I
Christopher Haigh

RICHELIEU
R. J. Knecht

GUSTAVUS ADOLPHUS (2nd Edn)
Michael Roberts

OLIVER CROMWELL
Barry Coward

ALEXANDER I
Janet M. Hartley

JUÁREZ
Brian Hamnett

LLOYD GEORGE
Martin Pugh

HITLER
Ian Kershaw

CHURCHILL
Keith Robbins

NASSER
Peter Woodward

DE GAULLE
Andrew Shennan

FRANCO
Sheelagh Ellwood

MACMILLAN
John Turner

CASTRO
Sebastian Balfour

. . . . .

MACMILLAN

John Turner

LONGMAN
London and New York

Longman Group UK Limited,
Longman House, Burnt Mill, Harlow,
Essex CM20 2JE, England
and Associated Companies throughout the world.

*Published in the United States of America
by Longman Publishing, New York*

First published 1994

ISBN 0 582 21880 2 CSD
ISBN 0 582 55386 5 PPR

British Library Cataloguing-in-Publication Data
A catalogue record for this book
is available from the British Library

Library of Congress Cataloging in Publication Data
Turner, John, 1949 May 18–
    Macmillan/John Turner.
        p. cm.—(Profiles in power)
Includes bibliographical references (p.) and index.
ISBN 0-582-21800-2 (CSD).—ISBN 0-582-55386-5 (PPR)
1. Macmillan, Harold. 1894–   . 2. Prime ministers—Great
Britain—Biography. 3. Great Britain—Politics and
government—1945–1964. I. Title. II. Series: Profiles in power
(London, England)
DA556.9.M33T87   1993
941.085'5'092—dc20
    [B]   93-11786   CIP

Set in 10½/12pt New Baskerville
Produced by Longman Singapore Publishers (Pte) Ltd.
Printed in Singapore

CONTENTS

· · · · ·

ACKNOWLEDGEMENTS

Like every academic author I have incurred many debts in writing this book, but I must particularly thank Kathleen Burk for advising on an earlier draft and Peter Hennessy and Matthew Jones for useful conversations. Lord Home of the Hirsel and Lord Sherfield were generous with their time and with background information, and I learned much from the Rt. Hon Enoch Powell, Sir Patrick Dean, and Sir David Pitblado at witness seminars at the Institute of Historical Research. For permission to cite unpublished material I am grateful to the Master and Fellows of Trinity College Cambridge, and to the Trustees of the Beaverbrook Foundation. My greatest debt remains to my wife for her remarkable patience throughout and at the last minute for making the index possible.

London, August 1993

INTRODUCTION
SUPERMAC 1894–1986

Harold Macmillan was one of the most successful actors to reach 10 Downing Street in the twentieth century. His career as a Member of Parliament ran for forty years from 1924, and when illness forced him to resign the premiership in October 1963 he had held the office for seven years, a longer continuous period than any of his twentieth-century predecessors had enjoyed. In the last fifteen years of his active career, and even more so in a long and occasionally mischievous retirement, he depended for power and influence upon a *persona* which was lovingly crafted to take advantage of the times. As the ever-unflappable Supermac, who invented the 'Middle Way' in the 1930s, built more houses than any Housing Minister before or since, invented Premium Bonds, told an electorate that they had 'never had it so good', and restored Britain's position in the world in the rôle of Greece to the new American Rome, he was also the 'last Edwardian in Downing Street' who sustained the grace and style of a lost generation at the summit of power. No historical reinterpretation can take this away from him; but no historical interpretation can now overlook the strenuous effort he expended on these displays of 'effortless superiority', the nervous tension which drove the 'unflappable' prime minister, the risks and disappointments which punctuated his relations with American presidents, or the self-seeking ruthlessness which governed his relations with colleagues and his approach to political issues, from the beginning to the end of a long and highly successful political career.

Like all truly successful politicians, Macmillan possessed a degree of ambition which could be lethal to competitors. Unlike many, he was able to turn this energy and ambition to political ends which seemed radical and constructive, even if hindsight

1

suggests that they were not enough to deal with the problems which he had identified. During his ministerial career he was preoccupied with Britain's changing circumstances, economic and political. Protecting British interests abroad and reshaping commitments to match resources were the watchwords of his overseas policy: they led him to retreat from the empire, cultivate the American connection and in due course seek British entry to the European Common Market. At home he was an ingenious but often unlucky manager of a declining economy, who saw clearly that structural renewal was needed but found his government buffeted by the short-term pressures of inflation and recurrent crises in the balance of payments. In his handling of domestic and foreign policy he was very often at odds with his party, and perhaps his greatest achievement was to lead the Conservative Party so far towards places which it never knew it wanted to visit.

Towards the end of his premiership he was widely criticised for preferring show to substance and for defending an *ancien régime* with cynical disregard for the country's real needs. Macmillan's reputation evaporated during the 1964 General Election. He was the real target of Labour's charge of 'thirteen wasted years': his was the economic policy of 'stop–go' which had discredited demand-management without putting anything useful in its place; his was the government which had subordinated British policy to the 'special relationship' with the United States and then bungled entry into Europe; his was the offhand political style which had alienated government from the rising generations, while condoning the depravity of the Profumo scandal. His memoirs, which began to appear in 1966, were an attempt to rebut these charges, if only by burying them under a mountain of detail, but it was an uphill struggle. The first examination of his full political career, by Anthony Sampson, appeared in 1967 with the sub-title 'A Study in Ambiguity', and retained the quizzical perspective which seemed natural for the 1960s. A brilliant essay by Larry Siedentop, published in 1970, was the first academic effort to analyse his whole career, and looked behind the *persona* to the working politician. Siedentop was no hagiographer, but he took Macmillan seriously, made an effort to distinguish style from content and to see style as part of political technique, and thereby set a new and useful tone for examination of his subject's contribution to politics and policy. By now, though, it was becoming apparent that Macmillan himself was well able to influence his own historical reputation by the weight of his own writing, and by merely staying alive. His major work of the 1930s, *The Middle Way*, was republished in 1966 with a polemical essay 'The Middle Way: 20 Years After', which combined a swingeing attack on the Labour Party with a bold claim that the Tories were the permanent rightful tenants of the political middle ground. His memoirs of his premiership appeared in the early 1970s, enabling reviewers to contrast an earlier Conservative government's competence with the uncomfortable experiences of the Heath administration; rumours even surfaced that Macmillan, only in his mid-seventies and renewed in health, was waiting to be recalled to the leadership if events took a turn for the worse.[1]

The election of Margaret Thatcher to the Conservative leadership in 1975 made it clear that the Conservative Party was not, for the moment, looking for a return to the Toryism of 'One Nation'. Yet the contrast between the new and the old party did no damage to Macmillan's reputation among the party's enemies and the new leader's few surviving opponents within the party. The self-conscious repudiation of the alleged post-war consensus has stirred critics to compare the economic performance of Macmillan's governments with the experience of the 1980s, and find in favour of Macmillan.[2] Macmillan himself was known to object to the Thatcher government's privatisation policy, which has endeared him to the Centre and to the Left. New information about the 1964–70 Labour government reveals the hollowness of Labour's criticism of its predecessors.[3] In this climate Alistair Horne's official biography, the appearance of which was postponed until after Macmillan's death, was eagerly awaited. In the event, despite the breadth of unpublished material from the Macmillan archives available exclusively to an official biographer, it is not clear that very much of the received interpretation will have been changed by its appearance. Horne has confirmed what many had suspected, and for an official biographer his personal judgements are unusually candid and sometimes acerbic. But he does not seek to alter the main outlines of Macmillan's own account of his political career, nor to reassess his position within the Conservative Party.

MACMILLAN IN PROFILE

As a 'Profile in Power' this book is not offered as a definitive biographical study, let alone as a substitute for the official biography. Its purpose is to assess Macmillan as a political leader, to explain his rise to power in its historical context, and to suggest a perspective on his achievements as a politician, Cabinet minister and ultimately as prime minister. It is based largely on the wealth of printed sources available on twentieth-century political history, but on occasion the temptation to use unpublished material has been irresistible, and it is therefore not merely a synthesis of existing knowledge. Because even political life is experienced chronologically, the book is laid out without apology as a narrative until it reaches the premiership, when it has often proved more convenient to follow themes through to their conclusion. As an account of the pursuit and use of power by one man it inevitably omits a great deal of importance even on the issues about which he was concerned. These gaps are partly filled by references to further reading.

Unlike many of the subjects of this series, Macmillan is a contemporary figure, who was still alive, though only just, when the book was commissioned. There are hazards in the striking parallels between the issues facing Macmillan's governments and issues which are central to contemporary politics. Anglo-American relations, Britain's relations with Europe, industrial relations and wage settlements, inflation and even the balance of payments are still the stuff of political debate. It is very easy to assume that the questions are identical, when in fact thirty years of rapid change has radically altered the context in which they appear. For an author whose first conscious memories of contemporary political events are of newspaper pictures of the Suez invasion, there are further hazards. Macmillan was prime minister when it was first explained to me what a prime minister was. I was first aware of the Conservative Party as the parliamentary supporters of Mr Macmillan and of the Labour Party as a body of people who criticised Mr Macmillan's government. This makes objectivity more difficult for anybody with even the most minimal political views, especially when those views are somewhat to the left of what I believe Macmillan's views to have been.

Fuller, and I hope objective conclusions about Macmillan as politician and statesman can be found in the Conclusion, but there is a place here for some observations about Macmillan as a person, since responses to him as a person have evidently coloured much of what has been written about him, and no doubt colour the chapters which follow. The contrast between the showman or actor-manager who became prime minister and the private individual has been emphasised by almost every writer since Emrys Hughes (who saw nothing but the showman). Often this has been taken as evidence of hypocrisy, and weighed in the scales against him. His ruthlessness is legendary, witnessed by innumerable episodes from his takeover of the Next Five Years group in 1936 to his dismissal of half his cabinet in the Night of the Long Knives in 1962, and his long and successful campaign to deny the premiership to R.A. Butler. His sarcasm, and his talent for Trollopian comedy, is evident from his diaries, published in part in his memoirs and in full for the war period.

Yet nowhere in this can be seen the hollowness and cynicism with which his enemies charged him. To the end of his premiership, if not to the end of his life, Macmillan seems to have been a shy, vulnerable and often unhappy man. He found it difficult to enter the bonhomous world of pre-war Conservatism, because he was too obviously cleverer than most MPs and at the same time lacked the social skill to conceal the differences between himself and his fellows. Understandably, he preferred books to people, and was an isolated man with few friends. His marriage was for a long time unsatisfactory and disappointing. He once openly explained his determination to get on in politics as an attempt to compensate for personal unhappiness. It was also a natural counterpart to a deep and unforced religious faith, which gave him a social conscience which he was sometimes at pains to conceal. His physical courage was proved during the First World War and on many recorded occasions later; his moral courage was tested repeatedly during his career, and not found wanting. It seems to me difficult not to sympathise with such a man, and in particular impossible not to admire his ability to continue a career and promote what he saw as the interests of his country and his party at enormous personal cost. Ruthlessness, egotism and disingenuousness are the stock in trade of politicians. They need them to get power, and without power they are useless. Macmillan had them all, but used them appropriately. Where they are remarked upon in later chapters, it is by way of explanation, not condemnation. They are the counterparts to the determination, inner self-confidence, patience and intelligence which brought Harold Macmillan to the top of the greasy pole.

. . .

NOTES AND REFERENCES

1. Anthony Sampson, *Macmillan: A Study in Ambiguity* (London: Allen Lane, 1967); L.A. Siedentop, 'Mr Macmillan and the Edwardian Style' in Vernon Bogdanor and Robert Skidelsky (eds), *The Age of Affluence* (London: Macmillan, 1970); Harold Macmillan, *The Middle Way* (London: Macmillan, 1938, reprinted 1966).
2. For example, Hugo Young and Ann Sloman, *The Thatcher Phenomenon* (London: BBC, 1986), p. 142, quoting Roy Jenkins: Britain in 1985 had eight times the number of unemployed, and six times the inflation rate, of 1960; the annual growth rate was 3.1 per cent compared with 5.5 per cent in 1960, the rate of investment in 1985 was 7.7 per cent, against 9.7 per cent in 1960. Whatever the explanations, and there are many, such comparisons did Macmillan no harm.
3. Clive Ponting, *Breach of Promise: The Labour Governments, 1964–70* (London: Hamish Hamilton, 1989).

Chapter 1

THE LAST EDWARDIAN

Harold Macmillan was, of course, a Victorian by birth, not an Edwardian, and the carefully cultivated *persona* of his years of power scarcely acknowledged the influences which formed his childhood and early youth. He was born in 1894, the son of Maurice Macmillan, a partner in Macmillan's publishers, and Helen (Nellie) Tarleton Belles, the daughter of an Indiana doctor. As a background for a future politician the Macmillan family had advantages and drawbacks. Harold Macmillan's own account of it is coloured by a strong sense that family tradition created expectations which he had to discharge. His grandfather, Daniel Macmillan, the son of a crofter on the Isle of Arran, set up in business as a bookseller and in 1843 as a publisher, with his brother Alexander. He died in 1857. His son Maurice, Harold's father, was educated at Uppingham and Christ's College Cambridge, and became a schoolmaster before marrying Nellie Belles and entering the family business. Family mythology was constructed around Daniel Macmillan's self-improvement and instinctive self-reliance. Despite the very adequate comfort in which the family lived, the emphasis on striving and seriousness discouraged any temptation to enjoy the fruits of affluence. Macmillans went to the best available schools and universities, but this was expected to be only the beginning of lives of solid achievement. Daniel Macmillan took his religion seriously and by the end of his life had become an admirer of Cardinal Newman; when Maurice was born he was keen on the Christian Socialists, and the boy's godfathers were F.D. Maurice and Charles Kingsley. Nellie Macmillan, who dominated her household, was fiercely ambitious for all her offspring and brought her own doctrines of self-reliance to complement the Macmillan doctrines she had married. She

7

was also rigidly Protestant, and a firm believer in the importance of education.[1]

Macmillan's childhood, by his own description, was understandably austere. The family house was in solidly affluent
Cadogan Place, in London. He went to school at Summer-
fields in Oxford, thence as a Scholar to Eton, thus beginning
an academic career which was distinguished, but not as distinguished as that of his elder brother Daniel. He remained at
Eton for three years, but in 1909 became extremely ill. When a
heart condition was diagnosed his formidable mother decided
to keep him at home, where he was to have private tuition to
prepare him for entrance to Oxford.

Macmillan was evidently a rather precious adolescent, not
perhaps as physically frail as a domineering mother would have
him believe, now thrust back into a family life marked by intense emotional stress. His departure from Eton was associated with a period of despondency and self-doubt. It was his
duty now to succeed, and he had a number of tutors, amongst
whom the most important was Ronald Knox, an Eton contemporary of his brother. Knox was already moving towards the
spiritual metamorphosis which was to make him, as the University Catholic Chaplain from 1926 to 1939, an influence over
many generations of clever Oxford undergraduates.[2] For the
moment he was an Anglo-Catholic, passionate in his conviction
and eager to proselytise. A deep affection sprang up between
the two young men: Knox was twenty-two and Macmillan was
ready to be instructed. Discovering this, Nellie ordered Knox
not to discuss religion with her son. When he refused, he was
put on the next train *sans* bicycle or laundry.[3] Apart from its
effect on Knox,[4] this episode seems to have confirmed the
contradictions in Macmillan's relations with his mother. He
later told a friend that 'I admired her, but never really liked
her.... She dominated me and she still [in the 1960s] dominates me.' It was with acknowledged relief that he escaped to
Oxford, taking a Classical Exhibition at Balliol.

Macmillan's biographer, perhaps predictably, has likened
the world which he entered in 1912 to the Oxford of Zuleika
Dobson. It was certainly a comfortable existence, with all the
trappings of privilege and, for the first time in Macmillan's
experience, a wealth of agreeable friendships. It was also a
period in his life when he applied himself conscientiously to
self-advancement. He was Secretary of the Oxford Union in

his fourth term and Treasurer in his fifth, and a member of many political societies. These activities established connections which he could revive later, such as a link with Walter Monckton, later a colleague in government. On the other hand, his spiritual preoccupations were intensified by the presence next door of Ronald Knox, still an Anglican and Chaplain of Trinity College, and by his close friendship with Guy Lawrence, who formed the third apex of a triangular relationship with Knox and Macmillan. Knox's pressure on his young friends was intense, though it cannot be established that this contributed very much to an apparent recurrence of Macmillan's nervous difficulties in the spring of 1914 which nearly brought him to withdraw from the university. Macmillan considered seriously whether he should become a Roman Catholic, and his eventual decision in 1915 that he was '*not* going to "Pope" until after the war (if I'm alive)' was a mortal blow to his intimate relationship with Knox, who had by then joined the Roman Catholic church. This relationship, together with enough academic work to get him a First in Classical Moderations, evidently occupied much of his time as an undergraduate. He was no more aware than anyone else of his generation that their world was about to be obliterated by the Great War.

The Archduke Franz-Ferdinand was assassinated at the beginning of the Long Vacation, and Macmillan did not return to Balliol to read Greats. He first enlisted in the King's Royal Rifle Corps, but was transferred to the 4th Battalion, Grenadier Guards, after his mother pulled the appropriate strings. Here, especially after his posting to the Western Front in August 1915, he confronted death and the working classes with an almost equal sense of novelty. His physical and moral courage as a young officer responsible for thirty men in action stands out even from the detached and ironical record in his memoirs. He was wounded in the hand in his first action, at the Battle of Loos, hospitalised and then sent back to ceremonial duties in London until he had fully recovered. In April 1916 he was sent out again, to the 2nd Battalion of Grenadiers. After a period in a quiet sector of trenches near Ypres, his battalion took part in the second wave of the Somme battle, and on 15 September he was wounded again while attacking a machine-gun post near Ginchy, in an engagement where Haig's premature and incompetent use of tanks had left the advancing infantry vulnerable to machine-gun fire from entrenched positions. Macmillan was hit in the pelvis at close range and spent most of the battle in a shell-hole, feigning death to discourage any passing Germans from despatching him, while, according to his own account, reading Aeschylus's *Prometheus* in the original when times were quiet. After some hours he was found by guardsmen from his company and eventually reached a field hospital in Abbeville. From there he was returned to England. His mother rescued him from the blundering ministrations of military surgeons, and he spent the rest of the war in a private hospital in Belgrave Square, suffering a series of unpleasant operations which left him with a slight limp and a lifetime of recurrent pain.

These were not experiences to leave a man unchanged. In May 1916 he had written to his mother that 'I never see a man killed but I think of him as a martyr', and his letters home are full of crusading imagery and an outspoken patriotism.[5] By the end of the war he had begun to show the sense of separateness which afflicted many who had seen action in that war. His irritation at the civilians who had stayed at home was not diminished, but his sense of loyalty to his comrades now took the form of a deep resentment against the incompetence of the generals and an almost romantic admiration for the personal qualities of ordinary soldiers as well as for his officer friends who had died. He never found it easy to like Germans, or men who had spent the war behind the lines or out of uniform; he did find it easy to like the common soldier, or people who might become soldiers, especially when they were his constituents in industrial Stockton.

After the Armistice, Macmillan, though secure in the offer of a job in the family firm, looked for employment abroad 'to be on my own'.[6] The state of his health prohibited a move to Bombay, where he had hoped to join his acquaintance George Lloyd, who had just been appointed Governor. Nellie once more intervened, arranging with her friend Lady Edward Cavendish that Captain Macmillan should go to Ottawa as ADC to the Duke of Devonshire, Lady Edward's son, who was the Governor-General of Canada. He travelled to Canada in March 1919 to embark on ten months of 'almost unalloyed enjoyment'.[7] His own description is of a long house-party, and indeed the functions of the Governor-General included a great deal of entertaining, both formal and informal, which occupied much of the ADC's time. Moreover, Macmillan's greatest single achievement during his period of duty in Ottawa was to become engaged to the Duke's daughter, Lady Dorothy Cavendish, whom he married in April 1920. This rather unexpected match, which later broke down in substance if not in form, marked Macmillan's adoption into an intensely political dynasty, as well as a striking forward move in his personal development. Into a life which had previously been spent between a sequestered home and a number of masculine institutions, with a heavy and rather precious overlay of religion and self-conscious morality, came an energetic, ill-educated, earthy young woman who immediately captured his affections. Rumour and biographers would have it that she was anxious to escape from a particularly domineering mother – Evie, Duchess of Devonshire – and had not reckoned on Nellie Macmillan,[8] and the basis of his attraction for her is still a matter of debate.

Nevertheless, the life of a Governor-General's ADC was not all play and flirtation, and it is significant that Macmillan's first practical experience of politics was at the very top. Canadian politics were in a state of flux. The ruling Conservative Party, which under Sir Robert Borden had staunchly supported the British war effort, was under pressure in the reconstruction period from social unrest in industrial areas and from the perennial discontent of the francophone majority in Quebec. It was also recognised that even if these problems were solved, Canada's relations with the British Empire and with the United States were bound to change. Simultaneously Borden and his chief lieutenant, Arthur Meighen, were trying to construct a peacetime coalition with some of their Liberal opponents to preserve the wartime governmental arrangements, rather as Lloyd George had done in Britain. This involved the Governor-General in a good deal of cross-party negotiation. It was his habit to discuss progress with his young ADC and although (perhaps because) nothing came of the various schemes proposed, the intricacies of policy at national and international level fascinated the young Macmillan.

Marriage seems to have dictated a return to England, and Macmillan finally entered the family business in 1920. His opportunity to make a mark was not great, since his uncles were still in firm control of editorial decisions and most aspects of the business, but he began to investigate the technicalities of book-production, which later and unexpectedly brought him an early brush with high politics. For a year or two his life seemed to settle into a steady pattern of business which had no intrinsic reason to change. But for an able young man with a well-connected wife and an intensely ambitious mother, this state of affairs could not long survive.

. . .

NOTES AND REFERENCES

1. A powerful but uneven discussion of the Macmillan family can be found in Richard Davenport-Hines, *The Macmillans* (London: William Heinemann, 1992).
2. One of them, Evelyn Waugh, wrote the official biography, *Ronald Knox* (2nd edn, London: Cassell, 1988).
3. Alistair Horne, *Macmillan, 1894– 1956* (London: Macmillan, 1988), p. 20.
4. Waugh, *Ronald Knox* p. 107.
5. Horne, *Macmillan 1894–1956*, p. 40
6. Ibid., p. 52.
7. Harold Macmillan, *Winds of Change* (London: Macmillan, 1966), p. 115.
8. Horne, *Macmillan 1894–1956*, pp. 56–8, citing Lord Sefton, another of the Duke's ADCs.

Chapter 2

LAUNCHING A CAREER
1922–40

Macmillan decided to 'try for Parliament' at some time before the election of 1922, though the date of this decision is
unknown.[1] The Duke of Devonshire, who had returned from
Canada in 1921, was Colonial Secretary in Andrew Bonar Law's
government and kept the office under Stanley Baldwin until
the Conservatives were defeated in 1923. With a father-in-law
in the Cabinet, it was difficult for Macmillan to avoid some
thought of political career, and when Baldwin decided at the
end of 1923 to call an election on the single issue of Tariff Reform, he applied to Conservative Central Office for a seat. He
was offered Stockton-on-Tees, a borough seat in a declining
shipbuilding area which was generally reckoned unwinnable,
and within days the local association had nominated him. Being rich enough to meet his election expenses he was glad to
accept, and he remained loyal to this rather unlikely political
base until after the Second World War, with the exception of
some flirtations with southern seats in the early 1930s.

Macmillan's first campaign at Stockton was a fair success,
about which he has written amusingly in his memoirs.[2] With
his wife he canvassed energetically, toured the steelworks, and
made the usual round of formal election speeches. He observed the Conservative Party's standard protectionist line with
positive enthusiasm, and laid about the Labour opponents he
was already learning to call 'socialists', as well as the Liberals
who had held the seat since 1910. As a stranger to industrial
England he was appalled by the level of poverty caused by unemployment in heavy industrial areas, and made this clear in
his campaign. Although he was generally recognised to be a
bad speaker and a shy man who found it difficult to talk to the
voters personally, he was reinforced by Lady Dorothy's com-

plementary enthusiasm and willingness to go anywhere and canvass anyone. The final result gave the Liberal 11,734 votes, Macmillan 11,661 and Labour 10,619.

It was Macmillan's misfortune that the Liberal Party in Stockton was taking an unconscionable time to die. Although he romanticised the working class, spoke movingly of its soldierly qualities, and repeatedly returned to the view that 'before the rise of the Labour Party, the working class had traditionally been Tory',[3] his main problem in Stockton was not how to appeal to the supposed old allegiances of trade unionists, but how to capture the Liberal vote (a great deal of it working-class) which throughout the 1920s swung the balance both nationally and in many northern constituencies. He failed to do this to a sufficient extent in 1923; he was luckier in 1924.

Though not yet in the Commons, Macmillan was fully engaged in politics during the brief tenure of the first Labour government which resulted from the election, kept informed by his brothers-in-law (Lord Hartington and James Stuart, who had married his wife's sister) and determined to fight again in Stockton. When the election was called in October, one of the first moves advised by his agent was to approach local Liberal notables to seek their support, which was thought to be influential with wavering Liberal voters. This he later scorned as being less important than personal canvassing, and indeed the notables probably had little direct influence; but the result illustrated how critical the Liberal vote was to be. In Stockton, as elsewhere, the Labour vote actually rose as the party's working-class supporters responded to the achievements of their own government. The Liberal vote collapsed, and most of the benefit went to Macmillan, who polled 15,163 against Labour's 11,948, with his Liberal opponent reduced to 8,751. His parliamentary ambitions had been achieved, by a comfortable majority, less than a year after he had first expressed a positive interest in standing. Luck, a skilful political wife, a plausible if not very warm speaking manner, and the stumblings of Ramsay MacDonald's government had all contributed to an early success in an unpromising constituency; but in the end it must be said that it had not been very difficult at all.

Macmillan had become a Conservative M.P. because it would have been unnatural for him to join any other party. Temperament, culture and family impelled him to it. Moreover, of the two parties which might have accepted him, the Liberal Party was destroying itself while the Conservative Party appeared to be the natural party of government for the foreseeable future. For an ambitious man with some wealth and excellent connections, it was the only choice. From his first campaign in Stockton, Macmillan identified the Labour Party as the most serious long-term threat, and teasingly labelled it 'socialist' to make sure the voters knew the difference between his brand of progressive thought and anything offered by the other side. He joined a party which first under Stanley Baldwin and then under Neville Chamberlain was to succeed in controlling that threat until the crisis of war in 1940.

· · · ·

AMBITION

Macmillan's memoirs give a clear and plausible account of his early career plans. He concentrated on home affairs, allowing his constituency knowledge to determine his own political agenda. Rather than seek early promotion, he persistently criticised the nerveless economic policies of his own front bench, and looked outside the Conservative Party for intellectual allies. Lloyd George was an early hero, with his readiness to experiment with novel methods of state intervention. Later, in the 1930s, Macmillan helped to convene the cross-party 'Next Five Years' group and contributed especially with his own writing to the definition of a 'Middle Way' between extreme free-market capitalism and the atavistic muddles of socialism.[4] In this way he anticipated the post-war consensus over which he was ultimately to preside as prime minister.

This account makes up in clarity and plausibility for what it lacks in strict fidelity to events. Macmillan had clearly not intended to remain so long on the back benches, and his interwar political career was determined by the need to make the best of a bad job. Baldwin's Conservative Party was secure in its dominance of the inter-war polity, largely because of the divisions among its opponents. After the upset of 1923, when Baldwin went to the country on a Tariff Reform platform and scared rather too many middle-class voters back into Liberal hands, most Conservative M.P.s could expect a reasonable security of tenure, and competition for junior office was intense. At most levels, but especially at the top, the 1924–29 government was riddled with faction. The major source of dissension within the Cabinet was the demand for protective tariffs, to which Leopold Amery, Neville Chamberlain, Philip Cunliffe-Lister and Arthur Steel-Maitland were committed, while Winston Churchill, as Chancellor, was fundamentally opposed. Challenges from protectionists, organised on the back benches through the Empire Industries Association, represented the strongest threat to Baldwin's leadership of the party in the dying years of the administration. Macmillan himself was a staunch protectionist, even though he had nothing to do with pre-war Birmingham, where Tariff Reform had been nurtured, and his wife's grandfather had been a leading Unionist Free Trader before the War.

Another source of dissent, noticeable even during the 1920s, was imperial policy, in which Baldwin's willingness to contemplate reform in India made him unpopular with Churchill and the political heirs of the pre-war Die-Hards. This was linked to disputes over naval policy which pitted Churchill against the First Lord of the Admiralty, William Bridgeman. On these two questions Macmillan also tended to oppose Churchill and support the Conservative Front Bench. At home, in its industrial relations policy, the Cabinet was driven by events and parliamentary passions. Its failure to solve the structural problems of the coal industry led inexorably to the miners' strike in 1925 and thus to the General Strike in 1926; reaction to this upheaval forced Baldwin and his colleagues to prepare a punitive Trade Disputes Act which divided his Cabinet. In this area, Macmillan was once again to be found comfortably behind the government, rather than boldly critical of his party: he voted for the Trade Disputes Act while complaining that it might presage an outbreak of extremism on Left and Right. Only in the area of industrial policy, where the government was weakest and least loved, did he make a very clear stand against the front bench. Nonetheless, a fellow Durham member, Cuthbert Headlam, remarked as early as July 1926 that he was 'easily the cleverest of the "coming men", though he is a trifle sententious and apt to be carried away into rather vague views which might lead him into other camps than the Conservative'. For all that, rumour was offering him a job at the Admiralty in December 1926.[5]

Assessments of Baldwin's second ministry have generally

stressed its successes and its moderation, though recent writers have questioned its unanimity of purpose and sureness of touch.[6] The modern view is more realistic: the parliamentary party which Macmillan entered was divided over so many issues that the administration which it supported was often directionless. As a young MP he therefore tried to make his name by attaching himself to distinctive positions, and it was no disadvantage that some of these positions should be different from those of his leaders. He made his maiden speech on the 1925 Budget and was suitably partisan, attacking the speech of the former Labour Chancellor Philip Snowden, with a lumbering wit.

> If he thinks that he and his party have only to offer us as true socialism a kind of mixture, a sort of horrible political cocktail, consisting partly of the dregs of exploded economic views of Karl Marx, mixed up with a little flavour of Cobdenism, well iced by the late Chancellor of the Exchequer, and with a little ginger from the Member for the Gorbals (Mr. Buchanan) – if he thinks that this is to be the draught given to our parched throats and that we are ready to accept it, he is very much mistaken.[7]

He then began to concentrate on housing and rating reform, which was unpopular and (more disadvantageously) rather dull. After the General Strike he came together with Robert Boothby, Oliver Stanley and John Loder to produce *Industry and the State*, an extended pamphlet on the relations between the state and the two sides of industry which foreshadowed in many important respects the arguments of *The Middle Way* which Macmillan published in 1935.

Industry and the State, though, is less important for the future than for the context in which it was produced. In the aftermath of the General Strike, while the Cabinet was manifestly unable to persuade the mine-owners to accept either a substantial reorganisation of their industry or a real amendment of their policy of reducing wages unilaterally, Macmillan suggested that the Government should legislate for compulsory amalgamations. While a Cabinet Committee was at work on the Trades Disputes Bill, during the winter of 1926–27, he began to speak on the need for 'a sense of partnership' in industry to be achieved by greater public control of utilities, such as electricity and transport, coupled with legislation for compulsory arbitration and conciliation in industrial disputes.

17

Industry and the State was the next step, published in April 1927 in anticipation of the Trades Disputes Bill which appeared the following month.

In later years Macmillan was to insist that 'what then seemed so visionary has now become commonplace and generally accepted' and likened his proposals to modern ideas of the mixed economy.[8] At the time he was probably more aware of it as a 'constructive alternative to Socialism'. He had been shaken by the General Strike; as well as participating enthusiastically in the distribution of *The Times*, he supplied a list of blackleg printers to the *Morning Post* for possible use in producing the *British Gazette*.[9] His aim was to defuse a dangerous conflict, and incidentally to nudge the government towards policies which might help him and some others with similar views to retain their seats in marginal industrial constituencies. At this stage there was little sign of centrism, and, although he was fairly liberal with his contempt, his sympathies were not evenly divided between the two sides. Speaking on the coal dispute as it dragged on into September 1926 he remarked that

> ... the leadership of the men throws discredit either upon the in-
> telligence or upon the patriotism of those leaders, and there is no
> explanation of their conduct which does not impute to them either
> the most extraordinary puerility or the most sinister motives. The
> leadership of the owners, it seems to me, in my humble judgement,
> has been unnecessarily harsh when it should have been pliable and
> obstinate when the time came to give way...

Later in the same speech he attributed 'the mentality of a Russian revolutionist' to the miners' leadership.[10]

During 1927 and 1928 he repeatedly expressed sympathy for the economic proposals which Lloyd George was developing through the Liberal Summer Schools. These finally took shape in the Liberal Industrial Inquiry (the 'Yellow Book') and in *We Can Conquer Unemployment*, and it became clear that Lloyd George was advocating a much higher level of expenditure than Macmillan envisaged. The official response (*Certain Proposals relating to Unemployment*, Cmd. 3331) criticised not only Lloyd George's proposal in direct detail, but also by implication the propositions of *Industry and the State*.

Besides *Industry and the State*, Macmillan soon busied himself with the notion of industrial de-rating. A simple idea in itself, it was to have potent consequences. Its essence was that industry in depressed areas was burdened with high fixed costs because local authority expenditures, often inflated by the consequences of high unemployment for the Poor Law, were met by rates levied on property. Macmillan proposed to replace this source of revenue by a partial Exchequer subsidy. As early as July 1925 he suggested that 'the whole system of raising local taxation is ... built upon an obsolete and mediaeval foundation ... [which] ... throws an undue burden on productive industry', and in late 1926 he raised the possibility of 'nationalising' certain services, by which he meant funding them directly from the Exchequer.[11] This was in due course taken up by Churchill at the Exchequer and eventually turned into the main proposal of the 1928 Budget and the centrepiece of his last year of office, the Industrial Derating Bill of February 1929.

Macmillan's place in the development of the idea is indicated by considerable detailed correspondence with Churchill over the winter of 1927–28, and Macmillan and his friend Robert Boothby, who was Churchill's Parliamentary Private Secretary, became outspokenly attached to it as a means of restoring the electoral fortunes of the Conservative Party.[12] It must be said, though, that Macmillan's 'chance remark' had undergone considerable development at the hands of Churchill and senior Treasury officials before it saw the full light of political day, and that the success of the scheme depended entirely on Churchill's ability to persuade Neville Chamberlain, the Minister of Health, to accept a bold scheme which, for all its merits, disrupted Chamberlain's own large plans for the reform of local authority finance.

All this is not to denigrate Macmillan's own part in the affair, nor to belittle its significance for his own developing political position. In December 1927 he was taken fully into the Chancellor's confidence, and wrote a lengthy political memorandum on the implications of the proposed combination of derating and a profits tax. This document is interesting because it sets a robustly partisan tone which coloured all Macmillan's dealings with de-rating. To the rhetorical question 'Will the Socialists raise the cry "You are letting off the rich employer & doing nothing for the poor working man"? Will this be a dangerous cry?', he answered shrewdly:

It will be more dangerous in prosperous areas than in distressed areas. It will be no good in agricultural areas at all.[13] We can in reply point to

1. Gold Standard for the Rentiers
2. Widows, orphans & old age Pensions Acts for the people
3. This scheme for depressed Industry. Industry is after all our 'father & mother'. On its prosperity we all ultimately depend.

I am not much afraid of this cry nowadays. It would have been more dangerous before 1920. But the 'slump' has left its mark & a great number of ordinary folk have begun to learn the lesson, in a hard school, of the mutual interdependence of all classes and interests.[14]

He challenged Neville Chamberlain's warning that without industrial rating local businesses would cease to have any interest in the soundness of local authorities' financial administration by remarking that 'These people will still be to some extent interested as *residential* ratepayers. Moreover, if the fat kine are taken away, the lean kine will have nothing left to devour but their own proletarian hides.' This was not entirely an emollient Conservatism.

Macmillan was further taken into Churchill's confidence when he was shown the whole Treasury file on de-rating on 21 December. His response was to describe Churchill's proposals as 'absolutely masterly and quite unanswerable .... We shall "dish the Whigs" & steal their clothes while they are bathing, in the true Disraelian style.' A certain amount of mutual flattery ensued, and it was clear that Macmillan saw many advantages in a political attachment to Churchill. Although the connection was to wither, for both political and personal reasons, it sustained Macmillan's career for a few important months, and when the de-rating measure was finally introduced he took a significant part in its parliamentary presentation.

* * *

CONFUSION AND DESPAIR

In 1929 Stockton fell to Labour, in a microcosm of the General Election result in which the temporary revival of Liberalism elbowed Conservative candidates out of marginal seats. It was ironical that Macmillan himself was probably as keen a supporter of Lloyd George's economic policy as the official Liberal candidate. Yet the election result could hardly be seen as a vindication of his policy prescriptions, and in the scramble to attribute blame which occupied the Conservative Party for the next two years Macmillan's voice was raised but rarely heard. As a convinced protectionist, he was naturally attracted by Lord Beaverbrook's Empire Free Trade campaign, and for a few months during the winter of 1929–30 he co-operated with Beaverbrook in attempts to overthrow Baldwin – an episode which he later attributed to youth and inexperience. He was present also at two meetings in November 1929, attended by, among others, Boothby and Walter Elliott, with blessings relayed from Amery and Oswald Mosley, which contemplated the formation of a new party but in the event could not agree on its form or its policy.[15] His journalism reiterated the themes of his earlier speeches, and in an attempt to combine criticism with loyalty he emphasised 'new directions' rather than directly attacking Baldwin's leadership. These consisted of 'modernisation of our economic methods, the humanisation of our industrial relations, and the expansion of our foreign, and primarily of our imperial markets'.[16] In 1930 his restlessness brought him temporarily close to Oswald Mosley: he wrote teasing letters to the press in support of Mosley's famous 'Memorandum' in May 1930[17] and later in the year considered joining the 'New Party' which Mosley launched after leaving the Labour Party. His wavering loyalty to official Conservatism was noted by, among others, R.A. Butler, who wrote to the press recommending that he find 'a pastime more suited to his talents', giving Macmillan something to remember and resent in years to come.[18]

Macmillan's brief relations with Mosley are important, not because they indicate any latent Fascism but because they illustrate both the strengths and the limits of political dissent in the early 1930s. Mosley himself had fallen from a position of potential influence because his ideas could not be carried either in Cabinet, where they were opposed by Philip Snowden, or in the Parliamentary Labour Party. He was quintessentially a victim of party discipline and committees. Macmillan, like many others who at first admired the direction of Mosley's thinking, decided that it was impossible to make a career outside an established party. This he later rationalised in a famous passage of his memoirs, remarking that 'It is a deep and, no doubt, a sound political instinct in our country, that men do better to stick to their own parties and try to influence their policies and their character from within.'[19] Although some writers on economic policy-making have argued that the parties had by this time abdicated much of their influence to organised interests such as the TUC and the Federation of British Industries,[20] working directly with the departments of government, the important negative power of the political parties should not be underestimated. Angry young men would always count the cost of dissent.

Moreover, the limitations of Macmillan's ideas must also be stressed. His constituency responsibilities and the electoral threat from Labour forced him to be most concerned with the results of unemployment. His ideas on the causes and cure of the disease were less fully worked out. He can hardly be blamed for this: J.M. Keynes, on whose journalism most of the novel economic ideas of the later 1920s were based, had at this point only a partial grasp of the problem, and his *General Theory* was still in the future. Politicians during the economic crisis of 1929–32 were for the most part reworking old ideas, such as public works expenditure (to relieve unemployment directly) and tariffs (to protect uncompetitive domestic producers). Lloyd George's ability, claimed on his behalf by Keynes, to 'Conquer Unemployment' was at first based mostly on a public works scheme aimed at the million or so long-term unemployed who were troubling politicians in 1928. Keynes's later gloss, that the famous 'multiplier effect' would create snowballing economic growth, had not been worked out; nor had the unemployment figure reached its final figure of three million. Most politicians were still relying on an upturn in international trade to revive the economy. Macmillan, as one of his articles in the *Saturday Review* shows, was among them, and he had not fully grasped the possibilities of expanding domestic demand, which was the centrepiece of Mosley's scheme. His contributions to *Industry and the State* were more obviously in the tradition of the 'productioneers' of the First World War: an appeal for the modernisation of business methods, and co-operation between big business and organised labour, backed by protection for the home market. His problem was that neither the state nor the organised interests were very interested, either in 1927 or in the early 1930s when he revived his proposals.

A further reason for Macmillan's limited political impact during the period of the second Labour government was that he was undergoing a profound personal crisis. Lady Dorothy

Macmillan began an affair with his colleague Robert Boothby which was to last for the rest of her life. It brought the Macmillans' sexual relationship to an end (Sarah Macmillan, born in 1930, was Boothby's daughter), subjected Macmillan to protracted humiliation in 'society', where everyone knew of the affair without needing to discuss it, and induced what his biographer calls 'a full-scale nervous breakdown' by 1931.[21] It also divided him from Churchill, of whose circle Boothby was a prominent member. In the long term, the effective collapse of his marriage is said to have strengthened Macmillan's political ambition, brought him to a more realistic and ruthless awareness of the limits of human happiness, and reinforced his religious faith. In the short term the benefits were less obvious, but the Macmillans' decision not to divorce appears to have been based on a mutual agreement that Lady Dorothy would continue her active and very useful support for her husband's election campaigns. This at least enabled him to pick up his political career at the 1931 election. During the political crisis of August 1931 he was in a sanatorium in Germany, where until the election was mooted Lady Dorothy was urging him to stay. On hearing of the election he wrote to his mother that 'I want to get into the H of C, because I think it wd. make my life much easier',[22] and he arrived back in England, walking with a stick, five days after the beginning of a campaign which his wife had already mounted.

. . .

RETURN AND CONFUSION

Returning to Parliament as part of a triumphant coalition in 1931 did not solve the problem of Macmillan's career. His victory in Stockton, like so many other Conservative victories in northern constituencies, was obtained by the withdrawal of the Liberal candidate; Labour's vote against him was only 800 fewer than in 1929. However, since both Labour and the Liberals were in disarray, both the government and Macmillan's own seat looked reasonably safe. The same could be said for dozens of other young MPs, and the prospect of political advancement was correspondingly small. All the worse for Macmillan was his lack of a patron, since the connection with Churchill, so carefully built up over de-rating, had been severed, partly because of Boothby and partly because Churchill's outspoken opposition to Baldwin's Indian policy had aligned him with the most reactionary elements of the parliamentary party, with whom Macmillan could not work. He therefore turned to further novelties, which led him during the next two parliaments to busy himself with pamphleteering and the promotion of cross-party movements. The climax of this effort was *The Middle Way*, a hasty compilation of economic ideas published in 1938. Only when Macmillan aligned himself once again with Churchill over appeasement did his progress towards office and power resume in earnest.

Macmillan was unusually literate for a back-bench M.P., and since he owned a publishing house it was easy for him to use print as a medium to convey his ideas. Co-operating with Allan Young, a former Mosleyite who had left the New Party because he detested Mosley's leanings to Fascism, Macmillan produced a short booklet on *The State and Industry* in March 1932. This was followed in May by *The Next Step*. These were welcomed by Keynes, which is unsurprising since the main economic recommendations for lower interest rates and an Investment Board reflected proposals which Keynes himself had inserted four years beforehand, and in rather more detail, in the Liberal Yellow Book and thus into the Liberal election campaign in 1929. A more substantial book, *Reconstruction: a Plea for National Unity*, published in 1933, added the detail which had been lacking in the pamphlets.

In these three works the concrete proposals built upon themes which Macmillan had outlined before in the 1927 pamphlet, *Industry and the State*, in particular the suggestion that economic policy should be decided by the state in association with 'representative bodies' drawn from both sides of industry, which would constitute a 'sub-parliament'. This suggestion had been made before from both Right and Left: G.D.H. Cole had proposed something rather like it in *Self-Government for Industry* in 1917, while the Federation of British Industries at the end of the Great War had suggested it as part of an elaborate scheme to retain the benefits of state intervention in the economy while avoiding state control of industry. In its most extreme form the FBI proposal would have had a Ministry of Industry directly responsible to the economic sub-parliament. This idea was predictably and firmly squashed by the Haldane Report on the Machinery of Government, but its attractions as a bulwark against state socialism remained.

The advantages, from the government's point of view, of shedding work and responsibility on to the shoulders of organised interests, were perceived particularly clearly by Lloyd George, and a prominent Lloyd George Liberal, Sir Alfred Mond, was responsible for a revival of the idea in 1927 in *Industry and Politics.* Mond, by then a Conservative, was also responsible for an interesting attempt to bridge the gap between employers and employees in the Mond–Turner talks of 1927, in which leading trade unionists and a number of employers, many in 'new' industries, discussed co-operation.[23] Mond's son, Henry Mond, entered Parliament as a Conservative in 1929 and succeeded his father as Lord Melchett in December 1930. In the 1930s he became one of Macmillan's political collaborators, in particular in the Industrial Reorganisation League which consciously promoted the idea of compulsory amalgamations and the 'rationalisation' of industry. Industrial reorganisation was in fact the core of Macmillan's politics from 1931 to 1937, succeeding industrial de-rating as an issue to which he could confidently return as an organising principle for speeches, writings, lobbying and coalition-making. Later writers have recognised him, together with Lord Eustace Percy and Raymond Glendinning of the Federation of British Industries, as being among the most prominent 'corporatists' in the Conservative Party in the 1930s,[24] giving a particular flavour to his well-known support for the idea of 'planning'.

Macmillan's contribution to the much-discussed political 'middle opinion' of the 1930s should be treated with caution. Certainly there was a large number of active and articulate individuals in and out of Parliament, but mostly outside it, who wanted to find an economic policy which would invigorate the declining British economy without resort to socialism. Their preferred method was generally known as planning, though the questions of who would plan, for what, and with what powers, very often divided 'planners' among themselves. One especially persistent group was Political and Economic Planning, an association of concerned individuals who came together to study both the political and economic system and the process of planning itself. PEP, whose members collectively mustered a wide range of expertise, eventually grew into an independent research institute. In its anniversary history a founding member remarked of Macmillan and his associates that 'we were essentially a research group; they issued political manifestos'.[25] This represented a real difference between Macmillan's middle position, which was rooted in party politics, and the middle position occupied by PEP, which included Labour supporters and addressed itself to concerns which had no immediate foothold in party debate. There was cross-fertilisation: Macmillan, with half a dozen other Conservative politicians including Melchett, Eustace Percy and Oliver Stanley MP, was present at PEP's first formal dinner and brought his Industrial Reorganisation proposals for discussion with the PEP Industry Group.[26] Nevertheless, Macmillan was attracted to 'planning' because he was an ambitious politician – ambitious to change the world but also to advance his own career. Headlam guessed that 'His idea ... may well be that, if he makes a nuisance of himself and can form a small and effective group to assist him in the job, he may persuade *hoi en Telloi* to offer him a billet to silence his opposition.'[27]

The prominence of 'planning' as a political idea made the competition for attention very intense. The Industrial Reorganisation League, established by Melchett and Macmillan in the summer of 1934, was one of many bodies promoting rationalisation in industry. Its early members included Sir Robert Horne, once Lloyd George's President of the Board of Trade, Lord Weir of Weir Engineering, who had also once been in a Lloyd George government, and Sir Harry McGowan of ICI. The rationalisation which it advocated was a chameleon concept. The *Economist* noted in 1929 that it was a neologism used 'as a cloak for confused ideas, and sometimes as a badge of respectability for processes of doubtful value'.[28] More often than not, it meant horizontal amalgamations of companies in similar fields of business in order to reap economies of scale. Sometimes it implied the closure of inefficient plant; sometimes it implied the development of new methods; sometimes it implied the extension of market control, in which case its protagonists often wanted to combine companies vertically so that, for example, steel producers and tinplate producers would join in a single company. The version favoured by Macmillan and Melchett was mainly horizontal amalgamation. To publicise this, as much as to effect real change, they arranged in November 1934 to introduce an Enabling Bill which would give statutory backing to compulsory mergers if 75 per cent of an industry approved of such a plan.

This proposal is interesting for a number of reasons. First, it harked back to the ideas of the 'productioneers' of the First World War, who believed that big business was the key to economic success, and that the government should reject the traditional prejudice against trusts and combines which was enshrined both in public policy and in the common law.[29] Second, it picked up points made in the Liberal Yellow Book about the need for public regulation of merger activity. Third, and most important, it was a means to rebuild Macmillan's career as a radical in politics.

Industrial Reconstruction coincided both in timing and in tone with Lloyd George's eruption into the politics of economic depression with a scheme for a New Deal, which was launched in January 1935. Lloyd George's New Deal was both opportunity and embarrassment for Macmillan: Headlam remarked that 'I fancy that [Lloyd George] is hoping to catch Harold Macmillan and his little band of earnest supporters and they may be silly enough to be caught'.[30] As a former prime minister and a consummate publicist, Lloyd George was able to force ministers to respond, despite the undying hostility of Neville Chamberlain, now Chancellor of the Exchequer. In May 1935 he had a meeting with a Cabinet committee to present his ideas. Sir H.P. Hamilton of the Board of Trade and Sir Richard Hopkins of the Treasury were commissioned to provide ammunition against Lloyd George's proposal of a National Development Board. In answering a hostile questionnaire drawn up by these officials, Lloyd George remarked that 'I am in agreement with the proposals for a general Enabling Bill as advanced by Mr Macmillan and his colleagues of the Industrial Reorganisation League.' Macmillan provided further notes in defence of this position, which were annotated unfavourably in the Board of Trade. On the afternoon of the meeting a Board of Trade official reported that Macmillan had rung him up to check the time and date of his meeting with the Cabinet committee.

> I replied that there seemed to be some serious misunderstanding. At the Meeting which Mr Lloyd George had this morning with Ministers, it had been agreed that Mr Lloyd George's experts on Industrial Organisation should confer with Board of Trade officials....
>
> Mr Macmillan took the strongest possible exception to his being regarded as 'an expert' of Mr Lloyd George. While it was true that he had been asked by Mr Lloyd George to answer certain questions

on Industrial Organisation and that he had prepared answers to these questions, he did not regard himself in any way as a 'Lloyd George expert'. He was sure that some of his friends would take the same line.

He had no intention of acceding to any request of Mr Lloyd George or his private secretary to attend a Conference with the officials of the Board of Trade, though he would of course gladly accept the invitation of the President of the Board of Trade to a Conference on this subject....

The President's delighted private secretary minuted 'This is almost too good to be true. I think we can now lie low until the row between LG and his chief expert is finished.'

A compromise was achieved, which hardly gave Macmillan all he wanted. On 30 May the Parliamentary Secretary to the Board of Trade, John Colville, received a deputation from the League which presented a memorandum by Macmillan reassuring the Board that 'the Industrial Reorganisation League is not a political organisation.... I might say that I am its Chairman more by accident than design. It merely happened that I had been expressing a similar view in speech and in writing at the time...'. The deputation was made up of politicians and industrialists, and a number of prominent businessmen sent written apologies and statements of support. From these, and the report of the discussion, it is possible to locate the Industrial Reorganisation League quite precisely in an industrial spectrum, but not so readily in politics. The businessmen – P.G. Donald of Clydesdale Builders Merchants, George Douglas of the Bradford Dyers Association, Malcolm Robertson of Spillers Ltd, H. Summers of John Summers (steel sheet manufacturers) and Sir William Firth, chairman of Richard Thomas and Baldwin's – were all deeply involved in major price-fixing associations which controlled large shares of their respective markets. Those sending apologies included Frank Platt of the Lancashire Cotton Corporation, one of the most ambitious attempts ever made in the interwar period to rationalise an invalid staple industry. Their complaints were uniform and predictable. They would have liked to be empowered by Melchett's Bill to buy up surplus plants for the purpose of closing them down. They had tried price-fixing, but they found themselves thwarted by outsiders trying to enter their trades, and despaired of preventing such undercutting. The politicians present, besides Macmillan and Melchett, included C.W.

Peat, MP, who was also a partner in Peat Marwick Mitchell. Sir Robert Horne sent a letter of support, as did Sir Valentine Crittall, a manufacturer of window-frames who had been a Labour MP for nine months in 1924. It is hardly surprising that officials should catch a whiff of Lloyd George in these connections, nor that Macmillan should have some difficulty in denying it plausibly; this was not a conventional rally of loyal Conservative back-benchers.[31]

The threat of being upstaged drove Macmillan to further efforts. The specific thrust of the Industrial Reorganisation League was complemented by the wider aspirations of the Next Five Years group. The progenitor of this body was Clifford Allen (Lord Allen of Hurtwood), a prominent conscientious objector in the First World War who had been active in the ILP in the 1920s, despite recurrent illness caused by his prison experiences. His socialism moderated during the later years of the decade, and he was content to take a peerage from Ramsay MacDonald in December 1931, to support the National Government in the Lords. One of his many services to the infant National Labour Party was to run a *News-Letter*, and his first contact with Macmillan seems to have been an invitation to him in April 1932 to write an article on the reorganisation of industry for this broadsheet.[32] Allen was soon writing to Ramsay Macdonald that 'I have been seeing a good deal recently of the younger Conservative Members of Parliament, and they are most emphatic in wanting the Government to lead and not allow itself to be frightened by possibly fifty to one hundred of the old fashioned Tories. They seem to me to be entirely at your disposal.'[33] At the end of 1933 Macmillan helped him in an unsuccessful attempt to buy the *Weekend Review* as a mouthpiece for 'vigorous action scientifically conceived' in both national and international politics.[34] Some of the parties involved, including Allen and Macmillan, put together a manifesto called *Liberty and Democratic Leadership*, published by Allen and signed by Macmillan, among other Conservative MPs, in February 1934.

This was a difficult period. Cuthbert Headlam noted in March 1934 that Macmillan

> ... is evidently still anxious for a political career, but realises that he has missed the boat. My advice to him was to go on pushing his ideas and developing them – but not to keep speaking and voting

against the Government – and, above all else, to find a safer seat than Stockton. His only chance is to make good while the Party is in opposition, and if we are really to have a smash at the next election, it is no good anyone who wants to have a political career to stand for a seat in Co. Durham.[35]

Within a couple of months Headlam found his strange friend 'now wrapped up in his plans for "reconstructing" everything and does not appear to grasp that reconstruction by Act of Parliament may lead to odd results'.[36]

A coherent group intent on 'reconstruction' was formed at an Oxford meeting in the late summer of 1934, and Macmillan joined a drafting committee which also included Clifford Allen, W. Arnold Forster, A. Barratt Brown,[37] Geoffrey Crowther, and Arthur Salter. The final product of their efforts was *The Next Five Years: An Essay in Political Agreement*, published in July 1935. Macmillan had helped to draft the first, economic section of this work. It is not certain that he played 'a leading role in the development of its economic themes', as his biographer believes, since that part of the book closely resembles earlier work by Arthur Salter,[38] but there is no doubt that its message was similar to what he had been saying and writing since 1927, or that it was a political statement which openly competed for attention with Lloyd George's 'Councils of Action for Peace and Reconstruction'. This was an excellent vehicle for the advancement of his own career.

Correspondingly, much of the later history of the Next Five Years group as a cross-party and non-party organisation was shaped by the political calculations of its leading members, of whom Macmillan was the most prominent and the most calculating. By the middle of 1935 he was a 'very bitter, poor man' because he had not been offered a job when so many of his parliamentary contemporaries were entering the ministry.[39] The election expected in the autumn of 1935 encouraged talk of a 'centre party', and some members of the Next Five Years group, including Macmillan, visited Lloyd George in August to sniff the possibility of co-operation with the Councils of Action. They decided against it, ostensibly because it would be incompatible with the 'spirit of our original constitution'; but Macmillan seems to have been in the minority.[40] Allen and other members supported Macmillan in his election campaign, even trying, without success, to persuade the Liberal candidate in Stockton to stand down.

Within weeks of the election Macmillan was ready with a new tack. He sent a long memorandum to Lloyd George on the new situation in Parliament:

> The Government is secure for four or five years. The attempt to create a group of progressives holding the balance of power has definitely failed. In these circumstances it seems to me that the Members who agreed to the Council of Action Questionnaire cannot attempt to compete with the opposition parties in doing the routine work of critical examination in the day to day activities of Parliament. An entirely different method is forced upon them by the secure position of the Government

Concluding that persuasion rather than parliamentary opposition was the only promising course, he went on boldly to suggest that

> The Council of Action group will find it difficult to enlist...co-operation from the Government side of the House. Under the pressure of Election necessity it has become quite definitely associated with the opposition as an anti-Government movement. Would it not therefore be better to allow the Council of Action Group *as such* to disappear and replace it with a Parliamentary Group working in consultation with the 'Next Five Years' organisation which has no association in the public mind with any electoral activity in the past?[41]

No response appears to have survived to this rather impertinent suggestion that the Council of Action should abolish itself.

The Next Five Years group was reformed in February 1936 as a pressure group committed to a 'practical programme of action' but emphatically not as a new political party. Within a few months, however, the establishment of a periodical to promote its ideas – *The New Outlook* – led to a fierce internal disagreement. Allen complained that Macmillan was trying to control all the group's activities. Macmillan wanted to co-operate with other groups, including Lloyd George; Allen in particular did not. The row over the form of the new publication led Macmillan to propose a radical reform of the group's function whose purpose was to remove Allen from any controlling influence. In this he was largely successful, but just to make sure he floated *The New Outlook* as an independent journal under his own chairmanship to run a simple programme of collective security, the abolition of the means test, action in the distressed areas, tariff reduction, and greater public control of industry.

At the end of 1936 Allan Young, acting as Macmillan's secretary, proposed to the Next Five Years group that it was time to unite the progressive opposition: and among the groups to be approached was Lloyd George's Council of Action. This move had been authorised by 'a number of private and informal conversations [which] have been held under the auspices of *The New Outlook* with regard to the possibility of achieving a unity of the progressive elements in the political life of Britain'. Macmillan returned to the themes of late 1935, urging on Lloyd George that a 'nucleus formed as a result of the co-ordination of the Next Five Years Group, the Council of Action, and others, would be able to enlist sufficient support to enable it to act as the midwife of the new alliance' of Liberals and Labour with progressive Conservatives.[42] Allen's fragile patience finally broke, and he wrote to a member of the Next Five Years Executive:

> You probably do not know what is behind this proposal of Macmillan's. It all dates back from the stupid squabble for power which first appeared when Macmillan was inclined to do a deal with L.G.'s Council of Action when it was formed, and when he and I went down to see L.G. . . . .
>
> The fact is that when Macmillan was a supporter of the National Government he took X view of the functions of 'The Next Five Years' Group. Now that he has cut his traces and has no political home, he looks at the work and functions of our Group in a new way, which is largely influenced by his own personal position.[43]

In these transactions Macmillan was, no doubt, behaving with ruthless self-interest; but that is what politicians do. Cuthbert Headlam reckoned at the beginning of the Group's existence that 'the one thing he is really hankering for is political success and I feel that he would accept any job that was offered him' and further that 'Harold is a strange creature . . . the longer you know him, the less intimate you become with him and his sole interest in life appears to be himself.'[44] Allen, by contrast, was an attractive figure, much loved by his friends on all sides of politics and widely respected for his sincerity. He had also shown himself in many contexts to be a difficult and prickly colleague, energetic but quick to take offence, and wedded to his own vision of truth and justice. A rift between the two men was not a surprise. By the end of 1937 both the magazine and the group were defunct, not because its policies were any less attractive to its members, but because it no longer offered Macmillan any interesting opportunities for political advancement.

．．．

THE MIDDLE WAY

Once separated, fairly amicably, from the Next Five Years group, Macmillan was free to make his own statement. He did so in *The Middle Way*, written with the help of his secretary Allan Young and published in May 1938. Distinctive and indigestible, it is now the best remembered of Macmillan's books, though it differs little in substance from his earlier pamphlet and polemic writing.[45] Allowing himself the luxury of an ethical position as well as a political statement, Macmillan constructed an argument very close to that of the New Liberals of his youth, believing like them that capitalism was in danger and that the greatest political threat in a democratic system was socialism:

> It should be the responsibility of society to find the means of granting to every one of its citizens a guarantee of security in the enjoyment of minimum standards of food, clothing, and shelter in return for their willing offer to share in the labour necessary to produce them. That is to say, society has the responsibility of creating the social and economic organisation for the continuous supply of these minimum requirements; society has *not* the right to abandon the individual because, as a result of faulty organisation, the labour which he is still willing to expend cannot temporarily be utilised.

To this Macmillan added certain other obligations of society, such as that to provide adequate care for mothers and babies, educational opportunities for children 'in so far as the parents are unable to provide these essentials', and, echoing a traditional Labour Party slogan, the requirement that 'If it fails to provide the citizen with work for his willing hands, then society must provide him with maintenance.'[46] At this point his argument moved beyond that of the New Liberals, for he urged that it was not enough merely to redistribute wealth through the transfer payments – pensions, sickness and unemployment benefits and the like – which they had hoped would fend off the wrath of the working classes. Arguing that 'we are approaching the limits of what can be accomplished by the negative procedure of transferring wealth through taxation or levy', Macmillan wanted society to 'achieve an increased production of wealth out of which to support the satisfactory minimum standards that so obviously are essential'.[47]

The solution was to lie through planning rather than socialism:

(a) A form of Industrial Organisation which curbs unwise, speculative over-expansion of any industry and assists, by an intelligent system of market anticipation, in guiding capital investment into the correct channels and in the correct proportions, to maintain a balance in the quantities of separate goods which, if stability is to be preserved, must exchange for one another.

(b) A method of ensuring that financial policy is conducted in such a way as to keep the factors of production at the highest possible degree of permanent employment.

(c) A method of insuring the consumer against a loss of purchasing power arising from unforeseen fluctuations, which, by maintaining his standard of life at an irreducible minimum by means of social provisions, would check in its early stages any tendency towards depression that might still arise. The proposals under this head will rest, therefore, not only upon the humanitarian arguments that have already been advanced, but upon the requirements of a comprehensive economic policy.[48]

Industrial organisation he proposed to deal with by a general Enabling Bill, reminiscent of his proposals for the Industrial Reorganisation League. On finance he was evidently influenced by the Liberal Yellow Book of 1928, by Keynes's *General Theory*, published in 1936, and to a lesser extent by Lionel Robbins's *The Great Depression* of 1934. He argued that 'the volume of credit and the quantity of money should be regulated in accordance with the needs of the productive system and not be dominated by irrational and anti-social speculation in the fluctuating value of securities'.[49] He also commented on the adverse consequences of excessive saving: the hoarding of idle balances because of investors' 'liquidity preference' which Keynes had put at the centre of his explanation of the current economic discontents. Macmillan therefore proposed a reformed Bank of England and, more tentatively, a National Investment Board to co-ordinate public borrowing and regulate capital issues and overseas investment. Unabashed at the number of authorities he was creating, he also proposed a foreign trade committee to manage the balance of payments through duties, subsidies and bulk purchasing of imports – a suggestion first made by the 1931 Committee on Finance and Industry.

By this stage in his argument Macmillan was ready to propose an overarching system of economic control. This was nothing if not comprehensive:

> The direction and guidance of a single national policy through the channels that our organisational structure would provide, would bring each branch of activity into a harmonious relationship with the others in the pursuit of a common aim.... The National Economic Council, with all the facts before it, would survey the whole field of economic activity, and, in consultation with the responsible representatives of the Government, formulate a comprehensive plan for general guidance. The Central Bank, the National Investment Board, the Foreign Trade organisation, and the Industrial Advisory Council would conduct their operations in accordance with this policy and seek to enlist the co-operation of industries or enterprises to assist in carrying it into effect.[50]

The National Economic Council was not to be an elected body nor, properly speaking, an executive agency either. Although it was expected to guide the subordinate organisations, its policy was supposed to be subject to ratification by the government. Its membership was to be appointed by the government, but drawn from the subordinate organisations and from the TUC, the National Confederation of Employers' Organisations, the Federation of British Industry, with 'representatives of every department of Government concerned with economic policy' and 'selected individuals of eminence in the fields of Economic Science and any other branches of learning from which expert assistance could usefully be recruited'. This bore disconcerting similarities to the Economic Advisory Council which Ramsay MacDonald had set up under the 1929–31 Labour government, and Macmillan offered no reason for thinking that such a group would not reproduce the internal disagreements which had crippled the earlier body,[51] but it seems clear that his main concern in describing it was to reassure readers that the sovereignty of Parliament would not be infringed. After the careful preparation of earlier chapters, there is a surprising contrast between the cautious description of the powers of the planning bodies and the bold assertion that through them 'the Government will be expected to achieve the full employment of the labour and capital resources of the nation'.[52]

The Middle Way was graciously reviewed, both by friends and opponents. Harold Nicolson in *The Observer* described it as 'an exhaustive and intelligent study of the means by which we can obtain economic liberty without sacrificing political liberty' and remarked that 'many progressive and puzzled people will hail this book with relief', while G.D.H. Cole praised it in the *New Statesman*. Judged by the standards commonly applied to books written by practising politicians, it is clearly far above average, though one must wonder whether it would have maintained its reputation had the author not subsequently become prime minister. An assessment of its originality and its place in the context of contemporary writing about economic policy cannot be so clear-cut. Every idea has a history, and every idea in *The Middle Way* can be fitted into debates about unemployment, foreign trade, industrial reorganisation and the structure of government which were pursued vigorously throughout the interwar period.

For the most part *The Middle Way* is a rather cautious compilation of the economic revisionism of the 1930s, written up so that Conservatives need not find it too unpalatable. Harold Nicolson's 'relief' seems to have been the intended effect. This is particularly noticeable in the passages dealing with macroeconomics in which Macmillan relies heavily on Keynes and Robbins. Economists are used in these passages to lend authority to some valid criticisms of the effect of existing economic institutions on the prospects for recovery. Some quite technical matters, such as Keynes's discussion of liquidity preference and the possibility that the economy, if left unmanaged, will reach equilibrium at a point where there is still substantial unemployment, are put firmly in front of the reader. But although Macmillan admits the possibility of counter-cyclical spending – 'Government spending would be reduced to a minimum when everybody else was spending freely, whether on consumption or investment, and it would be expanded to the maximum when any interruptions occurred in the flow of savings into effective demand for capital construction, or for use as working capital'[53] – even this is described as a 'reserve weapon' and relegated in significance by comparison with the major planning agencies. The concept of demand management does not emerge at all clearly in any part of the book. Given the rate at which Keynes's revolution in economic thought was by that time sweeping academic economics, and the remarkable speed with which even such bastions of orthodoxy as the Treasury and the Parliamentary Labour Party were to take up his views within the next ten years, it is misleading in the extreme to suggest either that Macmillan's book in 1938 was 'in many ways a revolutionary document' or that he was 'adhering faithfully to the doctrines of Keynes' in what he wrote.[54] Macmillan himself, in an otherwise unconvincing gloss on the book delivered as a lecture thirty years later, observed of it simply that 'it is along this line that the Tory tradition springs from the past and leads to the future'. This, rather than revolution, is the hallmark of *The Middle Way*.

. . .

IN THE WILDERNESS

The publication of *The Middle Way* was, though not a turning point in Macmillan's life, a convenient watershed for the historian. After 1938 the main theme of his political career was his reconciliation with Churchill and the Eden group of dissident Conservative M.P.s. Appeasement and rearmament were the main issues in his political repertoire, and in his disillusionment with the Conservative leadership he became an outspoken critic of Neville Chamberlain. These are the themes which begin the next chapter. The economic issues which he had made his own were of diminishing importance, both to him and to the political world at large. It is an appropriate point, therefore, at which to review the first stage of his political career.

In 1938 Macmillan was forty-four years old. He had entered Parliament at the age of thirty, and made an immediate impression. 'Janitor', one of the wittiest and occasionally most acute of commentators on politics in the later 1920s, wrote in 1927 that 'On the whole...if I had to "spot" the future leader of the Tory Party from the ranks of the Young Conservatives, my choice would fall...on Harold Macmillan.' This was for idiosyncratic but interesting reasons. Janitor made a neat comparison between Macmillan and Duff Cooper: 'Both joined the Brigade of Guards; both distinguished themselves rather unexpectedly in an uncongenial profession; and both have married Wives.' But Macmillan had been an unusually active constituency member, and moreover:

> In the House his reputation rests, not on a single effort, but on a sequence of thoughtful speeches, out of which emerges the germ of a constructive industrial policy. He knows his subjects. As a director of the famous publishing firm with which his family is associated, he is necessarily in contact with many of the business and industrial problems of the day; and having been A.D.C. to the Duke of Devonshire during his Canadian Governorship, he has some personal knowledge of the Empire.
>
> So sound a reputation has he made for himself in so brief a space, that to-day, when under-secretaryships fall vacant, people are beginning to mention his name as a candidate for office.[55]

But eleven years later he had not become even an under-secretary. Anthony Eden, who had entered Parliament only a year before (and quite failed to make an impact on 'Janitor') had already reached the Cabinet and resigned from it; R.A. Butler, who entered Parliament in 1929, had held two under-secretaryships in succession. Even Boothby, whose personal ambition was nullified by his epicurean tendencies, had come closer to the smell of power as Churchill's PPS at the Treasury. Macmillan was a political failure.

The historian must decide between his own account of his misfortune, which as outlined above was that he had deliberately chosen to pursue an unpopular principle and an unpopular attitude rather than grovel to the managers of his increasingly unsatisfactory party, and a more contingent explanation. The latter has the merit of explaining rather better than the former Macmillan's realistic and calculating attitude to political ideas. Under the second Baldwin administration, from 1924 to 1929, he behaved as a rationally ambitious politician should. He concentrated on his subject, worked on his parliamentary style, sought publicity in print as well as in the chamber, and attached himself firmly to a political patron. The choice of Churchill as a patron was, however, doubly unfortunate. Churchill's own unhappy relations with the large Tariff Reform element in the party forced him into increasingly tortuous manoeuvres after the government fell, culminating in a dramatic breach with Baldwin over India. This lurch to the Right left Macmillan without a patron. Any hope of restoring

relations was blighted by Boothby's presence in Churchill's co-
terie. On the other hand, Macmillan had singularly failed to
make an impression on Chamberlain, who was the rising star
in the party. The flirtation with Mosley's New Party was an
entirely natural response to frustration; his final rejection of it,
in favour of loyalty to the established Conservative Party, was a
rational decision which left scars.

During the 1930s it seemed clear that Macmillan could not
leave the Conservative Party, even if he had wanted to do so.
He was married, albeit unhappily, to a daughter of the Conservative establishment. He was a wealthy man, as he told Lord
Longford in 1938 in explanation of why he could not join a
Popular Front.[56] In the prejudiced but often very acute analysis
of 'Simon Haxey' in *Tory MP* Macmillan was identified as having 'shown on many occasions a vigorous independence and
respect for our democratic traditions',[57] by which the author
meant that he had spoken against appeasement, but he also
appeared as a railway director and as one of the six current and
nine former MPs related to the Cavendishes. The gravitational
force of these connections kept him loyal to the party, without guaranteeing him any preferment. His adventures across
party lines, with the Industrial Reorganisation League and especially with the Next Five Years group, were never intended
to detract from his political partisanship, and although circumstances forced him into conflict with the party's leaders,
especially Neville Chamberlain, these were not circumstances
of his own choosing. Macmillan in the 1930s was not so much
a natural rebel as a frustrated careerist, making outlets for his
natural energies. He was also unhappy in his private life, cuck-
olded by a former close friend and known in the Conservative
Party and in society at large as a conceited, rather introverted
bore.

.   .   .

NOTES AND REFERENCES

1. Harold Macmillan, *Winds of Change* (London: Macmillan, 1966), p. 129.
2. Ibid., pp. 140–6.
3. Ibid., p. 146.
4. Ibid., pp. 198–459.

5. Diary entry for 26 July 1926, in Stuart Ball (ed.), *Parliament and Politics in the Age of Baldwin and Macdonald: the Headlam Diaries 1924–1935* (London: The Historians' Press, 1993), p. 96; diary for 9 December, ibid., p. 107.
6. Compare R.K. Middlemas and J.A. Barnes, *Baldwin* (London: Weidenfeld and Nicolson, 1969), with Stuart Ball, *Baldwin and the Conservative Party* (London: Yale University Press, 1988).
7. *H.C. Debs.*, 1924–25, vol. 183, 30 April 1925, col. 405. The edited highlights of this speech in Macmillan, *Winds of Change*, pp. 206–7 give an impression of greater force and fluency than is apparent in the Hansard record.
8. Macmillan, *Winds of Change*, p. 220.
9. Stephen Koss, *The Rise and Fall of the Political Press in Britain Volume II: The Twentieth Century* (London: Hamish Hamilton, 1984), p. 455.
10. *H.C. Debs* 1926, vol. 189, 27 Sept. 1926, cols 305, 306.
11. *H.C. Debs* 1924–25, vol. 186, 6 July 1925, col. 181; ibid., vol. 199, 16 Nov. 1926, col. 1749.
12. Horne, *Macmillan 1894–1956*, pp. 82–3; see also Martin Gilbert, *Winston Churchill* Volume V (London: William Heinemann, 1976), pp. 242–97.
13. This was because there was already a scheme for agricultural rate relief.
14. Macmillan to Churchill, 11 Dec. 1927, Gilbert, *Winston Churchill*, V, 254.
15. TS note signed 'E.M.', 5 Nov. 1929, Beaverbrook Papers C/235. See *Winds of Change*, p. 240; Ball, *Baldwin*, pp. 160–2.
16. *Saturday Review*, 9 Nov. 1929.
17. As a junior minister Mosley had been assisting Tom Johnston and George Lansbury in devising proposals for the reduction of unemployment, and his memorandum had proposed the control of investment and foreign lending, and an emphasis on the home market.
18. Anthony Howard, *RAB. The Life of R.A. Butler* (London: Jonathan Cape, 1987), pp. 41–2.
19. Macmillan, *Winds of Change*, p. 247.
20. R.K. Middlemas, *Politics in Industrial Society* (London: André Deutsch, 1979).
21. Horne, *Macmillan 1894–1956*, pp. 84–90, 98.
22. Ibid., pp. 98–9.
23. Howard Gospel, 'Employer's Labour Policy: a study of the Mond–Turner talks', *Business History*, XXI (1979), 180–97; Michael Dintenfass, 'The Politics of Producers' Co-operation: the FBI–TUC–NCEO talks, 1929–1933' in John Turner (ed.), *Businessmen and Politics: studies of business activity in British politics 1900–1945* (London: Heinemann Educational, 1984), pp. 76–92.
24. L.P. Carpenter, 'Corporatism in Britain, 1930–1945', *Journal of Contemporary History*, XI (1976), 3–25.
25. Max Nicholson, 'The 1930s: Organisation, Structure, People', in John Pinder (ed.), *Fifty Years of Political and Economic Planning* (London: Heinemann Educational Books, 1981), p. 30.
26. Oliver Roskill, 'The 1930s: The Industries Group' in Pinder, *Fifty Years*, p. 64.

27. Headlam Diary, 18 July 1934, in Ball (ed.), *Parliament and Politics*, p. 308. The editor suggests that Headlam intended to render *hoi en telei*: 'those in authority'.
28. *Economist*, 7 Dec. 1929, p. 1073.
29. On productioneers see John Turner, 'The Politics of "Organised Business" in the First World War', in Turner (ed.), *Businessmen and Politics*, pp. 33–49; R.P.T. Davenport-Hines, *Dudley Docker* (Cambridge: Cambridge University Press, 1984), pp. 84–132.
30. Headlam Diary, 19 Dec. 1934, in Ball (ed.), *Parliament and Politics*, p. 317.
31. Correspondence and papers about this episode from 23 to 30 May 1935 are in PRO, Board of Trade papers, BT 64/10/IM1111.
32. Allen to Macmillan, 23 April 1932, Martin Gilbert, (ed.), *Plough My Own Furrow: the life of Lord Allen of Hurtwood* (London: Longmans, 1965), p. 255.
33. Ibid., p. 257.
34. Ibid., pp. 282–90.
35. Headlam Diary, 11 March 1934, in Ball (ed.), *Parliament and Politics*, p. 296.
36. Ibid., 3 June 1934, p. 304.
37. Principal of Ruskin College.
38. Especially *Recovery* (London: Bell, 1932).
39. Headlam Diary, 16 June 1935, Ball (ed.) *Parliament and Politics*, p. 333.
40. Macmillan, *Winds of Change*, p. 339; Gilbert (ed.), *Plough My Own Furrow*, pp. 304–9, 323.
41. Macmillan to Lloyd George, 22 Nov. 1935, House of Lords Record Office, Lloyd George Papers G/141/30/4.
42. Macmillan to Lloyd George, 16 Jan. 1937, Lloyd George Papers G/141/30/6.
43. Allen to 'a member of the Next Five Years Executive', 6 Feb. 1937 (misdated 1936), Gilbert (ed.), *Plough My Own Furrow*, p. 323.
44. Headlam Diary, 18 July 1934, 3 June 1934, Ball (ed.), *Parliament and Politics*, pp. 308, 304.
45. It was reprinted, with *The Middle Way: 20 Years After*, by Macmillan in 1966.
46. Macmillan, *The Middle Way*, p. 29.
47. Ibid., pp. 36, 37.
48. Ibid., pp. 187, 192–3.
49. Ibid., p. 257.
50. Ibid., pp. 289–90.
51. On which see Susan Howson and Donald Winch *The Economic Advisory Council* (Cambridge: Cambridge University Press, 1977).
52. Macmillan, *The Middle Way*, p. 300.
53. Ibid., p. 298.
54. Horne, *Macmillan 1894–1956*, p. 107.
55. Janitor, *The Feet of the Young Men* (London: Duckworth, 1928), pp. 39, 40.
56. Horne, *Macmillan 1894–1956*, p. 127, citing an interview with Lord Longford.

57. Simon Haxey (pseud.), *Tory MP* (London: Gollancz, 1937), p. 229. Haxey's work was 'A study of the personnel of the Tory Party and the opinions of leading Tories who have held the reigns of Government for eight years; its object is to show the true character of Toryism or Conservatism'. Though clearly partisan and published in the Left Book Club series, it is a valuable prosopographical source for the inter- war Conservative Party.

Chapter 3

THE SECOND WORLD WAR
1938–45

The Second World War dramatically put an end to the unproductive frictions of the 1930s, though not before the Chamberlain government had made an unsuccessful bid to carry on political business as usual. In 1940 the Conservative Party, which had dominated the Commons and the country since 1922, was forced to yield to a Coalition government in which Labour held a commanding position in home affairs. Within the party, Churchill's succession to the premiership restored a number of the political casualties of the 1930s to the eminence which they might have expected to enjoy but for Chamberlain's displeasure. Macmillan was one of these. As a supporter not only of the overthrow of Chamberlain but also of Churchill's succession, he was rewarded by his first taste of office, the Parliamentary Secretaryship at the Ministry of Supply. From there he moved on to the Colonial Office as a junior minister, where he took responsibility for the economic section. Finally he became a Minister of State with Cabinet rank (whatever that meant) as Minister Resident in Algeria, from January 1943. His political responsibilities finally extended to the whole of the Mediterranean theatre of war, and he was responsible for the political arrangements which brought the war to a close in Italy, Greece and Yugoslavia. This was a 'good war' for a middle-aged civilian, especially for one whose political ambition had for so long been thwarted. Although his own very full recollections concentrate on his achievements as a diplomatist, the more notable lesson of these five years is that he was able to establish a reputation for energy and organising ability in economic matters, concealed behind an ironical and patrician façade.

APPEASEMENT

In a political sense, Macmillan's war began with Appeasement. His rôle in the fall of Chamberlain was therefore important for his own career as much as for the history of politics. He was associated with a number of anti-Chamberlain groups within the House of Commons. The 'Eden group' in particular acted together after Munich, with Leopold Amery and Lord Cranborne prominent among its members, and Macmillan tried to act as a link between it and Churchill's more particular followers such as Duncan Sandys and Boothby. He also kept in touch with Chamberlain's Labour opponents, especially Hugh Dalton, and this led him naturally to co-operate with the all-party 'action group' convened by Boothby and Thomas Horabin, a Liberal, in the early part of the war. His public commitment as an anti-Munich Conservative came with his support for A.D. Lindsay, the anti-Munich Independent candidate, in the Oxford by-election of October 1938.

Yet the eruption of feeling after Munich had been long prepared. Macmillan's commitment to 'collective security' dated back at least to the Liberty and Democratic Leadership manifestos which he had signed in 1934, and which prepared the ground for the Next Five Years group. He had criticised the Hoare–Laval pact in 1935, on the ground that it nullified the League of Nations sanctions against Italian action in Abyssinia. When Hitler marched into the Rhineland in March 1936 he condemned Baldwin and MacDonald for 'elevat[ing] inactivity into a principle', and after a foreign affairs debate in June 1936, again over Abyssinia, he voted against the government and a week later resigned the Whip, which he was only to accept again a year later. By the time Chamberlain had been to Munich and abandoned the Czechs to their fate, Macmillan was recognised by the Whips as a 'habitual suspect' on foreign affairs, and a collaborator, albeit a somewhat distant collaborator, with Anthony Eden, who had become Foreign Secretary after Hoare's resignation in 1935 and had himself resigned in February 1938.

Macmillan's foreign policy views were closely linked with the economic proposals of *The Middle Way*: in a pamphlet on *The Price of Peace*, published in October 1938, he argued that the necessary armaments could only be produced by careful eco-nomic planning if they were not to disrupt the civilian econ-omy. This point was taken further in February 1939 in *Economic Aspects of Defence* which sold widely because of its relevance to the European crisis but whose main interest in retrospect is its powerful defence of industrial reconstruction, control of in-vestment, and state-backed foreign trade. In both pamphlets, and in the House of Commons, he emphasised the achieve-ment of the German government in reducing unemployment. He was one of only three Conservatives – the others being Churchill and Brendan Bracken – to vote against the govern-ment in a Liberal and Labour call for a Ministry of Supply in November 1938. By the middle of 1939 he had challenged the Chamberlain government's policy with a critique which was unusual both for its breadth and for its cogency.

Nevertheless, dissent was a forlorn road, and it was often dif-ficult for the dissidents to maintain coherence and determina-tion in the face of Chamberlain's relentless news management and large, loyal parliamentary majority. Despite the best efforts of Churchill and Eden the back-bench opposition to Chamber-lain's foreign policy was tiny, perhaps twenty reliable members compared with around eighty who consistently opposed the party leadership's India policy in the early 1930s. It was eas-ier to be right about Germany than to do anything to correct the government's errors, and many of the anti-appeasers were conscious that they had somehow to get back into office if they were going to achieve anything. Eden in particular seemed inhibited by his natural ambition to return to the Cabinet. Macmillan, having less to lose, was more outspoken, but his decision to accept the Whip again in June 1937 was a recogni-tion that no-one could stray too far from the Conservative Party and still hope to influence events. His practice of remaining somewhat closer to Eden than to Churchill was realistic. In later life Macmillan was to make much of the psychological gulf between supporters and opponents of Munich, as indeed was Eden, but in the last two years before the war the disparity in size between the pro and anti groups restrained the anti-appeasers from full-blooded action.

Macmillan himself was among the most energetic, espe-cially in October 1938, immediately after Munich, when he welcomed Duff Cooper's resignation and tried hard to set up what he called '1931 in reverse', with the Tory minority joining Labour in an anti-appeasement government. He approached Dalton on 3 October, after seeing Churchill, and got the friendly assent of Clement Attlee and Herbert Morrison for exploratory talks. But, as Eden pointed out, the arithmetic was wrong; Parliament was behind the government, and if Chamberlain went to the country he would be supported strongly, so there was nothing except destruction to be gained from splitting the Tory Party on that particular line of cleavage. Macmillan's hopes of reconstructing party politics were dashed.[1]

* * *

WAR

At the outbreak of war the Conservative dissidents stepped up their efforts, but in vain. Chamberlain's serenity was hardly disturbed by continual military and political failures, and the inclusion of Churchill in the government at the beginning of the war as First Lord of the Admiralty did little to cheer the critics, since they feared that he would be dragged down in the inevitable collapse. Like most of his political collaborators, Macmillan was confined to the back benches. He used up his energy in constituency work, Commons interventions on matters of industrial production and supply, and a semi-official mission in support of the Finnish government, which was negotiating for covert British support in its war against Russia.[2]

The collapse of British operations in Norway in early May 1940 precipitated action by the Conservative rebels. Macmillan was present at meetings of the Salisbury group, the 'Eden group' – now chaired by Amery – and the all-party group, all of which decided that the government must be brought down. The announcement that Churchill was to be 'spokesman' of all military departments in the War Cabinet did not deflect them, and Amery's Cromwellian appeal to Chamberlain on 7 May 1940 – 'In the name of God, go!' – precisely expressed Macmillan's view as he later recalled it. Macmillan did not speak in the debate; his main contribution was to urge, in a number of meetings of the dissident Conservatives, that Churchill rather than Halifax should be the next prime minister.

On assuming office Churchill constructed a ministry which included not only Labour and Liberal members, but also a broad range of Conservatives including Chamberlain and some of his closest supporters. He could hardly do otherwise, since few of the anti-appeasers were administratively experienced or competent and in any case it was important to maintain the unity of the party. Macmillan was offered a lowly office, the Parliamentary Secretaryship at the Ministry of Supply, working first under Herbert Morrison, then under Sir Andrew Duncan, and finally for a period under Beaverbrook. In the circumstances this was not a flattering appointment.

At first his rôle at the Ministry was to devil for his ministers and answer for them sometimes in Parliament; he would take on any job from the management of a glut in salvaged oily rags to the winkling out of unused drop-forging capacity in Manchester.[3] When Beaverbrook took over, in July 1941, Macmillan took full responsibility for representing Supply in the Commons. Although none of this gave him the independent executive responsibility which he wanted, he was fully occupied with administrative detail and gained an intimate knowledge of production problems. By the beginning of 1942 he was able to write a detailed proposal for the establishment of a Ministry of Production to take full responsibility, as a super-ministry, for all the factors of production and allocate them between all the producing departments. The aim was to overcome the handicap faced by the Ministry of Supply, which was the same as that faced by Lloyd George's Ministry of Munitions in the First World War: although Supply was responsible for equipping the army, the Admiralty jealously maintained its own production organisation and the supply of aircraft was in the hands of an independent Ministry of Aircraft Production. This would have involved integrating the control of manpower with the control of capital equipment and raw materials; it would have trodden on the toes of Ernest Bevin, the Minister of Labour; it was therefore politically unworkable. But the proposals were accepted, in a modified form, in February, and Beaverbrook became Minister of Production.[4]

Macmillan's work at the Ministry of Supply depended for its texture on the character of his successive ministers. Morrison, whom he respected as a politician but not as an administrator, left him alone to develop the machinery of industrial planning and the control of raw materials. Sir Andrew Duncan had greater administrative confidence but no political instinct, and Macmillan's growing competence in the House of

Commons began to yield results. Beaverbrook was an elemental force, who applied to the Ministry of Supply the energy, though rather less of the genius, which Lloyd George had applied to the Ministry of Munitions in the previous war. Because Beaverbrook sat in the Lords, Macmillan had full responsibility for representing the department in the Commons, and this he finally came to enjoy. The job expanded after Russia's entry into the war in June 1941. Because Beaverbrook, unlike his predecessors, had the will and the capacity to spend time abroad in high-level negotiation, Macmillan assumed more and more responsibility for the running of the department. These valuable experiences, which of course complemented what he had already learned as a businessman, confirmed Macmillan's confidence in his own abilities. In addition, they exposed him to senior politicians. Morrison, after a pounding received from Macmillan during the post-war debates over steel nationalisation, eventually turned against him. Beaverbrook, too, found himself in the 1950s horrified at the changes Macmillan was making in Conservative policies. Both men, even so, claimed to have recognised in their Parliamentary Secretary a considerable administrative and political talent, and Macmillan was one of many younger politicians who found themselves having to make a conscious effort to resist Beaverbrook's undoubted personal magnetism.

Macmillan's reward for his work at Supply and his part in designing the new Ministry of Production was a Privy Councillorship and a transfer to the Colonial Office. The Minister of Production was given no Parliamentary Secretary, and since Sir Andrew Duncan was chosen to return to Supply from the Board of Trade, Macmillan could not find a parliamentary rôle there. The Colonial Office, where Lord Moyne was Secretary of State, provided a convenient opening. Three weeks after Macmillan's arrival Moyne was replaced in a Cabinet reshuffle by Macmillan's old friend Lord Cranborne,[5] and in a working relationship which lasted nine months Macmillan took on the economic organisation of the colonial empire. The main object was to increase Empire production of strategic materials such as rubber, tin and wolfram, and of vital food products such as palm oil and peanuts, and to arrange trade in these commodities so as to use scarce shipping most effectively. Macmillan, who later admitted freely that his 'knowledge of the Colonies was very limited',[6] simply applied, with considerable success, the methods he had learned in the Ministry of Supply. Imperial economic contributions to the war effort did improve,[7] and at the same time the Colonial Office took some preliminary steps towards economic reconstruction of the colonies after the war, with discussions – never in the event to come to anything – on land reform in East Africa and industrial development elsewhere. This stage in Macmillan's rise ended when Oliver Stanley was appointed to succeed Cranborne.[8] Preferring not to serve under a member of the House of Commons, Macmillan contemplated resignation but was dissuaded by Churchill's confidant, Brendan Bracken. Within a month he had been invited to take on a new rôle as Minister of State in Algiers, sent to influence the North African campaign and the evolution of French politics in the liberated territories in the directions determined by British interests. He was the prime minister's second choice, after Harry Crookshank.[9]

. . .

NORTH AFRICA

Macmillan began his new mission with enthusiasm. As he later wrote, 'Although neither I nor the Prime Minister had really the slightest idea what I was going to do, I would do it with the utmost diligence and perseverance.' Within days of the appointment Admiral Darlan, the representative of Vichy France who had become the effective civilian authority in Algeria under Allied occupation, was assassinated by a sympathiser with the Free French. Macmillan's immediate reaction was to fear that 'the fact that Darlan had been eliminated might so simplify the French situation that a new Minister would not be needed'. Fortunately there was no prospect of simplifying French politics-in-exile, and the rôle of the Minister of State expanded steadily. Besides acting as a buffer between Churchill, the American government and de Gaulle, until de Gaulle was installed, in August 1944, as *de facto* leader of the provisional government of a liberated France, Macmillan managed the transfer of power from the invading forces to a pro-Allied government in Italy, and also exercised local political control over the liberation of Greece in 1944 and British intervention in the Greek rebellion. Finally, he was responsible for British policy in the Balkans, where British, French, American, Soviet and Yugoslav forces were fighting alongside one another by the Austrian border and in the Venezia Giulia. Here, in a brief encounter with the problem of anti-communist Cossack prisoners of war, he became involved with the 'Klagenfurt conspiracy' which has overshadowed discussion of his activities in the Mediterranean theatre.[10] For most of the time, his work in the Mediterranean was coloured by the need to align British and American policy in a theatre of war whose political complexity increased as its military significance declined.

The problem of France occasioned Macmillan's mission to Algeria and dominated his first year's activity. After the surrender of the French army on 22 June 1940, the Germans had divided France into an Occupied Zone under German military government and an Unoccupied Zone in the south, which from July 1940 was governed from Vichy by a new administration under Marshal Pétain. General Charles de Gaulle, who had been a junior defence minister in the last independent French administration, left France on 18 June and launched the Provisional French National Committee, which stood for the continuance of the war and was supported by the British government. De Gaulle's 'Free French' won the support of the administrations of some of France's minor colonies, but the major settlements of West and North Africa, and the French mandated territory in Syria, resisted temptation: their governors took the view that the Vichy regime was the legitimate government of France. An assault on Dakar in September 1940, supported by the British, was a failure. In February 1942 another combined operation, against Syria and the Lebanon, succeeded, and Madagascar was invaded by British troops in May 1942. By this time the Vichy regime and the Free French were deadly enemies. The emergence of Admiral Darlan as Vice-President and Foreign Minister at Vichy was an important development. He was much more inclined than Pétain to co-operate with Germany – it was at his instance that Vichy agreed to the operation of German and Italian forces from Syria, which precipitated the Allied attack in 1942 – and he was associated with the introduction in Vichy France of repressive and anti-semitic legislation, to conform to German policy.

Vichy had no diplomatic relations with Britain, but until December 1941 the United States maintained an ambassador to the Pétain government, and afterwards retained some hope that Vichy would eventually co-operate in the liberation of metropolitan France. Correspondingly, the Americans were suspicious of de Gaulle. The Allied landings in North Africa in November 1942, the main purpose of which was to eliminate German and Italian troops from Libya and Tunisia, were commanded by an American, General Eisenhower, even though most of the troops involved were British. The Americans had insisted that de Gaulle's forces be excluded from the campaign, and indeed even from its planning, on the grounds that French colonial administrations who were still attached to Vichy detested the Free French and were more likely to co-operate if a different French figure were available. Their choice had fallen on General Giraud, a cavalry commander who had recently escaped from a German prison camp and who had no connection with either Vichy or the Free French.

After the landings, which were resisted by French forces in Algeria, Giraud was spurned by the local French commanders, and the Allies found themselves dealing with Admiral Darlan, who was by chance in Algiers when the landings took place. An agreement was quickly reached, and Darlan ordered a general cease-fire in North Africa and assumed control of all French forces and civil administration in the area. He also ordered the French fleet at Toulon to join the Allies. At this point, fearing the collapse of their hegemony in southern France, the Germans occupied the Vichy area, sent troops to Tunisia (then controlled by Vichy) and forced Pétain to repudiate Darlan. The naval commander at Toulon, though hostile to the British, scuttled his ships rather than let them fall into German hands. De Gaulle, already bitterly offended by his exclusion from the planning of the campaign, was cut to the quick by the deal with Darlan, and refused to co-operate with Allied forces in North Africa until the 'guilty men' were eliminated.

The agreement with Darlan had caused bitterness in both Britain and the United States, where public opinion tended to share de Gaulle's view of Frenchmen who collaborated with Germany. The British government was attacked in Parliament, and a Secret Session on 11 December required all Churchill's powers of persuasion.[11] Churchill was particularly concerned to retain the support of the Americans in the Mediterranean, and therefore did not wish to fall out with them. Nevertheless, de Gaulle's forces had a great and growing potential in the overseas colonies, and his support was also important. On Christmas Eve, 1942 Darlan was assassinated. This cleared the air somewhat, but it was soon obvious that where there had once been two French factions at daggers drawn, there were now three: the Free French, the Vichy regime and its supporters in France, and the colonial administrators and military and naval officers in North Africa who believed that the Darlan agreement, and only that agreement, had legitimated their repudiation of Vichy and their co-operation with the Allies.

It was Macmillan's unenviable job to bring about a political settlement in French North Africa which would serve Britain's ends in both the long and the short term. After getting rid of the Comte de Paris, who showed some signs of introducing a fourth warring element by launching a Royalist campaign, he began to work for an agreement between de Gaulle and Giraud. At first, although his presence in Algiers and regular intercourse with assorted French officers and politicians was important, the initiative lay higher up. At the Casablanca Conference (15–29 January 1943) Roosevelt and Churchill spent some time trying to resolve their own differences about the future of French politics, and it was at Casablanca, after considerable effort, that de Gaulle and Giraud were persuaded to shake hands in public, though de Gaulle did not get the recognition he wanted as an equal participant in Algerian government.[12]

In March, acting with Robert Murphy, President Roosevelt's political representative in North Africa, Macmillan managed to get Giraud to accept Gaullist representatives into his 'Comité de Guerre', which was in effect to be the core of a reunified French resistance to Germany, in which de Gaulle's French National Committee, based in London, would participate in a single government-in-exile. His next move was to secure the allegiance of 'Force X', a detachment of the French fleet interned in Alexandria harbour. The final arrangements, both for the fleet and the political union, took until the end of July, with numerous resignations and counter-resignations on the part of de Gaulle, Giraud and their followers; by 26 August, de Gaulle was prime minister of a single, unified French government-in-exile which had been recognised by Britain and, more reluctantly, by the United States. This outcome, the French National Committee of Liberation, owed a great deal to Macmillan's diplomatic skill and his willingness to 'interpret' his instructions from Churchill and the Foreign Office. The affair also gave him important personal contacts with de Gaulle and Jean Monnet, which he was to use later when managing Britain's policy towards the European Economic Community.

Macmillan had by now made himself an important figure in inter-Allied politics, taking initiatives without undue concern for the torrent of instructions which emerged from Churchill and Anthony Eden, the Foreign Secretary. His exchanges with London over Force X are particularly revealing. His plan was to force the commander, Admiral Godfroy, to acknowledge Giraud's authority as the legitimate head of the French state by ensuring that the subsidies advanced to Godfroy by the Allies were henceforth paid through Giraud. Godfroy, though a devoted Anglophile and hater of Germans, was inclined to stand on the letter of his loyalty to the regime in Vichy. Macmillan finally persuaded him that Pétain was no longer a free agent and therefore that the French state was now in other hands; meanwhile he had authorised the payment of a small subsidy through Giraud before Godfroy's agreement was confirmed. Churchill exploded.

Prime Minister to Minister Resident, Algiers, 12 April 1943 [telegram]
What you propose is exact opposite of what was explained, through you, to Giraud in my telegram.... No pay of any kind should reach recalcitrant squadron...until they definitely come over to Giraud.

Minister Resident to Foreign Office 4 May 1943
From your telegram[s].... I judge that you consider that I have not followed out the plan agreed on....
I am afraid Admiral Godfroy will never rally in the full-blooded sense of that word. The most that he could do would be to make dainty and decorous approaches in the nature of the steps of a minuet. I think he has already taken steps in the direction of his partner and is in fact committed.... Throughout all this I have had not as much help as one might have expected from our Ally, partially because – quite frankly – State Department policy has been vacillating, obscure, and none too straightforward. I cannot believe, therefore, that it would be wise at this juncture to risk throwing away all that we have achieved, largely by our own efforts, by quarrelling with Giraud on this comparatively minor point.[13]

Churchill continued to grumble, but Macmillan's policy was vindicated.

. . .

ITALY

The peculiarity of Macmillan's position became more evident as the North African campaign was concluded (on 13 May, with the surrender of all German and Italian forces in Tunisia) and Allied attention turned to the invasion of Sicily. He had originally been sent to establish an arm's-length relationship with Allied Force Headquarters (AFHQ) the military body which had planned and executed the Torch campaign in North Africa with Eisenhower as supreme commander. His job was to give political advice to the commanders on the spot and to represent the British government with ministerial authority. In practice he had become a skilled mediator between the commanders in North Africa and their masters in London and Washington. 'London' was an entity in which there were some conflicts of view between Churchill, Eden at the Foreign Office and the War Office planners; but the manipulation of 'London' was relatively simple when compared with the problem of 'Washington', where conflicts between the State Department, the War Department and the White House were endemic, with all three elements becoming involved in the political work of dealing with the French in North Africa and, later, the Italians in Sicily and on the mainland. A typical episode in June 1943 illustrates the nature of Macmillan's job:

> General Eisenhower showed me some further telegrams from the President, and I showed him mine from the P.M. General Eisenhower then said, 'What do you think I should do?' I said, that as he observed from my telegrams, my instructions were to give him absolute support in carrying out the President's instructions. He said, 'Oh yes. But as a friend, what would you advise me to do?' I said that was quite a different question, and that I thought we might interpret these instructions in our own way. Finally he sent a very sensible reply to the President, which he dictated in front of us. He asked me to suggest amendments, and I made a few.[14]

The meeting was attended only by Macmillan, Robert Murphy, Roosevelt's own representative, and General Walter Bedell Smith, Eisenhower's Chief of Staff.

Macmillan's influence over events in the Mediterranean theatre was increased as the invasion of Sicily got under way. The landings were commanded by a British officer, General Sir Harold Alexander, with whom Macmillan had a close and admiring relationship. As the campaign proceeded AFHQ developed a more prominent rôle in the Mediterranean, which was not diminished even when Eisenhower left the theatre (to take over command of the operations in north-west Europe) and was replaced by General Sir Henry Maitland Wilson ('Jumbo'), with whom Macmillan also struck up a good relationship, despite having pushed Alexander for the job. Increasingly Macmillan's claim to influence was his ability to understand and work with the Americans, a skill which was especially important as the purely British command in Cairo, which had its own Minister Resident, became less influential.

Macmillan's readiness to stretch his instructions was demonstrated to even greater effect during negotiations for the surrender of Italy. Allied forces landed in Sicily on 10 July 1943. On 25 July it was learned that Mussolini had stepped down, to be replaced by Marshal Badoglio; it was later discovered that he had done so after the Germans had refused to promise to defend Italy south of the River Po. The immediate priority for the Allies was to persuade the new Italian government to join the war against Germany, thus reversing the existing balance of forces in the Italian peninsula. The British and American governments wanted to impose comprehensive peace terms on Italy; the local commanders and Macmillan, as the local political adviser, wanted a quick and acceptable armistice to prevent the need for a costly invasion of the mainland. In the midst of a seven-way telegraphic correspondence, a policy was worked out during July and August. Macmillan's experience of balancing military and political needs in liberated territories was evident from the first: early in the turmoil he reflected that 'if the King and Badoglio do *not* within a few days ask for an armistice, we can get up a real revolution in Italy against them. But it would suit us better *not* to be stimulators of revolution, which we shall only have to suppress later.'[15] Negotiations were carried on through the British Embassy in Lisbon and in direct conversation between Italian and Allied officers at the Allied headquarters in Palermo, and an armistice signed on 3 September. Meanwhile German forces had been rushed to Italy, so that on 8 September Badoglio's government tried to postpone the armistice, but this was firmly squashed and on the same day Allied forces landed at Salerno, opposed by German but not by Italian troops. Macmillan described the armistice as 'the biggest bluff in history'.[16]

Badoglio's government left Rome for Brindisi on 9 September,taking with it the king and the crown prince but leaving behind much of the civilian administration; Macmillan's task was to define Allied relations with this government. Eventually it was decided to impose the 'long terms' which had been drawn up by the Allied governments in July as an Instrument of Surrender. Badoglio accepted them, with some reluctance, at the end of September, and Italy henceforth had 'co-belligerent' status with Britain, France and the United States – an indication of being on the same side in the war against Germany without the benefit of a full military alliance.

These negotiations were delicate and exhausting in the short term, but the long term held the greater difficulties. Macmillan wanted an early and complete return to an 'indirect rule' through a properly constituted Italian administration, while the Americans at first preferred to govern directly through an Allied Military Government in Occupied Territory (AMGOT). It was later agreed that AMGOT should be confined to the area immediately behind the advancing armies, with an Allied Control Commission to support local administrations indirectly in areas further to the rear. The problem of establishing a legitimate and stable government in the Control Commission area was not straightforward. The American government wanted to force the King of Italy into abdication; Macmillan and the British government did not. Macmillan also feared the growing influence of the Communist Party, a fear compounded by the unilateral action of the Soviet Union in exchanging diplomatic representatives with the Italian government in March 1944. King Victor Emmanuel was forced to abdicate in April, after a stiff interview with Macmillan, and it was learned with considerable relief on 21 April that 'an infant government had definitely come into the world and was expected to live. The P.M. will be pleased because Badoglio remains P.M. and Foreign Secretary.... Moreover, the Interior [Minister] is a Christian Democrat (moderate), *not* a Communist.'[17] Even so, he was dissatisfied with the general drift of policy. He believed that Eden and the Foreign Office were inclined to be harsh with the Italians out of a sense of retribution, while he preferred 'a positive policy based upon the desire to rescue the Italian people and help them to preserve their general social, economic and religious life, and thus prevent them, perhaps, from falling into the hands either of the extreme Communist movement on the one hand or of Fascist reaction on the other.'[18]

By now his responsibilities extended beyond France and southern Italy. In December 1943 the Allied military commands in the Middle East and North Africa were unified (under 'Jumbo' Wilson) and Macmillan took over political responsibility for the whole area, relinquishing the embryonic French state to Duff Cooper who became Minister Resident in Algiers. Just as the Italian situation took a further twist in June, with the enforced retirement of Marshal Badoglio in favour of Bonomi, Macmillan took on the political problems of Yugoslavia and Greece. In Yugoslavia Marshal Tito's (communist) partisans were fighting the Germans and also the (Royalist) Chetnik underground forces under Mihailovic. The Chetniks, an exclusively Serbian group, were supported by the Americans, but not by the British who suspected them of collaborating with the Germans and Italians in their campaign against Tito. Macmillan proposed to repeat the pattern of negotiation he had adopted with the French and the Italians. He would allow the rival groups to wrangle with one another until they sought help from the Allies, while making it difficult for either side to get what it wanted without Allied help. This angered Eden, who by the middle of 1944 had determined to reduce Macmillan's independent political activity in the Mediterranean.

Eden's antipathy was hardly surprising, and it was reciprocated. Macmillan had earlier complained of the 'very tired and very unimaginative' policies of the Foreign Office and insisted that 'I am not an ambassador, and am not the servant of Mr Eden, or the P.M., or anyone else.'[19] In early 1944 most of the tension between Macmillan and London concerned French politics, and relations between Churchill and Macmillan were strained, the prime minister being heard to urge General Wilson to 'Keep Harold up to the mark. He is much too pro-French. He will not carry out my policy or my wishes. I rely on *you*.'[20] The success of Macmillan's activity in Italy, and the steady consolidation of French politics, improved his stock with the prime minister, but Eden was not consoled. In June 1944 Macmillan visited London briefly to discuss the next stage in the Mediterranean campaign – whether to attack in southern France or north-east Italy – and found Eden and the Foreign Office very hostile, and Churchill very friendly. In a farewell visit to the Foreign Secretary he found Eden 'still adamant, and he seems to think I want to be Foreign Secretary everywhere. I quite see his point of view; I told him, frankly, that if I were Foreign Secretary I would secure the immediate liquidation of all Ministers Resident wherever and whoever they might be.'[21] This clearly struck Eden as a good idea, for in August he sent his private secretary, Pierson Dixon, to Italy with that very aim. Macmillan's response was to 'resent being got out by the back door, and I have told Bob Dixon so. I shall now fight for my position to the bitter end.' He succeeded, by persuading Churchill that he and not Sir Noel Charles, the ambassador to the Italian Government, should take responsibility for the Allied Control Commission.[22]

. . .

YUGOSLAVIA AND GREECE

Yugoslavia and Greece were now the most taxing problems. Macmillan wanted Dr Subasic, the exiled Ban (Governor) of Croatia and a Royalist, to be allowed to come to an agreement with Tito to merge the Royalist army with the partisans, and encouraged Subasic to return to Yugoslavia to try to form a political combination. In Greece, the main problem was to re-turn the *emigré* government of Papandreou to Athens as soon as the German army was out of the way, to prevent a vacuum of power which might be filled by the communist partisans in the ELAS resistance movement. Papandreou's government included representatives of communist, socialist and miscella-neous bourgeois parties. As with Yugoslavia and Italy, the ten-sion between Royalist and anti-Royalist parties was already evi-dent, and although London was, as usual, broadly sympathetic to monarchy as a principle, Macmillan was concerned to keep both the King and the Crown Prince of Greece out of Greek affairs. The basis for co-operation with Papandreou was that, although he was a socialist, as a Greek nationalist he was deter-mined to resist 'Slavic' – Soviet – aggression in the Balkans. He was therefore willing to take a firm line against the resistance movement which in both its manifestations – the political Na-tional Liberation Front (EAM) and the paramilitary National Liberation Army (ELAS) – was dominated like many European resistance movements by the Communist Party (KKE).[23]

In October the Papandreou government was taken to Athens in a British flotilla to re-enter Greece, formally under British military protection. Macmillan accompanied them, and im-mediately began work to stabilise the Greek currency and disarm the communist guerrilla forces in areas evacuated by the Germans. He was to be engaged in this characteristic rôle of civilian manager of war for the rest of the year. The currency was stabilised on 11 November and the new National Guard planned; but on 3 December civil war began with the withdrawal of communist politicians from the Papandreou government and a major riot in Athens. British troops supported the Papandreou government, to the horror of the Americans and of the House of Commons. Macmillan, by chance, was in England during the debate, and recorded his view that 'If we yield now, we shall be committing the first act of appeasement in the liberated countries to the Fascism of the left.'[24]

The Greek civil war did play an important part in the evolution of the Cold War, and the eventual success of the (Labour) government in persuading President Truman to extend the 'Truman doctrine' to Greece in 1947 helped to align the territorial division of Europe into 'spheres of influence' with the ideological division between Communism and the Western world. Macmillan's foresight reflects the depth of experience he had gained in the complex and fast-moving politics of the Mediterranean war. His remarks also reflect a well-rooted suspicion of the United States and of some opinion-makers in Britain, which had grown during his efforts to make a useful settlement in Italy and were now brought into the open. His dismay at the apparent perversities of American policy had begun in Algiers. When Anglo-American co-operation worked, as it sometimes had done during the reconstruction of the French polity-in-exile, he found it an enormously powerful political weapon, and he was keen to protect it from muddles imposed from afar by the Foreign Office. A change of personnel in Washington, bringing Edward Stettinius to the State Department, reinforced a streak in American diplomatic activity at all levels which was profoundly suspicious of the British Empire and also of Britain's apparent sympathy for the tattered remnants of the European royal houses. Macmillan was criticised by the Americans for encouraging British military action in the oppression of Greek resistance fighters, and for supporting a Regency, and he realised that American sympathy for his approach to Mediterranean politics would always be limited. While negotiating with the Greek factions in late December 1944 he noted that 'the President has let us down badly',[25] and he frequently had occasion to complain of the over-organisation, and consequent inefficiency, of the American political presence in Italy. Afterwards he always emphasised the importance of Anglo-American co-operation, but took care to represent himself as a skilled craftsman working with a particularly obdurate material to achieve good results.

Even with his determination to take a flexible view of the possible outcome of Greek factionalism, Macmillan found it hard to bring about an orderly settlement, and at various points had to bring in reinforcements in the shape of the army and Churchill. He returned to Greece on 11 December, to find the rebels holding more than four-fifths of Athens, including the port, the power station and the water supply, and also the commanding positions in the hills around the city. With Rex Leeper, the Ambassador, he resolved on the plan of making Archbishop Damaskinos into a Regent for King George of Greece, who was in London. The king objected, and Macmillan, with Leeper and General Scobie, the C-in-C, spent many hours persuading Papandreou to tender formal advice to induce George to change his mind. By 17 December he was recording in his diary that 'It is clear that the politicians have double-crossed us (and each other) completely',[26] but the ingenuity of squabbling politicians was steadily overhauled by Macmillan's counter-ingenuity and the exercise of considerable force by the army and the RAF, which used rocket and machine-gun fire against the rebels in Athens to expand the area in which the British writ could run.

On Christmas Day Churchill and Eden arrived to meet Damaskinos, and after an initially difficult interview Macmillan was able to overcome Churchill's suspicion of an arrangement which appeared to attack the interests of the monarch. The Archbishop became Regent; General Plastiras, a robust former dictator, became prime minister of a coalition government including the Royalist and Venizelist parties together with some Liberals, Progressives and indeed most of the non-communist factions with the exception of some socialists sympathetic to ELAS and EAM. This gave Macmillan, now commuting between Greece and Italy to oversee his many responsibilities in the Mediterranean, an unparalleled opportunity to exercise his skills in writing political comedy, which can be read in his *War Diaries*. It also exercised his political talent to restrain Plastiras from counter-revolutionary excesses, such as imposing his will through former associates who had been involved in the anti-communist 'Security Battalions', which were tainted by association with the German occupation. The ultimate purpose was to arrange a truce between the government and EAM/ELAS, which required an amnesty for political offences committed since 3 December 1944. This was finally consummated in the early hours of 12 February 1945, and blessed by a conference between Churchill and the Greek government two days later. Though much credit is due to Leeper and to General Alexander, the resolution of the immediate crisis in Greece was Macmillan's greatest political achievement up to that date, and contributed much to his political self-confidence.

Attention now turned to the northern Adriatic, where the political problem of liberating Europe flowed even more directly into the political problem of the Cold War. Greece and Italy, and to some extent France, posed difficulties for the British and American governments because the best-organised elements of the resistance movements were the communist partisans. To avoid communist domination of the post-war regimes, the liberating armies were therefore obliged to make deals with anti-communist elements in the resistance movements and even with politicians and groups with a record of collaboration with Germany. In France and Italy this was successful, though it was not without complications. In Greece, the complications were not resolved without considerable bloodshed, but the result attained by February 1945 was generally satisfactory to British policy. These were Macmillan's main political achievements as Minister Resident. By contrast, Russian policymakers concerned with the areas of Eastern Europe liberated by the Russian armies were equally determined to impose an acceptable post-war regime, and lacked any inhibition about using considerable force against political opponents, including civilians, to impose communist governments. The Yalta agreements of 4–11 February 1945 embodied high-flown resolutions about the independence of a liberated Europe, and did not acknowledge the Soviet Union's full territorial claims in Eastern Europe. Within a month the Russian armies had imposed communist-dominated regimes in Bulgaria, Romania and Hungary, while the Czechoslovak government was forced to accept more communist members. Britain and America were powerless to prevent these developments, much as the Russians had been unable to prevent the temporary effacement of communism in Italy.

In north-east Italy and Austria, though, the Western Allies had substantial forces deployed, and confronted the communist Yugoslav partisans led by Tito, who was determined to expand his sphere of operations to the province of Venezia Giulia and even into Austria. Russian forces, pushing German troops back across a wide front in Eastern Europe, arrived in Austria themselves, and the competing liberators found themselves side by side. The crisis blew up suddenly after German forces surrendered to Alexander on 2 May 1945, though the problem of Tito's territorial claims to areas inhabited by ethnic Slavs had been recognised since 1943. On 4 May Macmillan noted in his diary that 'a fresh headache is developing – Yugoslav armies are advancing into Venezia Giulia and Austria – in a fierce race with the Eighth Army'.[27] With 'as usual ... only vacillation or silence' from the British and American governments, Macmillan and Alexander had to devise a practicable scheme to contain the situation. Macmillan had previously wanted to negotiate a military settlement with Tito, holding over any discussion of political sovereignty until after the war, but with the war in Europe now over he had no choice but to look for a political settlement. On 10 May Macmillan and Alexander received Tito's proposals, which assumed that all territory east of the River Isonzo belonged to Yugoslavia. This, with the implication that Italian claims to sovereignty over Trieste would have to be abandoned, posed an acute political problem. With Togliatti, the Italian communist leader, supporting Yugoslav claims to the Venezia Giulia, there was a full-scale political crisis in Rome, threatening the existence of the Bonomi government, whose inherent instability Macmillan had foretold when it overthrew Badoglio in June 1944. To nip trouble in the bud, Alexander referred the matter to the British and American governments (on the grounds that Tito had turned a military question into a political one) and ordered his staff to estimate the forces needed to drive Yugoslav troops out of the Venezia Giulia.

This was another episode of political untidiness created partly by political scheming and partly by military necessity. In 1944 the Allied troops advancing in northern Italy had to choose between going westwards or eastwards round the Alps to enter Germany. The westward method, finally adopted, was Operation Anvil, which was eventually chosen by the Allied governments partly in response to Stalin's desire that Anglo-American offensives should tie down German troops as far to the west as possible. The other proposal, known inelegantly as Operation Armpit, was favoured by Alexander and Macmillan, and would have sent an Anglo-American force north-eastwards through the Venezia Giulia and through the 'Ljubljana Gap' towards Vienna. The decision to give 'priority' to Anvil removed four American and four French divisions from Alexander's forces by the middle of 1944. The result of this decision was that, at the end of hostilities with Germany, British forces in Venezia Giulia were outnumbered by the partisans. To make matters worse, the British forces which had finally moved forward into Austria to occupy the British Zone agreed at Yalta found themselves jostling with Russian troops who spilled over rather too readily into the British Zone, and another arm of Tito's forces which had raced into Carinthia with thirty or forty thousand troops in an attempt to seize Klagenfurt. Russian forces were known to have installed heavy anti-aircraft emplacements in their own zone even after the Luftwaffe had ceased operations on the Eastern Front. With the Germans defeated (but not, unfortunately, out of the way), the full complexity of the situation was dropped into Macmillan's experienced hands.

Because Macmillan was plucked from the middle of this situation to return home as Secretary of State for Air, he was unable to follow through the political developments which resulted: a treaty provision of 1947 giving most of Venezia Giulia to Yugoslavia, and a settlement in 1954 ending the partition of Trieste, which became an Italian city. He is therefore remembered less for his small contribution to balancing relations between Tito and the Italian government than for his efforts to solve the immediate military problem for Alexander. The commander of the Eighth Army needed safe lines of communication from northern Italy to his advanced positions in Austria, in case he had to fight either Yugoslavs or, in the most extreme circumstances, Russians, to preserve the British presence in Austria. So long as Tito's partisans held the hinterland of Trieste, his operations in Austria could be endangered, which was why he had attempted to make a military deal with Tito. Furthermore, it was not certain that the rank and file of the Eighth Army would cheerfully set upon the Yugoslavs when ordered to do so, now that the European war was over. The availability of American forces was in doubt, because Washington changed its mind frequently about its priorities. Against this background of confusion and changing priorities, Alexander and Macmillan had to make the best of their options. An entry in Macmillan's diary for 13 May 1945 records a problem and its resolution on a brief visit to the Klagenfurt headquarters of the British V Corps:

> ...in addition to the Yugoslavs, to the order of 30,000 to 40,000, General Keightley has to deal with nearly 400,000 surrendered or surrendering Germans, not yet disarmed (except as to tanks and guns) who must be shepherded into some place or other, fed and given camps, etc. On his right flank Marshal Tolbukhin's armies have spread into what is supposed to be the British zone in Austria, including the important city and road centre of Graz. With the Russians are considerable Bulgar forces. Moreover, among the surrendered Germans are about 40,000 Cossacks and 'White' Russians, with their wives and children. To hand them over to the Russians is condemning them to slavery, torture and probably death. To refuse, is deeply to offend the Russians, and incidentally break the Yalta agreement. We have decided to hand them over...but I suggested that the Russians should at the same time give us any British prisoners or wounded who may be in his area....
>
> To add to the confusion, thousands of so-called Ustashi or Chetniks, mostly with wives and children, are fleeing in panic into this area in front of the advancing Yugoslavs. These expressions, Ustashi and Chetnik, cover anything from guerrilla forces raised by the Germans from Slovenes and Croats and Serbs to fight Tito, and armed and maintained by the Germans – to people who, either because they are Roman Catholics or Conservative in politics, or for whatever cause are out of sympathy with revolutionary Communism and therefore labelled as Fascists or Nazis. (This is a very simple formula, which in a modified form is being tried, I observe, in English politics).[28]

The 40,000 Russians among the German prisoners were a very mixed bag. Some were prisoners taken on the Eastern Front who had volunteered to fight against the Soviet Union. Many of these were part of the Russian National Army, led by General Vlasov; there was also a Cossack Corps. Others were *emigrés* who had left Russia during or after the Civil War and joined the German army either as individuals or in organised formations such as the Rogozhin Corps, which had fought against Tito in Yugoslavia. Some were Russians only in the sense that they had fled from the Russian invasion of the Baltic States, or that they originated from parts of prewar Poland which were to be transferred to Russia under the Yalta agreements. The Western Powers had agreed at Yalta to repatriate only 'Soviet citizens', and these were defined as 'persons coming from places within the boundaries of the Soviet Union as constituted before the outbreak of the present war'; the Foreign Office confined this definition further by excluding White Russian *emigrés*, who had left between 1917 and 1939, from Soviet citizenship. Enormous controversy arose at the end of Macmillan's life because among the Cossacks and White Russians handed over to the Russians were a number of these *emigrés*, accompanied by their wives and children. Nikolai Tolstoy has explicitly alleged that Macmillan deliberately engineered this outcome, and in so doing misled Alexander and other senior British officers.[29] Moreover, British troops were also handing over anti-communist Yugoslavs, in all their varieties, to Tito, and Tolstoy has held Macmillan responsible for their ultimate fate.

These episodes have received a great deal of scholarly attention, quite apart from polemics and litigation. The official biography gives Macmillan the benefit of the doubt, arguing that although he almost certainly consented to the wholesale transfer of Russians, including White Russian *emigrés*, into Soviet hands, he neither initiated the process nor consciously frustrated the intentions of the Yalta agreements, which had been to protect the old *emigrés*. Macmillan himself is quoted as remarking robustly that 'I may well have said "we'd better send them all back"...' and to have been prepared to take the blame for sending them back by mistake, but not for a deliberate conspiratorial plot to send innocents to their deaths.[30] This interpretation is entirely compatible with the conclusions reached by independent scholars working on the tangled military and political history of operations by V Corps in Austria. Historians also emphasise the hurry with which decisions had to be taken: Macmillan's visit to Keightley allowed no more than thirty minutes' discussion of the problem of dealing with prisoners of war.[31] None of Macmillan's critics can explain why he should have wanted to increase the slaughter deliberately, nor why he would have deceived Alexander in order to do so.

In the event the first priority was to reduce British responsibilities for feeding and clothing prisoners of war, and in the case of the Yugoslav Chetniks, to remove from British lines of communication a large body of doubtful individuals towards whom the British (at any level from field commanders to the Foreign Office) felt no pressing political or moral obligations. Both the White Russians and the Yugoslav right-wingers had fought against Britain and her Allies, upholding as they did so the worst traditions of murder, rape and pillage associated with inter-ethnic warfare in Eastern Europe and the Balkans. After Macmillan's visit, and without further intervention by him, V Corps headquarters decided to clear its area of prisoners-of-war by handing back all Russians except the Rogozhin Corps to the Soviet army. Some divisional commanders protested, though their protests were aimed at protecting the whole of the Cossack formations, not just those few who were 'old *emigrés*', from Soviet revenge. The moral dilemmas which faced British forces in Carinthia in May 1945 arose not only from Yalta, and the pragmatism of Macmillan's advice to Keightley, but also from the fact that there was little if anything to chose between the inhuman brutality of some of Stalin's forces and the inhuman brutality of some of the Cossacks, White Russians and Chetniks. Military necessity dictated an unsparing policy towards former enemies, and military necessity, rather than Macmillan, sealed the fate of the 'Victims of Yalta'.

. . .

RETURN

Macmillan returned to England on 26 May, to become Secretary of State for Air in the all-Conservative 'Caretaker Government' which held office from the end of the European war to the General Election of July 1945. For a man who had been an ageing and frustrated back-bencher on the outbreak of war, this promotion represented a just reward for outstanding political service to the coalition government. Macmillan's old association with Churchill had now paid off; as Churchill rose to the highest office, his client also rose to an appropriate station. But this simple *politique* explanation is far from adequate to explain Macmillan's progress. On the one hand, he was not promoted above some of the surviving 'Munichois' whom Churchill had kept on after Chamberlain's fall; R.A. Butler, soon to be a rival as well as a colleague, was promoted from the Ministry of Education to the Ministry of Labour and National Service. There was a shortage of obvious talent in the upper echelons of the Conservative Party, and while Eden was established as the heir apparent, Churchill had to make do with surprisingly large number of old Liberals from the

National Government and non-partisan figures such as Lord Cherwell. That Macmillan did not rise to the very top in this politically mixed company suggests that more than just political friendship and old loyalty determined Churchill's choice of colleagues, and, furthermore, that although Macmillan clearly doted on Churchill as a political mentor, this admiration was not fully reciprocated. On the other hand Macmillan had established a claim based on proven political competence in his dealings with the governments in exile and successor governments in liberated southern Europe. Not only had he kept a clear sight of British and Allied political objectives in his area of responsibility, he had shown himself able to act on his own initiative and to maintain constructive relations with the Americans in the Mediterranean theatre, as well as with the liberated governments. He was often closer to his own Americans than the two governments were to one another. He had also seen off Foreign Office attempts to curb his independence by sending Sir Noel Charles to Rome as ambassador. This was an excellent first assignment for a man whose ambition was to mould the fate of nations, above all because it convinced him that political management was well within his powers.

.   .   .

NOTES AND REFERENCES

1. Adrian Smith, 'Macmillan and Munich: the open conspirator', *Dalhousie Review*, LXVIII (1988), 235–47.
2. Discussed at length in Harold Macmillan, *The Blast of War* (London: Macmillan, 1967), pp. 23–47.
3. See Minutes of Daily Conferences of Minister, Secretary and Parliamentary Secretary, Ministry of Supply, in PRO, AVIA 22/172: Minutes of 20 Aug. 1940, 5 Sept. 1940.
4. J.D. Scott and R. Hughes, *The Administration of War Production* (London: HMSO, 1955), pp. 431–2.
5. Moyne was asked to resign to make way for Cranborne, who was moved from the Dominions Office in the reshuffle occasioned by Beaverbrook's resignation from the ministry.
6. Macmillan, *Blast of War*, p. 124.
7. See M. Cowen and N. Westcott, 'British imperial economic policy during the war' in D. Killingray and R. Rathbone (eds), *Africa and the Second World War* (Basingstoke: Macmillan, 1987).
8. Cranborne succeeded Stafford Cripps as Lord Privy Seal in September 1942.

9. Crookshank, a friend of Macmillan's since the First World War, later reached minor office in Churchill's last government.
10. Nicholas Bethell, *The Last Secret*, (London: André Deutsch, 1974); Nikolai Tolstoy, *Stalin's Secret War*, (London: Cape, 1981); Nikolai Tolstoy, 'The Klagenfurt Conspiracy', *Encounter*, LX (May 1983), 24–37; Robert Knight, 'Harold Macmillan and the Cossacks: Was there a Klagenfurt Conspiracy?', *Intelligence and National Security*, I (1986), 234–54.
11. But for the favourable response of an MP not closely connected with the question, see James Chuter Ede's reaction in Kevin Jefferys (ed.), *Labour and the Wartime Coalition* (London: Historians' Press, 1987), pp. 113–14.
12. See also the discussion of the unfortunate 'Anfa Memorandum' in which the United States seemed to have conceded primacy to Giraud without consulting the British.
13. Telegrams in PRO, Foreign Office Papers, FO 660/91.
14. Diary for 18 June 1943, Harold Macmillan, *War Diaries* (London: Macmillan, 1984) p. 125.
15. Diary for 29 July 1943, Macmillan, *War Diaries*, p. 169.
16. Diary, 9 Sept. 1943, Macmillan, *War Diaries*, p. 211.
17. Macmillan, *War Diaries*, p. 427.
18. Diary 1–23 May, ibid., p. 444.
19. Diary, 5 Oct. 1943, Macmillan, *War Diaries*, p. 249; 3 Oct. 1943, p. 247.
20. Diary, 23 Dec. 1943, ibid., p. 335.
21. Diary, 27 June 1944, ibid., p. 476.
22. Diary, 15 Aug. 1943, ibid., p. 502
23. See E.D. Smith, *Victory of a Sort: the British in Greece, 1941–1946* (London: Hale, 1988).
24. Diary, 7 Dec. 1944, Macmillan, *War Diaries*, p. 598.
25. Ibid., p. 618.
26. Ibid., p. 608.
27. Ibid., p. 750.
28. Ibid., pp. 758–9.
29. Nikolai Tolstoy, *The Minister and the Massacres* (London: Hutchinson, 1986). The first public discussion of the episode by a historian was in Bethell, *The Last Secret*.
30. Alistair Horne, *Macmillan 1894–1956* (London: Macmillan, 1988), p. 261.
31. Robert Knight, 'Harold Macmillan and the Cossacks: Was there a Klagenfurt Conspiracy?', *Intelligence and National Security*, I (1986), 234–54.

Chapter 4

THE GREASY POLE
1945–55

Macmillan returned to the twilight of wartime politics. The 'caretaker government' might chafe under the title, but it was a cruelly accurate one. Macmillan himself took temporary charge of the Air Ministry ('How odd!', he noted),[1] his first full departmental responsibility, but this occupied little of his time and correspondingly he did nothing of interest for the Air Force or air policy. Most of his days were given to electioneering. He found the campaign in Stockton ominously calm, and predicted the defeat which was awaiting him. He lost by 8,664 votes, a mighty reversal of his 1935 majority of 4,068.[2] He quickly decided to remain in politics, and re-entered Parliament after a by-election in November, as the member for Bromley, Beckenham and Penge. He was fifty-one. His belated but very rapid rise in the Conservative Party was to bring him over the next eleven years to the threshold of 10 Downing Street.

Macmillan's post-war progress was both an ideological and a personal triumph. He had to persuade the party to accept him as a potential leader, and to reconcile his complex social, economic and foreign policy ideas with the visceral instincts of a great political movement. This he did in two stages, first in opposition and then as a minister under Churchill, but it was really a continuous process in which he was able to take advantage of political and personal circumstances which favoured his own advancement. As a member of Churchill's Shadow Cabinet he played a full part in the day-to-day leadership of the party in opposition, and also contributed to the *Industrial Charter* which in 1947 redefined the party's public attitude to state intervention in the economy. In foreign affairs he took a more prominent part, supporting Churchill in his commitment to the European Movement, and he was one of the Conservative members of the first Assembly of the Council of Europe at Strasbourg in 1949. This was more than a symbolic commitment to a pious aspiration. By taking part, Macmillan was promoting the concept of European political unity as a defence against communism; he was identifying himself more closely with Churchill, in contrast with the surviving traditions of the pre-war party; and he was distinguishing himself from Eden, who was markedly cold towards the European Movement, and from Butler, who was not interested in it.

His work in opposition helped to promote his career, but even by the time Churchill returned to power in 1951 Macmillan had only established a limited position in the party. He was appointed to the Ministry of Housing and Local Government, with the appalling task of meeting an electoral commitment to building 300,000 houses a year. This was a poisoned chalice concocted, rather casually, by Lord Woolton at the 1950 Conservative Conference. Few of his colleagues thought it could be done, and Butler as Chancellor of the Exchequer thought that it ought not to be done, but Macmillan obstinately did it by 1954. This perhaps weakened the country's economic recovery from the war, by diverting capital from industrial investment; on the other hand it provided Macmillan with 'three of the happiest years of my life' and considerably increased his political clout, for which he was rewarded in October 1954 with the Ministry of Defence. In this rôle he suffered, as Ministers of Defence usually do, from the superordinate enthusiasms of the prime minister and Foreign Secretary. Defence and foreign policy are inseparable, and the issues of 1954 were the independent nuclear deterrent and the military evolution of NATO; neither of them subjects from which Churchill or Eden could remain detached. Nevertheless Macmillan made an impression with the 1955 Defence White Paper, and was a plausible candidate for the Foreign Office when Eden appointed him, as second-best choice after Lord Salisbury, in April 1955. This marked his entry, really for the first time, into the list of possible candidates for the succession to Eden. He was never a front-runner: since Churchill had entered Downing Street in 1940 it had been obvious that Eden, among Conservatives, was his most likely successor, and during Churchill's last administration Butler held the unusual and not always dignified position of heir-apparent to the heir-apparent. Macmillan's final lunge to the premiership was based on his record as Foreign Secretary and then as Chancellor of the Exchequer, and belongs in the next chapter.

. . .

OPPOSITION

As an opposition politician Macmillan was faced, even more acutely than most front-bench Conservatives, by the embarrassment of opposing a government which held a parliamentary majority and apparently a popular mandate. Attlee's matter-of-fact handling of the House punctured any attempt by Churchill to capitalise on his wartime reputation; Labour's robust attitude to Soviet expansion deflected any serious attack on foreign policy issues; the rapid erection of a Welfare State was unassailably popular with the voters; even the nationalisation of coal, railway transport, gas and electricity merely concluded processes begun by Conservative and National governments before the war. In attacking the government, Macmillan had the further handicap that his pre-war writings, especially *The Middle Way*, were stout arguments for the public ownership of major industries, especially coal. They were much quoted by Labour politicians in the House and outside.

One way through the thicket was to strike dramatic poses. Just before the 1946 party conference he proposed that the Conservative Party should rename itself the New Democratic Party. This move, though it won some support, came to nothing.[3] Another response was to be prepared to oppose very robustly whenever a real opportunity arose. In one such case, that of the nationalisation of road haulage, the government's plans went far beyond anything which could be pinned on *The Middle Way*, since Macmillan's proposals had been confined to public utilities, natural monopolies, and industries which had demonstrably failed under private enterprise. Here, Macmillan could easily slip into staunch resistance, casting aside the work of a party committee which had recommended 'reasoned opposition' to the nationalisation proposals.[4] His parliamentary performances were energetic and witty enough to annoy the Labour benches, though unfriendly critics found them tiresome and later made them the basis of the common charge that he was obsessed with poses and indifferent to real results.

71

The other string to his bow was the possibility of shifting the party's attitudes to coincide more closely with his own. His opportunity came when a committee was set up by Churchill in response to rank-and-file discontent about the absence of any substantial policy which could be set against triumphant Labour. This was called the Industrial Policy Committee; chaired by Butler, who was Chairman of the Conservative Research Department as well as the most prominent Conservative with experience of domestic policy, it included Macmillan, Maxwell-Fyfe, Oliver Stanley and Oliver Lyttelton and a number of back-benchers. Butler evidently intended it to produce a document to rival Peel's Tamworth Manifesto, to be a 'rallying point for Conservatism' during a rather grey patch in its history, and appropriately called *The Industrial Charter*.[5] Macmillan did not disagree with this purpose, but his idea of the possible substance was considerably more radical than Butler's.

The most interesting feature of the *Industrial Charter*, though, is its careful avoidance of excessive detail within a document whose tone was progressive enough to alarm a substantial minority of the Conservative back bench and to annoy Churchill, whose step-child it supposedly was. Promising a Conservative Party which would 'reconcile the need for central direction with the encouragement of individual effort', the *Charter* recognised that the major public utilities would have to remain in public hands, that demand-management on Keynesian principles would be necessary to maintain full employment, and that public opinion favoured a 'Workers' Charter' to 'humanise, not to nationalise' the labour process. Specific policies were not spelled out, even though the discussion of demand-management was allowed to imply the possibility of a prices and incomes policy, and the discussion of industrial relations hinted at the withdrawal of government contracts from uncooperative companies. Although all this was enough to raise the hackles of right-wing back-benchers such as Sir Waldron Smithers, it committed the party to very little even after it was endorsed, after careful stage-management, at the 1947 conference. It was the tone rather than the content, the political meaning rather than the economic planning, which was most significant about the charter, and this enabled Macmillan to take particular credit for it, even though his was by no means the only hand in its making.

This was because the tone was easily linked by outsiders with

The Middle Way and thus with Macmillan, even though it was Butler who had managed the launch of a carefully designed reconciliation between the Conservative Party and modern political conditions. Butler succeeded in preventing Macmillan from leaking the main points of the document as his own work in a by-election speech a week before it was published, but he could hardly stop the *Sunday Express* remarking, in anger, that 'This report is a triumph for Mr Harold Macmillan. [He] once wrote a political treatise called *The Middle Way*. This is the second edition.'[6] Macmillan followed this with a number of speeches which enabled him to be recognised as an equal progenitor, with Butler, of a new conservatism. In part this was just: his pre-war record had been far more 'progressive' and imaginative than Butler's and he had been proclaiming the need for new policies for longer. On the other hand he had been only one of a number of contributors to the new policy, and not the main inspiration of it, while some of the details of *The Middle Way*, such as its emphasis on 'self-government for industry' and state-backed restrictive practices, would have been badly out of place in the *Industrial Charter*.

EUROPE

While working his way through the policy-making process within the Conservative Party, Macmillan further developed his interest in foreign affairs. Where before the war his foreign interests had been confined to the single issue of policy towards the European dictators, and even that as a minor counterpoint to his preoccupations in domestic economic policy, he now took on board the whole world. This was to be expected. His Mediterranean experience had given him both a taste for constitution-making and an appreciation of the endless fascination of multilateral diplomacy. Towards the end of the war, he had faced the problems of the Soviet Union's European ambitions and the political fragility of the post-war European nations, and even more fundamentally the problem of Britain's vanishing capacity to behave like a Great Power. In opposition he could do little directly about the retreat from Empire. He visited India and took part in the debates on British withdrawal;

he commented (in his memoirs at some length) on other imperial problems. Even on Europe he could do no more than make speeches. It was in Europe, though, that his more constructive effort was made, as a member of the Council of the European Movement, a creation close to Churchill's heart, and ultimately as a parliamentary delegate to the European Assembly. Although his memoirs reflect on this point the concerns of the 1960s, there is no doubt that European unification, of a sort, became an important goal for him and that his attitudes were formed in part in the late 1940s and early 1950s.

The political problems facing Europe after the war had been predictable, and indeed predicted, since 1943. Soviet policy was predicated on the need to establish a *cordon sanitaire* between the Russian homeland and Western Europe, whether by occupying territory directly or by creating client states. From the first military operations in southern and Eastern Europe, Britain and the United States had tried to balance the need for Soviet co-operation against their fear of excessive Soviet penetration. Stalin, Roosevelt, Churchill, Truman and Attlee wrestled with these problems at Yalta and Potsdam; Macmillan, at a humbler level, had tackled them on the ground in Italy and Greece. After the European armistice the main problems were the reconstruction of Germany – first its economic development, then the question of reuniting the Occupied Zones in a single administrative unit – and the stabilisation of regimes in Eastern Europe. British foreign policy under Ernest Bevin followed the pattern laid down by Eden before the election: a careful attempt to limit Soviet expansion by negotiation, coupled with efforts to keep the United States engaged in Europe to maintain a realistic balance of forces. 'Hasn't Anthony Eden grown fat?', remarked a Labour MP.[7]

The agreement between Eden and his Labour successor about foreign affairs was more striking, and much earlier to develop, than the notorious sympathy of view between Butler and Hugh Gaitskell over the economy. At first, it also created a rift between Eden and Churchill over European policy which led directly to Churchill's espousal of the European Movement; Macmillan's involvement placed him for the time being on the hawkish wing of the party. Churchill's consistent line, expressed most forcefully in a speech at Fulton, Missouri, was that the Soviet Union intended a totalitarian domination wherever 'the Communist fifth columns are established and

work in complete unity and absolute obedience to the direc-
tions they receive from the Communist centre'.[8] To counteract
this it was important to consolidate democratic government in
Western Europe and provide a framework for a common defence and economic policy. This was the aim of the United
Europe movement, launched by Churchill in May 1947, which
despite its ostensibly non-party character was held together in
Britain largely by Churchill, Macmillan, Boothby and Duncan
Sandys.[9] It became part of the wider European Movement in
December 1947, and took part in a well-publicised meeting at
the Hague in May 1948.

Though widely supported, both in Britain and Europe, the
European Movement was no more than a pressure group: the
substance of policy was made by governments. In March 1948
Britain, France and the Benelux countries set up the 'Brussels Treaty Organisation' with a formal secretariat to discuss
economic and occasionally military matters; a month later the
Organisation for European Economic Co-operation (OEEC)
was set up to discuss the common concerns of the fourteen
European countries receiving Marshall Aid; and during 1948
military negotiations leading eventually to the North Atlantic
Treaty Organisation (NATO) were undertaken, with Britain
and the United States taking the lead. In all this, British policy was shifting steadily towards the line taken by Churchill
at Fulton, and Eden was duly following Bevin. Churchill and
Macmillan, though, were now looking for a more fundamental
reform of European affairs. Their opportunity came in the
Council of Europe, a body set up in 1949 after the Brussels
Treaty countries had invited Italy, Ireland, Norway, Denmark
and Sweden to participate in a European Assembly. Bevin had
insisted that it should not be empowered to deal with defence
or economic questions; and it was understood that the Con-
sultative Assembly should consist of parliamentarians selected
by their governments, while the Council's main business was
left to a committee of Foreign Ministers. Nevertheless, it was
an important forum for raising controversial questions, and
Churchill and Macmillan seized their opportunity.

By late 1949 it was possible to say that the question of Eastern Europe had been settled, in that the satellites on Russia's
western borders had all succumbed to pressure and embraced
communist governments and formal alliances with the Soviet
Union. The Fulton speech had, in effect, been proved right;

Britain and America had responded with NATO; the greatest test was no longer the problem of borders and spheres of influence, but the military balance between East and West. There could no longer be any reasonable doubt that the Cold War was happening. The rearmament of Germany – that is of the Federal Republic – was now a rational object of policy, to be accompanied by the inclusion of Germany in the Council of Europe. Despite objections from the British government, and a marked lack of enthusiasm on Eden's part, Churchill and Macmillan pursued this in the European Assembly, to the accompaniment of wide publicity in Britain and Europe. Closely associated with the reintegration of Germany into Western Europe was a broad, and, as it then seemed, almost visionary plan for the creation of a common, regulated market for the production of coal and steel in Europe, which was put forward by the French Foreign Minister, Robert Schuman. These two issues crystallised the differences between Churchill and Macmillan on the one hand and the Labour administration on the other; they also emphasised the differences between Macmillan and Eden on European matters, and maintained the personal tension between them.

The 'Schuman plan' was to pool the coal and steel resources of France and Germany under a single authority which other European countries could in due course join.[10] From the first his aims were explicitly political: he wanted to prevent the revival of hostility between France and Germany by creating an economic partnership. Schuman was assisted by Jean Monnet, whom Macmillan had met in Algiers and who was convinced that a supranational league in Western Europe, stopping short of federal union, was both possible and desirable.[11] The official British reaction was extremely cool, partly because the French government demanded agreement in principle as a precondition of entering the talks, partly because a substantial section of the Labour Party, including Bevin and Dalton, distrusted the whole thing as an anti-socialist plot. Macmillan's immediate reaction was that 'The situation created by M. Schuman may well be a major turning-point in European history. It is certainly a turning-point in the fortunes of the Tory Party. This issue affords us the last, and perhaps only, chance of regaining the initiative.'[12] The Conservatives put down a critical motion, which was moved by Eden in a speech which made it fairly clear that he was being prodded rudely from behind, but the majority of Conservative speakers were more sympathetic to Churchill, who closed the debate with the ringing declaration that 'the Conservative and Liberal Parties declare that national sovereignty is not inviolable, and that it may be resolutely diminished for the sake of all the men in all the lands finding their way home together'.[13] For the moment, the Conservative Party was taking a leading part in foreign policy innovation, and Macmillan was prominent in the vanguard.

. . .

OPPORTUNITY

The Attlee government was by late 1950 winding down towards a long-awaited defeat. With its first nationalisation programme finished and the foundation of a welfare state in place it could find no energy to redefine its social mission; its leading members were exhausted by years of crisis management in diplomacy and external finance, and divided by the consequences of the Korean War, which seemed to demand rearmament on a huge scale. The narrow election victory of February 1950 had encouraged no one and left the government with a majority of six. The struggle between Gaitskell at the Exchequer and Aneurin Bevan in defence of the National Health Service symbolised a deeper conflict between consolidators and enthusiasts, and between Right and Left in the party, which grew more serious when Bevan (with Harold Wilson) resigned in April 1951. Attlee's decision to call an election in October had long been expected, and was not, as his opponents alleged, provoked by the government's embarrassment about troubles brewing in Iraq and Egypt.[14] For a demoralised and directionless party, Labour performed remarkably well in the 1951 election, winning 48.8 per cent of the popular vote against the Conservatives' 48 per cent, and returning 295 MPs against the Tories' 321. It was the end of an extraordinarily productive period in the Labour Party's history, yet it hardly seemed to signify a new dawning of Conservatism.

Churchill's leadership in oposition had been intermittent and unpredictable, and there were significant divisions within the party and within the leadership over most of the important issues which had been faced in the six years of Labour's administration. The party did not gain a seat from Labour

77

at any by-election between the general elections of 1945 and 1951, and enormous efforts went into reforming the party's organisation and refining its policies. Macmillan's rôle in Conservative politics, and the development in his career during this period, must be seen against this background. He was not in the very first rank of Tory leaders. Eden was Deputy Leader; Butler was chairman of the Conservative Research Department and acknowledged as the midwife of a new Conservative social and economic attitude. Other senior figures, such as Oliver Lyttelton and Lord Woolton, had important and very public jobs. Macmillan was distinctive because he had an aggressive parliamentary style, albeit with 'too many jokes', and because the partial and rather slow intellectual conversion of the party to an interventionist social and economic policy conveniently matched his past record. His efforts to rewrite Conservative attitudes had caused friction which proved difficult to overcome: when he tried his hand at a manifesto in 1951, as a draft for what became *The Nation's Choice*, his efforts were castigated as 'exaggerated', 'trite', 'thin' and 'cheap' by the Research Department, even though the content was if anything more critical of planning than the party machinery wanted it to be.[15] It was also clear by 1950 that he owed allegiance neither to Butler nor to Eden; he was above all Churchill's man.

Macmillan's personal relationships with Butler and Eden were later to determine the shape of his own career, and their origins lay well before the war. Butler was not a politician to Macmillan's taste. Ever since his entry to Parliament in 1929, when he had made a minor stir by lampooning Macmillan's support for Mosley, he had been identified with a cautious Conservative establishment. First Baldwin, then Chamberlain, had found him a loyal servant, and his contribution to the Education Act which bears his name had been the work of a cautious, consolidating administrator with an eye to the main chance.[16] When Macmillan had been writing radical tracts before the war, Butler had been Halifax's Under-Secretary at the Foreign Office, fetching and carrying for Chamberlain's policy towards Germany. This was not the basis for a firm and lasting friendship. With Eden, Macmillan had a longer tradition of co-operation, but Macmillan was more flexible than Eden and had cooler nerves. Their disagreements during Macmillan's service in the Mediterranean had convinced Macmillan not only that his own diplomatic instincts were sounder but also that his own view of European development was superior to Eden's. Personal tension, amounting eventually to jealousy, was perhaps inevitable between two such highly-strung men. After the war Macmillan was quite content to differ from Eden over the Soviet Union and Europe, confident that he was following Churchill's lead with greater assurance.

During the period of opposition Macmillan was competing with Butler and Eden as well as co-operating with them. In February 1946 his old friend Hugh Dalton cheerfully noted that Eden 'was not doing very well as acting Leader. Many of the rest didn't like him and several, including Macmillan and Butler, were trying to oust him.'[17] He could hardly hope to supplant Eden as the heir-apparent – neither could Butler – but it was to his advantage to establish a strong and independent position. In doing so he made himself a name in foreign affairs to which Butler, for all his experience at the Foreign Office, did not aspire. At the same time he continued to trade on the innovations in Conservative social thought which he had helped to launch before the war, and thus acquired a reputation on social and economic matters to which Eden, in turn, could not aspire. From this activity flowed backbench support, a prerequisite for advancement in any party. Though older than Butler and Eden, Macmillan was now behaving like a young man in a hurry, and with the formation of Churchill's last government came his first and last chance to establish himself as a potential leader of his party.

For all his energy and ambition, Macmillan still had no automatic claim on office, and he had to wait for nearly a week after the election to learn that he was to be Minister of Housing and Local Government. This appointment had a double significance for him. First, it was an opportunity to do something. Building houses had been a high priority for the Labour governments, but their policies had been frustrated by shortages of materials and skilled labour; Conservatives claimed also that the policy of promoting local authority building at the expense of private housebuilding tended to limit progress. Labour had failed, and it was an opportunity for Conservatives to show that non-socialist policies could succeed. Second, he had the inestimable advantage of an unequivocal electoral commitment to housebuilding. The promise to build 300,000 houses a year had been made by Lord Woolton at the 1951 party conference in response to an extraordinary display of rank-and-file discontent. It was set at that figure to contrast with the 200,000 target adopted by Bevan, and its achievement depended directly on the willingness of the Treasury to permit the necessary diversion of labour and imported materials to housebuilding rather than general building. This forced Macmillan to confront Butler, but also gave him the weapon with which to win.

Dalton, who had been Minister of Health in the outgoing government, confidently predicted that 'He won't be able to build any more, if as many as I.'[18] The greatest threat to Macmillan's plans was the economic situation. The new government had inherited the economic consequences of rearmament: inflation and shortage of skilled labour. At the Treasury Butler responded by substantial cuts in imports to protect the balance of payments, buttressed by an increase in the Bank Rate from 2 to 2.5 per cent. Both these measures threatened the housebuilding programme. Macmillan briskly proposed to raise the rate of building from 230,000 houses in 1952 to 300,000 in 1954.[19] With the support of Lord Swinton, who was in charge of raw materials, he was able to prevent a cut in the import of timber[20] but pressure on the interest rate grew steadily, so that by the time of the first Budget, in March 1952, the Bank Rate had to be raised to 4 per cent to protect the reserves. It is a measure of Macmillan's political success as a spending minister that he was able to maintain his programme, in which he spent much of his energy persuading local authorities to borrow money to fund housebuilding, and much of the energy left over into keeping up the flow of imports, while fully aware that both borrowing and imports put the Chancellor's economic policy in jeopardy.

Macmillan's methods at Housing were adapted from what he had seen during the war at the Ministry of Supply – he called it 'modified Beaverbrookism' – with the additional spur of decentralisation and deregulation. As a minister he had no direct power to build houses; if central government did take a direct housing initiative, it would be through the Ministry of Works. Macmillan had to work, like Addison after the First World War and Bevan after the Second, through the local authorities. The tools he had were building licences, which controlled the flow of labour and raw materials, and subsidies, which were direct annual payments from the Exchequer to the local authorities to cover a proportion of the interest which had to be paid on loans raised to cover the cost of building.

He brought in Sir Percy Mills, a Birmingham engineering manufacturer who had once been a temporary civil servant at the
Ministry of Supply, as an unofficial adviser, and used him to
set up Regional Housing Production Boards whose brief was to
overcome local shortages of land, labour and materials. The
principal bottlenecks in housing production were the supply
of steel and of timber for framing; Ernest Marples, Macmillan's junior minister, a civil engineering contractor, pushed
forward the development of all-concrete houses to save timber,
while Macmillan put immense political pressure on Swinton to
provide extra steel. Private housebuilding was encouraged by
relaxations in the allocation of materials, and by changes to
the system of building licences which allowed local authorities
to permit private building to the extent of one in two houses
built. Macmillan also repealed the Development Charge on
land, which had been part of the 1947 Town and Country
Planning Act, though his Bill was only enacted in 1954 and
therefore had little to do with the enormous increase in the
number of houses built during his tenure of office.

With Mills and Marples, whose help he fully acknowledged,
Macmillan saw the rate of house completions rise faster than
he had predicted, from 195,000 in 1951 to 240,000 in 1952
and 318,000 in 1953. He had every right to remind the party
conference in 1954 that at an earlier conference Lord Woolton
had 'stopped the bidding' at 300,000. 'He might have made it
guineas. We could have managed that all right.'[21] His achievement was substantial, without being miraculous: the houses
did not spring from nowhere. By a combination of exhorta-
tion and careful deregulation Macmillan got the best out of
the housebuilding section of the building trade, especially the
small builders who were allowed automatic licences to build
up to twelve houses on a plot as speculative developments,
or to build for clients provided the houses were small. The
Ministry of Housing helped to encourage large contractors to
economise in materials and to switch to concrete instead of
steel for structural work. For council building, steps had been
taken by Dalton to reduce the minimum size and specification
for family houses. Macmillan took this further, so that the
houses built later in his regime used 10 per cent less materials
than the sturdy dwellings favoured in Aneurin Bevan's grand
housing drive in the late 1940s. The ministry under Macmillan accelerated the long, and ultimately disastrous quest for

economy in land and construction costs through the use of high-rise building and prefabricated ('system') building methods. During his tenure, though, most of the gains in output came about because of increases in inputs, such as steel and bricks, which he succeeded in wringing out of other sectors of the economy. Like Beaverbrook at the Ministry of Aircraft Production, he achieved great things by concentrating on his own mission, ignoring any consequences this might have for anything else. In pressing for money, he was reliably supported by Churchill against Butler.[22]

These very impressive results do not tell the whole story of housing achievement. Like all Ministers of Health and Ministers of Housing before him, Macmillan was aiming at a moving target. Britain before the First World War had been short of adequate housing. The ill-fated Addison programme of 1919–21, followed by ambitious public schemes in the 1920s and the huge increase in private-enterprise housebuilding for sale in the 1930s had just about built enough houses to replace those lost in the war and to house the growing number of households which appeared as part of the demographic changes of the interwar years. Then the Second World War broke out, postponing repairs, exposing many areas to bombing raids, and further jolting the demographic pattern. As a result even the 300,000 target was not enough to shorten the waiting lists, and Macmillan needed to embark on a large programme of slum-clearance and renovation in order to prevent the housing situation actually deteriorating during his tenure, despite the enormous achievement in new building. His most positive measure was the Rent and Repairs Act of 1954, which was to work mainly by lifting some current restrictions on rents to allow landlords to make repairs. Its rather complex provisions were the result of a political judgement by Macmillan which restricted rent increases to what was necessary to pay for repairs which landlords had actually undertaken: civil servants observed that this was not enough to stimulate widespread improvements, while the Opposition predictably complained that it favoured the rack-renting landlord. Its full impact was delayed until after Macmillan had left the ministry.

Besides its direct link to an electoral pledge, Macmillan's housing programme had a fundamental political significance. Defending his new policies in December 1951 he avowed that 'We wish to see the widest possible distribution of property. We think that, of all forms of property suitable for such distribution, house property is one of the best.' To work at all, this policy depended on a massive diversion of resources from other forms of capital formation. Consequently economic policy, particularly in relation to external finance, was the one area of general government business in which Macmillan took an interest during his three years at Housing. In 1952 he began to press a policy of increasing home production and concentrating on finding supplies and markets in the Sterling Area, to avoid the continuing debilitating need for dollars. This had recognisable intellectual links with the policies he, and Mosley, had favoured in the 1930s. It was also coupled in Macmillan's exposition with the proposal to establish closer economic links with what were now becoming known as the 'Schuman Plan countries': France, Germany, Italy, Belgium, Holland and Luxembourg. The alternative, favoured by the Treasury, was to persist in the liberalisation of world trade which was embodied in the General Agreement on Tariffs and Trade (GATT).[23] GATT required signatories to reduce tariffs progressively and accord equal treatment to all signatory nations, and it was designed quite explicitly to prevent the re-establishment of Britain's pre-war Imperial Preference policies or the creation of a European economic community with a common external tariff. Macmillan was therefore treading on sensitive ground, and he found no allies in the Treasury and few in the Cabinet. In December 1953 he recorded his defiance in his diary: 'the great Treasury Dream is over! We had better get back to Tariffs and to the Commonwealth–Europe plan.'[24]

Most of Macmillan's concerns with economic policy were, for all that, the simple instrumental needs of a spending minister to get money for his own projects. As Chancellor of the Exchequer Butler had been reluctant in the early years of the ministry to allow the levels of spending which Macmillan required, but in successive discussions on the Estimates the Treasury position had been over-ruled by considerations of political advantage. By the time the housing drive was in full swing, Butler was committed to rapid economic expansion and could hardly resist the Housing Minister's demands for more and more funds. Later judgements on Butler's management of the Treasury have generally been unfavourable,[25] blaming him for an over-rapid expansion of the economy which had to be checked abruptly by his successors. Butler is said to have reduced taxes too far, allowed expenditure to climb, and relied too much on the manipulation of interest rates. Macmillan, who had to pick up the pieces as Chancellor and later as prime minister, contributed stoutly to this policy by his spending plans and praised the inflationary budget of 1953 for cutting income tax and ending Excess Profits Levy: 'This, of course, will be called a "Capitalist" Budget. But then we believe in Capitalism as the best instrument for the prosperity of the people.'[26] No irony was ever apparent in his subsequent discussion of economic affairs in the 1950s.

.   .   .

DEFENCE

In October 1954 Churchill reorganised his rather tired government, and Macmillan was promoted from Housing to Defence. This was a recognition of his political achievements in the housing drive, but hardly a reward, since the Ministry of Defence under a dominant prime minister was a particularly thankless office. Nevertheless, Macmillan's place in the inner circle of Conservative leadership was assured, and like most in the circle he devoted much of his energies in 1953 and 1954 to the delicate task of getting rid of Churchill. Churchill's advancing age – he was seventy-seven when he took office in 1951 – had worried those closest to him since the beginning of his premiership. In June 1952 Harry Crookshank, the Leader of the House, Patrick Buchan-Hepburn, the Chief Whip, James Stuart, the Scottish Secretary, and the Marquess of Salisbury, the Commonwealth Secretary, decided to ask the prime minister to resign. When Buchan-Hepburn approached him, he refused.[27] In December of the same year Eden asked when he intended to go, and what arrangements he would make for a smooth succession.[28] He was gently rebuffed. In June 1953 Churchill had a serious stroke, just as Eden was undergoing a major operation in Boston. The gravity of his illness was concealed from the public, and in an extraordinary episode Churchill's entourage suggested that if the prime minister was unable to carry on Lord Salisbury should become acting prime minister to keep Butler out and allow Eden to claim his rightful inheritance when he was himself recovered.[29] Churchill was back at work in August, and Macmillan was among those who called on him to discover whether he was really fit to continue for long.[30] By the end of the year he was convinced that 'we shall drift on to disaster'[31] without a change of leader. By the middle of 1954, with the press and his wife combining to urge retirement, Churchill was faced by a near-simultaneous approach from Eden and Macmillan, seeking a handover by the end of June. Macmillan repeated his advice in writing on 18 June, and was rebuffed.[32] Angered, he noted in his diary that 'All of us, who really have loved as well as admired him, are being slowly driven into something like hatred. Yet we know that illness has enormously altered and worsened his character. He was always an egoist, but a magnanimous one. Now he has become almost a monomaniac.'[33]

The reshuffle, when it came in October, had only a minor impact, and Churchill clung on to office until April 1955, not without alarming his colleagues as late as March with the disclosure that he was considering a postponement until July. Macmillan therefore had six months as Minister of Defence, knowing from the beginning that even if Churchill was extraordinarily obstinate the job would probably last for less than a year. For this and other reasons, the service at the Ministry of Defence had more influence on Macmillan than Macmillan had on defence policy. The issues of the day were the extent and nature of European contributions to NATO's conventional armed forces, and the way in which Britain would procure and use nuclear weapons for defence against the Soviet Union. Macmillan's predecessor had been a 'non-political' appointment in the shape of his old friend Field Marshal Alexander. Alexander had never mastered politics, and the initiative in the high politics of defence had passed to Eden and Churchill, while the job of running the armed services had remained with the ministers responsible for each separate service. This left Macmillan, who had mastered politics a long time ago, with relatively little to do. He went to NATO meetings in October to talk about financial contributions and in December to talk about the control of the alliance's nuclear weapons, but on both occasions the lead was taken by Eden. With high policy of this sort settled for him, he was left to manage and present the Defence White Paper which set out the government's spending decisions. Although the detailed proposals had emerged from the elaborate decision-making processes of the separate services, and the priority between them was ultimately settled by the Cabinet according to its lights, Macmillan was left in the middle to absorb the lessons for future policy.

The defence problem of the middle 1950s was in one sense the same as Britain's defence problem since the turn of the century: how to ensure stability in Europe while defending a global empire. The details had changed, in that the Empire was smaller (by the subtraction of India and Palestine in 1947 and 1948) than it had been at its height, and the major threat to European stability came from the Soviet Union and the Eastern bloc, rather than from Germany. After the Second World War the favoured solution, of involving the United States in West European defence, had been tried again and on this occasion succeeded. Nevertheless, the cost of European and imperial commitments to a small and struggling economy was prohibitive. Under Churchill's government, even after the Korean War was over, British forces were committed to active service defending imperial power in Kenya and Malaya; garrisons were maintained in Singapore, Hong Kong and Cyprus, and in Egypt until the provisions of the Egyptian Treaty of 1953 were in force; at the same time troops were committed to the British Army on the Rhine (BAOR) as part of the NATO forces defending Western Europe against possible Soviet attack. The establishment of SEATO (the South-East Asia Treaty Organisation) created obligations to have troops ready for action in that area. All this required armed forces of about 800,000 in 1954. The development of nuclear weapons demanded greater civil defence expenditure to cope with fallout as well as fire and blast damage. To do all this, Defence was given a budget of £1,525 million for 1955–56, except that it was still hoped that Germany would pay some or all of the costs of BAOR forces.

By the time Macmillan reached the Ministry of Defence the outlines of a solution to the problem had been sketched. Like the Americans, British policy-makers had decided that nuclear weapons were more cost-effective than conventional forces. The decision to build an independent nuclear deterrent had been taken by the Attlee government, and the Conservative government had decided to include the hydrogen bomb as part of this development. NATO strategy was to use tactical nuclear weapons in an early stage of a European land battle, to deny Warsaw Pact forces the advantage of overwhelming numbers of men and tanks. Macmillan summarised the political significance of this soon after taking office:

I fear that the public will be rather alarmed to discover that we really cannot fight any war *except* a nuclear war. It is quite impossible to arm our forces with *two* sets of weapons.... From a purely military point of view, there is no way out. We should be utterly crushed in a conventional war. But, politically, it is full of danger, at home and abroad, and may lead to a fresh outburst of defeatism or neutralism.[34]

Even in conventional armaments new hardware with greater hitting power was preferred to the maintenance of large forces of infantry. It was Macmillan's job to preside over the implementation of these decisions. He had to confirm the abandonment of the Supermarine Swift – a jet fighter which even in its seventh version had never fulfilled its specification – in favour of the Hawker Hunter, and commission the Blue Sky air-to-air missile, which like so many British missile projects was never to enter service. Ominously, he also ordered an American surface-to-surface missile, the Corporal, to enable BAOR to deliver tactical nuclear weapons, since no British equivalent could be manufactured. At the same time he was pressing the Cabinet to face the fact that distant garrisons could not be maintained indefinitely, and that when they were cut 'There would be no safety margin for anything like another Korea.'[35]

Macmillan did not introduce the 1955 Defence White Paper in Parliament. It was Churchill's last opportunity for a major parliamentary appearance, and the most important decision to be announced was the building of the British hydrogen bomb, which was Churchill's decision rather than Macmillan's. Macmillan resented his exclusion from the limelight, but there is no reason to think that he dissented from the philosophy or the details of the policies presented. He was therefore closely associated with the formal recognition that the British Empire had to be defended in Europe, and that defence problems had to be solved through NATO by nuclear means. His commitment was to recognising and winning the Cold War; he noted in 1954 that '...we are not really winning it, and the Russians have a central position...and a well-directed effort, with strong representation (through the Communist Party) in every country'.[36] His fear of Soviet expansion led him directly to an instrumental view of European integration. He wanted an effective European defensive system, but did not want the European Defence Community, a plan for a European army which had first been floated in 1951, and was therefore pleased when the EDC project collapsed at the end of 1954 with the incorporation of German forces in a confederal command structure. He remarked in his memoirs:

> This was a proud moment for Britain. The federal solution of European unity, of which E.D.C. was the supreme example, was dead, the confederal concept represented by Western European Union was very much alive. Out of this maze of confusion Britain had guided Europe.[37]

This determination to match commitments to resources, while maintaining British interests throughout the world, was to mark his premiership as well as his brief tenure of the Ministry of Defence. It also gives a clue to the otherwise paradoxical twists of his attitude towards European integration, which baffled and often irritated colleagues and Europeanists during his years of office and afterwards. Macmillan's commitment to European integration during his opposition years has been explained above as a political tactic, to distinguish himself from Eden and Butler, as well as a constructive policy for the future.[38] His approach to Europe became more complicated as soon as specific institutional change was proposed. He had successfully urged Churchill to put pressure on the Labour government to become involved with the Schuman Plan; but when the Plan developed, without British participation, into a tightly-organised Coal and Steel Community with definite supranational features, his ardour was cooled.

He responded in much the same way to the Pleven Plan, which was the basis of the short-lived European Defence Community (EDC) idea. René Pleven, the French Defence Minister, had launched his plan for a European Army in October 1950. It had been received well in the Council of Europe, and the necessary treaties had been prepared by the summer of 1951. The Labour government had rejected the idea of participation for the same reason as it rejected participation in negotiations over the Schuman Plan: it would restrict British sovereignty in matters of vital national interest. When Eden entered the Foreign Office in October 1951 he openly supported his predecessor's view. Macmillan opposed him, but, significantly, his opposition was not based on enthusiasm for the Schuman or Pleven Plans.

The Foreign Office view, approved by Eden and Churchill,

was that 'We want a united Europe.... It is only when plans for uniting Europe take a federal form that we cannot ourselves take part, because we cannot subordinate ourselves or the control of British policy to federal authorities', and in December 1951 Churchill told Schuman that the British 'should be with [Europe] though they could not be of it'.[39] This was very close to Macmillan's view. The difference came in the tactics by which it might be achieved. Eden and Churchill were happy for France, Germany and the other participants in the Schuman Plan to set up their arrangements, and for these to include the EDC if that was wanted. Macmillan feared that in that way Britain would be excluded from a European political organisation which would steadily increase its power. His 'hope' was that both the EDC and the Schuman Plan would fail; his proposal was that Britain should enter negotiations to create a confederal structure which, apart from being more acceptable to France as a form of co-operation, would allow Britain to stay with Europe but maintain its current relations with the Commonwealth and the United States. He put this point to the Cabinet in February 1952, and continued to press Eden not to go on encouraging the French and Germans to form a close alliance which would exclude Britain. He even suggested that

> With the Commonwealth behind us and holding, as we should, a balance between France and Germany, Britain would be the unchallenged leader of the European Confederation. This, in itself, would further strengthen our position in the Commonwealth. As the leader, moreover, of both the Commonwealth and Europe we should be able to establish a more equal partnership with the United States both in the immediate task of containing Russia and in the long term.[40]

In this he had no success at all. Throughout the negotiations, lasting until September 1952 when the European Assembly confirmed the EDC plan, he was a frustrated observer, with no power to influence events. For the next two years, while Eden was trying to get the French, now the reluctant party, to ratify the EDC proposal, Macmillan bombarded him with warnings about the dangers for Britain of a European federation of six countries 'with a common army, a common coal and steel industry, and eventually ending with a common currency, monetary policy and free trade area'.[41]

Macmillan's one success in this area came after the French Assembly had finally defied British and American pressure and refused to accept the EDC proposal. In August 1954 he suggested a new treaty to replace the 1948 Brussels Treaty, which had been agreed between France, Britain and the Benelux countries. The new deal would bring Germany into a military arrangement with the other Western European powers, without a supranational organisation, and would make German rearmament more acceptable to the French. This scheme was better attuned to the current of events than Macmillan's previous interventions. On 23 August Mendès-France, the French prime minister, had raised the possibility of a new organisation to include Britain and Germany, because he feared that the imminent French rejection of the EDC would destabilise Konrad Adenauer's government in Germany. Eden and Churchill had not taken this up, but after the rejection Eden was more sympathetic to Macmillan's plan, and carried it round the European capitals.[42] The result was the Western European Union (WEU), accepted at last by the French Assembly in December 1954. To get it, Eden had had to offer a permanent British military presence in Europe, including four divisions and the Tactical Airforce – a commitment which was to strain the defence budget in the later 1950s.

Macmillan's delight, even as an observer, at the ratification of the WEU is explained by this history of heavily qualified enthusiasm for European integration. Although he was not an isolationist, and criticised both Eden and Churchill for their failure to recognise the dangers of allowing Europe to develop without British participation, he was a very early subscriber to the notion of a *Europe des patries* in which supranational institutions would have no part. On European matters his view was therefore remarkably close to that of his old associate, Charles de Gaulle; and, ironically, he was to find his own efforts as prime minister to enter such a Europe thwarted by de Gaulle's intransigence.

. . .

TO THE FRONT RANK

When Churchill at last resigned, in April 1955, Eden asked Macmillan to take the Foreign Office. The new prime minister had wanted Lord Salisbury for the job, but recognised with reluctance that a peer would have difficulty defending the Foreign Office in Parliament. Macmillan thus entered the inner circles of power, very nearly on even terms with Butler, who retained the Exchequer, but still not the automatic choice for the highest office. It was a just reward for ten years of political effort, in which the early promise of 1945 had been converted into solid political and administrative achievement, with widespread public recognition to match. His elevation calls for an interim explanation of his political career to this point.

Macmillan's progress since the war emphasised how important the war had been in his career, as a discontinuity breaking a run of bad luck. His early success in Conservative politics had been as a protégé of Churchill, and when Churchill had been out of favour or Macmillan out of Churchill's circle, his career had languished, despite his ever-active attention to economic policy problems. Then he was taken up in 1940 as a loyal Churchillian, and given a succession of offices of growing importance in which to demonstrate his skills. At the end of the war this gave him an entrée into the Conservative leadership, but he had to remake his political position. During the years of opposition he was careful to stay close to Churchill and to differentiate himself from Eden and Butler, his chief rivals for the master's ear. Europe provided the issue on which this strategy could be based. Increasingly he emphasised the international dimension of Conservative politics, drawing upon his wartime experience in the Mediterranean. Even while Housing commanded most of his attention, he urged the importance of European unity as a counterweight to Soviet expansion. On the threshold of the Foreign Office he was a robust and plausible Cold Warrior.

At the same time, despite the euphoria over Housing, he was setting himself apart from his pre-war radicalism. Admittedly his first attempts to win public recognition harked back to the pre-war Macmillan: the futile attempt to rename the Conservative Party, and the rather more successful bid to garner the credit for the *Industrial Charter* by linking it to his own writings. Thereafter he ceased to use his radical background as a foundation for further advance. This was in part because the economic climate had changed. Years of post-war change, good luck and good management had reduced the problem of unemployment, and Butler's too-relaxed management of the

economy had fostered rapid expansion. This was no time to demand a resurrection of planning and state ownership after the
model of *The Middle Way*. Moreover, as argued above, Macmillan had been less radical in the 1930s than he later suggested.
The continuity between his pre-war defence of the free market
and his post-war defence of capitalism is at least as important
as the discontinuity in his attitude to public ownership. Yet,
for all these caveats, there was a real movement in his position, which brought him closer to the Conservative centre of
gravity than he had been in 1939. Without it, his ambition to
stand on his own feet unsupported by Churchill's patronage
would have lacked plausibility. By becoming a firm advocate
of NATO as well as a staunch defender of non-socialist policy at
home, he endeared himself to a party which had moved, albeit
only slightly, from the complacent rigidity of the Chamberlain
years.

. . .

NOTES AND REFERENCES

1. Diary, 26 May 1945, Harold Macmillan, *War Diaries*, p. 764.
2. The Liberals had polled 5158 votes in 1935, but did not stand in 1945.
   In his memoirs Macmillan coined the great examination question 'It
   was not Churchill who lost the 1945 election; it was the ghost of Neville
   Chamberlain.'
3. For Eden's delight at Macmillan's flop, see David Carlton, *Anthony Eden*
   (London: Allen Lane, 1981), p. 269.
4. John Ramsden, *The Making of Conservative Party Policy* (London: Longman, 1980), p. 119.
5. Ramsden, *Making of Conservative Party Policy*, pp. 111–13.
6. Anthony Howard, *RAB. The Life of R.A. Butler* (London: Jonathan Cape,
   1987), pp. 157–8; *Sunday Express*, 15 May 1947.
7. Carlton, *Anthony Eden*, p. 260.
8. The 'Iron Curtain' speech at Fulton, Missouri, quoted ibid., p. 263.
9. The most prominent non-Conservative members were Sir Walter Lay-
   ton and Lady Violet Bonham-Carter, both Liberals.
10. See John W. Young, 'The Schuman Plan and British Association', in
    John W. Young (ed.), *The Foreign Policy of Churchill's Peacetime Adminis-
    tration* (Leicester: Leicester University Press, 1988), pp. 109–34.
11. Note of 7 July 1944, cited in Harold Macmillan, *Tides of Fortune* (Lon-
    don: Macmillan, 1969), p. 188. In Monnet's recollection, 'C'est là,
    devant la mer, au cours de promenades dans les ruines romaines,
    que nous préparions tranquillement l'avenir.' Jean Monnet, *Mémoires*
    (Paris: Fayard, 1976), p. 281.

12. Memorandum to Churchill, June 1950, quoted in *Tides of Fortune*, pp. 193–5.
13. *H.C. Debs* 1950, vol. 476, 27 June 1950, col. 2159. Eden's speech on 26 June is at cols 1907–24.
14. In Iraq Mossadeq was nationalising the oilfields at the expense of the Anglo-Persian Oil Company; the Egyptian government was busy repudiating the Anglo-Egyptian treaty of 1936, which guaranteed a British presence on the Suez Canal.
15. TS draft of *The Nation's Choice* by H.M., n.d., but by internal evidence 1951, Bodleian Library, Conservative Research Department papers, CRD 2/49/23.
16. Howard, *RAB* pp. 40–1; Kevin Jefferys,'British politics and social policy during the Second World War', *Historical Journal*, XXX (1987), 123–44.
17. Dalton Diary, 25 Feb. 1946, Ben Pimlott (ed.), *The Political Diary of Hugh Dalton 1918–40, 1945–60* (London: Cape, 1986) p. 367.
18. Dalton Diary, 29 Oct. 1951, ibid., p. 565.
19. 'The Building Industry and the Housing Programme. Memorandum by the Minister of Housing and Local Government', 14 Dec. 1951, CAB 129/48, C(51)43.
20. In Cabinet on 6 March 1952, CAB 128/24, CC(52)26.
21. Harold Macmillan, *Tides of Fortune* (London: Macmillan, 1969), p. 459.
22. See e.g. the Cabinet discussion of 24 July 1952 in CAB 128/25, CC(52)73.
23. GATT was signed by twenty-three nations at Geneva in 1947, at the instance of the United States whose post-war economic policy had been based on a 'full-blooded thrust for convertibility [of currencies] and multilateral trade'. Kathleen Burk, 'The international environment' in Andrew Graham and Anthony Seldon (eds), *Comparative Economic Performance*, (London: Routledge, 1990).
24. Diary entry of 29 December 1953, quoted in Macmillan, *Tides of Fortune*, p. 394.
25. See in particular J.C.R. Dow, *The Management of the British Economy* (Cambridge: Cambridge University Press, 1964), *passim*.
26. Diary for 13 April 1953, quoted in Macmillan, *Tides of Fortune*, p. 392.
27. Bodleian Library, Crookshank Diary, 16 and 23 June 1952. Crookshank had been at Eton with Macmillan; Stuart and Salisbury were Macmillan's brothers-in-law.
28. Martin Gilbert, *'Never Despair': Winston S. Churchill 1945–1965* (London: Heinemann, 1988), p. 781.
29. Howard, *RAB*, p. 199.
30. Lord Moran, *Winston Churchill: the struggle for survival* (London: Constable, 1966), pp. 468–70.
31. Alistair Horne, *Macmillan 1894–1956* (London: Macmillan, 1988), p. 352.
32. Macmillan to Churchill, 18 June 1954, cited Gilbert, *'Never Despair'*.
33. Horne, *Macmillan 1894–1956*, p. 353.
34. Diary, 25 Nov. 1954, quoted in *Tides of Fortune*, p. 567.
35. Memorandum of 2 February 1955, quoted Horne, *Macmillan 1894–1956*, p. 345; the Defence White Paper was presented to colleagues as 'Statement on Defence', 4 Feb. 1955, CAB 129/73, C(55)29.

36. Diary for 30 November 1954, quoted in *Tides of Fortune*, p. 572.
37. Ibid., p. 566.
38. Above, pp. 73–7. This is not to belittle it: politicians who have principles but no tactical sense rarely succeed in advancing their principles.
39. Eden to HM Representatives Overseas, 15 Dec. 1951, FO 953/1207, *Documents on British Policy Overseas* Series 2, Vol. I (London: HMSO, 1985), Doc. 416, p. 791; 'Extract from a record of a meeting held in Hotel Matignon, Paris, on 17 Dec. 1951', ibid., Doc. 418, p. 796.
40. H. Macmillan, 'European Integration', 16 Jan. 1952, WV 10712/42, *Documents on British Policy Overseas*, Series 2, Vol. 1, Doc. 424, p. 815.
41. Quoted in Macmillan, *Tides of Fortune*, p. 478. On the EDC issue in general see John W. Young, 'German Rearmament and the European Defence Community', in Young (ed.), *The Foreign Policy of Churchill's Peacetime Administration*, pp. 81–107.
42. Parenthood of the scheme is contested. Eden claimed that the idea of a 'diluted EDC' originated in the Foreign Office and that the use of the Brussels Treaty to achieve it had come to him 'In the bath on Sunday morning' (6 September 1954). Richard Lamb attributes the WEU to Mendès-France at Chartwell. Macmillan's claim in his memoirs is supported by the survival of his memorandum. Anthony Eden, *Full Circle* (London: Cassell, 1960), pp. 149, 151 (which misdates the Brussels Treaty to 1946); Richard Lamb, *The Failure of the Eden Government* (London: Sidgwick & Jackson, 1987), p. 67.; Macmillan, *Tides of Fortune*, p. 481.

Chapter 5

THE OPPORTUNITY
1955–56

It is a useless but interesting speculation to ask what would
have happened to Macmillan's career if the Cabinet had forced
Churchill to resign in July 1953 and abandoned the attempt
to 'protect Anthony'. Butler, as acting prime minister, would
have succeeded to the premiership. The rest is fantasy: but
it is a matter of record that Butler's physical fitness and mental stability far exceeded Eden's. Unless he had handled the
Suez crisis even more incompetently than Eden did, it is hard
to think that he would have been forced to resign at the beginning of 1957, leaving the field clear for an older man such
as Macmillan. To that extent, the nineteen months of Eden's
premiership must be seen as an uncovenanted opportunity for
Macmillan to step up, ready to seize the great prize. He held
in succession two of the great offices of state, the Foreign Office and the Treasury. He was at the Foreign Office for nine
months, and evidently found it no more comfortable than he
had found Defence under Churchill, though the day-to-day
work was more to his taste. At the Treasury he regained some
of the initiative from Eden and began on a course of retrenchment and reform which also characterised the early years of his
premiership. But the key to his career, and to all of British political history in these years, was the developing crisis over the
control of the Suez Canal. Suez was to Macmillan what Norway was to Winston Churchill: an avoidable humiliation for
British arms, to which Macmillan by his own acts of policy had
contributed, and from which developed the political situation
which brought him the premiership. He did not scheme to
overthrow Eden by humiliating him, any more than Churchill
had schemed to overthrow Chamberlain. Nevertheless, Eden's
humiliation led rapidly to Eden's collapse and downfall, and

by then the only barrier between Macmillan and 10 Downing Street was R.A. Butler.

. . .

A GREAT EUROPEAN

Eden's official biographer has noted that the new prime minister's 'dominant concerns and interests...remained in foreign affairs'.[1] During 1955 this preoccupation finally destroyed what little sympathy was left between Macmillan and Eden and corroded the morale of the new Cabinet. A convincing election victory, increasing both the share of the vote and the number of seats won by Churchill in 1951, was widely attributed to Eden's own personality; yet the new prime minister lacked the self-confidence to leave his ministers alone to run their departments. Macmillan was the greatest sufferer, because foreign affairs was the only subject upon which Eden felt wholly at ease. Although much of the tension between them was caused by petty and detailed interference from 10 Downing Street, there were two major areas of conflict. Macmillan was much more sympathetic than Eden towards the strengthening of Britain's involvement in a European polity, and he was much more reluctant to throw Britain's weight around in the Middle East. In the event he was able to do little more than to press on with the policies bequeathed to him by Eden. After nine months Eden moved him sideways to the Treasury, either because of jealousy (as Macmillan himself believed) or because of a real need to replace Butler. It was a short and none too successful episode which neither posterity nor Macmillan himself have been able to praise.

Macmillan's first test was the sudden surge of activity in the European Coal and Steel Community which led to a meeting at Messina of the foreign ministers of the six ECSC powers at the beginning of June 1955 to discuss what was called a 'Common Market'.[2] No British minister or official attended the Messina meeting, at which Paul-Henri Spaak, the Belgian Foreign Minister, was appointed to lead a committee to set up a full customs union in Europe. Spaak, with his Dutch counterpart Beyen, came to London on 21 June to discuss these proposals with a ministerial team chaired by the Chancellor, R.A. Butler (Macmillan was not included: the Foreign

Office was represented by Lord Reading, the Minister of State). This meeting was followed by a Cabinet discussion on 30 June to which Butler reported. Advice from officials was consistent with British policy since 1951: the Messina powers wanted supranational institutions for political as much as economic reasons, the creation of a customs union would damage worldwide economic development through GATT, and Britain had more to lose than to gain in areas such as atomic energy. The Cabinet decided to send officials to the first meeting of the Preparatory Committee in Brussels on 9 July, and accepted Macmillan's suggestion that these should be 'representatives' rather than 'observers'. His argument, reflecting his earlier position on the EDC, was that it was desirable for Britain to be fully involved in these discussions from the start, in order to have the best chance of preventing the development of a supranational Europe from which Britain would necessarily be excluded. The Foreign Office disagreed.

Britain's representative in Brussels, a Board of Trade official, reported from the early meetings that the Messina powers were not moving very fast towards a Common Market, and that it seemed likely that France would reject a supranational organisation, in a repeat of the EDC performance. In London both officials and ministers rehearsed the disadvantages to Britain of entering a customs union: not only would economic relations with the Commonwealth and the United States be weakened, but Britain would be exposed to damaging European competition in textiles and chemicals and probably the engineering industries as well. None of this was new, and the decision to make a *démarche* against the Messina proposals in a regular meeting of the OEEC in December 1955 was an entirely logical consequence of British policy since the war.

Macmillan himself, who made the decision with Eden, saw no conflict between the desire to strangle the Common Market in its cradle and his previous fervent Europeanism.

> our responsibilities and our associations ruled out British participation in the Common Market.... Our declaration was not condemnation of the six power plans but it was a warning that we must not divide Europe in the course of trying to unite it. We felt that it would be useful to ... see how the six power plans could be recognised and harmonised with the activities of the OEEC.[3]

Translated into the language of British interests, he meant that he preferred, as he had always done, to see Britain involved both in Europe and in association with the United States and the Sterling Area, and that it was against British interests for any grouping to exist in Europe which was closer-knit than the grouping to which Britain could subscribe. This reasoning lay behind his heartfelt desire to see the end of the EDC, and distinguished him from Eden, who was at first happy to stand completely aloof and let the Europeans form whatever closer organisations they wanted, without British participation. The British ambassador in Washington, charged with the job of cooling American enthusiasm for the Messina proposals, assumed in a letter to Macmillan that 'your real object is to hasten the end of the Common Market'.[4]

Macmillan inevitably carried his European concerns over to the Treasury when he was reshuffled in December 1955. January 1956 saw a further burst of intense activity on the part of the Messina powers, some of whose representatives were clearly angry at Britain's *démarche* and determined to press ahead anyway. Without much affecting the general distaste for supranational arrangements, this divided official opinion in London between those who thought that the Common Market would collapse under its own weight and those who feared that it would grow so fast that Britain would be obliged either to come to an accommodation with it or to take positive steps to subvert it. Although the Treasury tended to discount progress towards a Common Market, Macmillan was persuaded by the views of his former subordinates in the Foreign Office that something strenuous might have to be done to protect British interests, and set the Treasury to work in February to make plans for 'an advance which would be recognised as such'.[5] At this point he still wanted to frustrate the Messina proposals. The outcome was an interdepartmental working party which by 13 April had produced a set of options. In May, the Messina powers met in Venice and agreed to draft a treaty, inviting other OEEC countries to attend a conference in Brussels at the end of June. Britain stayed away from Brussels. Nevertheless, the invitation spurred the Cabinet to choose from the working party's alternatives a proposal for a partial Free Trade area which would include the (six) Messina powers and other members of the OEEC, which would not cover foodstuffs and would thus protect Commonwealth interests. This became known as 'Plan G', and was circulated on 27 July.

Plan G's principal backers in Cabinet were Macmillan and Peter Thorneycroft, the President of the Board of Trade. Their defence of it was both economic and political: it would 'open the way to those competitive pressures which would force the economy to become more efficient', but also 'We have a chance which might not recur of gaining the general support of what might be described as both the European and the Imperial wings of the Conservative Party.'[6] To a business observer, it seemed that:

> ... political hunches more than traders' assessments had led Thorneycroft and Macmillan to their present line of thought. The political factors influencing them seemed to me to have been the probable decline of Commonwealth trade on the basis of the preferences, the desire to have Britain rather than Germany dominant in European influences and the conviction that without U.K. in, Germany would in fact dominate, and finally the belief that Britain alone would prove too small in size to match U.S.A. round the council table but Britain as acknowledged leader of West Europe plus Britain as centre of the Commonwealth might exert a not inconsiderable influence on the world stage.
>
> With such thoughts on the political side it only needed that they should be at heart Liberal Free Traders and opposed to protection for industry or feather-bedding for business men to bring Thorneycroft and Macmillan round to where they were now. It was those two, I felt, almost alone who were swinging the government.[7]

Though 'Liberal Free Trade' was stronger in Thorneycroft (whose conversation prompted this summary) than in Macmillan, this was an inspired summary of the political logic of Plan G.

The last stages of Britain's fruitless engagement with the evolving Common Market were overshadowed by the Suez crisis, whose first stages coincided almost precisely with the appearance of Plan G. Macmillan's position remained consistent in its analysis of British interests. His tactics, though ultimately unsuccessful, were at least based on reasonable premises. Indeed, during October 1956 it seemed possible that the French would repeat their EDC rôle and smash the Common Market's pretensions to supranationality by asking for too many concessions. But by November the Messina powers were proceeding at full speed to draft what became the Treaty of Rome (finally signed on 27 March 1957), including the outline of an agricultural policy which would make it impossible for Britain to join in without sacrificing Commonwealth interests. On 20 November the Cabinet plumped for Plan G, but found that the Six were unwilling to negotiate on it, either directly or through the OEEC. Britain's bluff was called, and the worst case envisaged by the Foreign Office – that the Messina powers would succeed in setting up their Market with no British participation at all – came to pass. In all this Macmillan had been just as much, or as little, a European as he had been in 1950; he had foreseen difficulties a few months before many of his colleagues, but had not been able to do much about them.

. . .

CYPRUS

As Foreign Secretary, and then as Chancellor of the Exchequer, Macmillan was presented with a series of problems in the Middle East of which the Suez crisis was merely the last and worst. All of them ultimately concerned the clash between British strategic interests and local nationalism, though none was ever quite so simple. To the basic problem the case of Cyprus added the extra dimension of a fierce ethnic conflict within the territory, and competition between two neighbouring countries, Greece and Turkey, to inherit Britain's suzerainty.[8] Cyprus had been borrowed from the Turks in 1878 as a convenient subsidiary base for the defence of the route to India. The island was annexed during the First World War, and made a Crown Colony in 1925. Nearly 70 per cent of the population were Greek-speaking Christians, many of them refugees from Turkish atrocities during the Graeco-Turkish war of 1920–22, and the rest Turkish Moslems. The Greek Cypriot population wanted union with Greece – Enosis – and the Turkish Cypriot minority duly feared massacre and pillage, which had been the normal accompaniments of political change during the collapse of the Ottoman Empire. Although Britain had proposed some constitutional advance after the Second World War, it was assumed that the strategic importance of the Cyprus bases would forbid total independence. The decision to evacuate the Suez Canal bases, taken by Churchill's government in 1953, placed further value on the retention of Cyprus, especially as an airbase. In April 1955 General Grivas's EOKA movement began a terrorist campaign to drive the British out of the island, supporting an outspoken civil campaign led by the acknowledged political leader of the Greek Orthodox community, Archbishop Makarios.

Macmillan inherited a policy devised by Eden with the former Colonial Secretary, Alan Lennox-Boyd, providing for definite but quite slow progress towards internal self-government. Faced with explosive evidence that this was not enough he took the bold step of engaging Greece and Turkey in discussion about the future of the island. This initiative brought Turkish and Greek representatives, and Archbishop Makarios, to London in August. Macmillan engaged in the subtle exercises which he had practised so well in Italy and Greece a dozen years before. His main aim was to identify 'moderates' on each side and try to persuade them that they needed British help against their own extremists. This worked reasonably well for Greece, whose Foreign Minister, Stephanos Stephanopoulos, seemed reasonably anxious to deflect Greek-Cypriot pressure from the shaky government of Field Marshal Papagos in Athens. The Turks – 'confident, assertive and tough'[9] according to Macmillan – offered no such foothold, and Macmillan could do nothing to prevent Makarios from withdrawing noisily. He had, nonetheless, made detailed proposals which went further than the Lennox-Boyd plan: a new Assembly to which all departments except defence, foreign affairs and the police would be responsible, a quota of seats and of ministerial portfolios for the Turkish minority, all to be introduced with the help of a tripartite commission appointed by Britain, Greece and Turkey.

Meanwhile the Governor, Sir Robert Armitage, asked to be supplied with police officers with Malayan or Kenyan experience. Armitage, whom Macmillan curtly described as 'ineffective, even for a Wykehamist', was in fact in a difficult position. He had warned the government in June that straightforward repression would not be enough without a declaration in favour of 'self determination', on which Eden had minuted 'No'.[10] He had then been denied permission to impose a state of emergency, which left him very few options. Nevertheless, Macmillan was so exasperated with Armitage's performance that he asked Eden to appoint a new Governor 'with guts and imagination', suggesting Fitzroy Maclean MP, whom he had known as a British agent with Tito during the War.[11] Against the Foreign Secretary's advice, Eden instead chose a soldier,

Field Marshal Harding. Harding, as expected, was a robust Governor who eventually declared a State of Emergency in November, which enabled him to be tougher still. While negotiations continued with Makarios over whether Britain could offer self-government (with foreign policy, defence and the police reserved to Britain) or self-determination, the terrorist campaign continued unabated. In due course Makarios was deported (in March 1956), and released soon after Macmillan succeeded Eden as prime minister. The Cyprus troubles lingered on until 1959 when a settlement was reached, but Macmillan's direct connection was interrupted on his translation to the Treasury in December 1955.

Although Macmillan neither started nor finished the Cyprus episode, it throws an interesting light on his position in Whitehall and in the Cabinet in the early months of Eden's government. It was only his business because he made it so. The Colonial Office was formally responsible for the Crown Colony, and hitherto the co-operation between Lennox-Boyd from the Colonial Office and Eden at the Foreign Office had been conducted on that assumption. Macmillan's opinion of the Colonial Office was very poor, and his criticisms of 'Byzantine incompetence' ring true.[12] To deal with the foreign policy issues raised by the troubles, Macmillan openly made the Foreign Office the leading department on the subject. It had always been interested because of Britain's delicate relations with Turkey and Greece over NATO; now it began to take initiatives to solve the problem by diplomatic action. As with Macmillan's efforts in Europe, that fact that this initiative did not work does not automatically mean that it was a bad idea, or that some other procedure than the Tripartite Conference would have done anything more to pacify Greek and Turkish Cypriots. Nevertheless, the business did nothing for his reputation.

. . .

EGYPT, 1955

To a greater extent even than Cyprus, the Egyptian question was inherited by Macmillan rather than begun during his tenure, and during all his work on it as Foreign Secretary he was subject to constant interference from Eden. Like Cyprus, Egypt had British sovereign bases, due for evacuation in 1956, international and strategic significance because of the Suez Canal and the proximity of oilfields around the Persian Gulf, and bitter local suspicions based on racial hatred, in this case between the Arab states and the state of Israel. The state of play when Macmillan took over in April 1955 had been determined by the flux of nationalist feeling in the Middle East and the steady retreat of British power. The British invasion of Egypt in 1882 had been sanctified by a series of special arrangements of which the most recent was the 1936 'perpetual' Treaty of Alliance which allowed British forces to be stationed in Egypt for twenty years. In 1951 the 1936 treaty was denounced by Egypt, and internal pressure to remove British bases immediately was so intense that King Farouk was overthrown in July 1952.

The new regime, though stridently nationalist, was a modernising military dictatorship which was prepared to make rational bargains to achieve its ends. The first of these was to drop any claims to the Sudan in return for British agreement to withdraw from the Suez base. Since British policy-makers had recognised that the base was strategically obsolete, this was accepted by Eden. In further upheavals in February 1954 General Neguib was supplanted by Colonel Nasser, who in July negotiated the terms of British withdrawal from the bases. Nasser, though apparently willing to co-operate with Britain and the United States, was determined to make Egypt, as the most populous modern state in the Middle East, the effective leader of an Arab bloc: he was therefore particularly suspicious of the Baghdad Pact, by which Britain in 1954 formed an anti-Soviet alliance with Turkey, Iran, Iraq and Pakistan. The other major element in Middle Eastern politics was Israel, whose occupation of the Negev Desert since 1948 was contested both by Egypt and by Jordan.

Macmillan's first task at the Foreign Office was to implement a plan worked out by Eden and John Foster Dulles, the American Secretary of State, to provide a link between Jordan and Egypt across the Negev. 'Project Alpha' did not quite suggest a corridor: two triangles of territory in the Negev, one with its base on the Egyptian border, the other with its base on the border of Jordan, would meet at their apexes on the road connecting the main Israeli settlements with port of Eilat on the Gulf of Aqaba. Thus Israel would maintain access to Eilat, while a land route would be established between Egypt and Jordan. The package included an internationalised zone in Jerusalem, financial help from Britain to enable Israel to compensate Palestinian Arab refugees, and other economic support for Israel from the Western Powers. Although Eden had brought this plan to life, and Macmillan compared it with his own initiatives in Cyprus –'Cyprus is *my* plan. *Alpha* is really an *inherited* plan'[13] – he was an enthusiastic and effective protagonist. In June he visited the United States, urging Dulles to continue to press it in Washington despite objections from the Jewish lobby during the presidential elections. Obstacles to progress included shooting incidents in the Gaza Strip, in which the Israeli army was condemned for violating the 1949 Armistice, and a running dispute over a scheme to divert the Jordan to irrigate the Negev. Macmillan and Dulles worked closely together, so that in August Dulles committed the United States in public to support a territorial rearrangement, in a speech which had been agreed by Macmillan. Eden's behaviour at this point brought Macmillan close to despair: up to the day before the speech he bombarded his Foreign Secretary with comments, mostly directed at what he thought was an American tendency to concede too much to Israel. Macmillan commented 'I might as well give up and let him run the shop.'[14]

It was essential to Project Alpha that the full details of the financial package, and the direct intervention of Britain and the United States, should be kept secret. Covert diplomacy left room for many pressures and enticements, including the possibility of arms supplies from the Western powers to Egypt. In September it was suddenly revealed that Nasser had concluded an arms deal with Czechoslovakia, and lost interest in Alpha; in October, while the Cabinet was still recovering from the shock, it was learned that Russia had offered to fund the Aswan High Dam project, with which Nasser intended to provide an infrastructure for Egyptian industrialisation. Alpha was obsolete, if only because the intended beneficiaries were no longer interested, but Eden and Macmillan continued to press both sides to make concessions, up to and beyond the end of Macmillan's tenure of the Foreign Office. There were no apparent differences between them on the fundamentals of policy. Both were more concerned to secure British oil supplies in the Middle East than to win any advantages over Egypt. Both underestimated the intensity of anti-Western feeling in the Arab world.[15] Where they did differ was over the responsibility for the details of foreign policy, and their personal relations, never easy, were further soured by the Middle Eastern problem.

Middle Eastern affairs before 1956 also created a political situation within the Conservative Party which had consequences for Macmillan's future. During the negotiations of 1953 about withdrawal from the Suez base a caucus of Tory back-benchers, subsequently known as the Suez Group, had dissented very openly. They were supported within the Cabinet by Lord Salisbury, and even Churchill had some sympathy with them, though he had loyally supported Eden. The Tory Right was sensitive to Middle Eastern issues, and pressed Macmillan when he was Foreign Secretary to conclude a defensive treaty with Israel simply in order to put further pressure on the recalcitrant Nasser. Although he never appeared to concede to this pressure, Macmillan in private was consistently hostile to Nasser's ambitions, remarking for instance in September 1955 that 'We really cannot allow this man, who has neither the authority of a throne nor of a Parliament, to destroy our base and threaten our rear.'[16] Though never more than about thirty in number, and as few as fifteen by the end, the Suez Group was the spearhead of a tendency in the party which reacted against the débâcle over the Canal Zone in 1956 and reinforced the demand for a strong prime minister to succeed Eden. When that demand came, it very clearly discriminated between Macmillan and Butler, even though Macmillan towards the end had usually been on the side of concessions to Egypt. It was an irony, but an important one, that Macmillan was to be helped into office by men whom he had often thought a political nuisance when he was trying to manage British foreign policy.

. . .

THE TREASURY

Macmillan left the Foreign Office under protest. Eden asked him on 23 September to take over the Treasury from Butler, in whom the prime minister had lost confidence. In some way this had been a prepared move: Eden had invited Macmillan in August to write a Cabinet Paper on the economy, and he had responded with a fairly optimistic piece, proposing marginal measures to choke off incipient inflation and a resort to a floating exchange rate to take pressure off sterling. He noted that between the wars the strain had been taken by unemployment, but 'we can't do that again and survive politically'.[17] At the time this made him seem both more level-headed and more imaginative than Butler, who had evidently mishandled the pre-election budget. But it was almost certainly not his virtues alone, or even Butler's failings, which caused Eden to seek a change, but the prime minister's urgent need to have a compliant Foreign Secretary. Macmillan believed that jealousy, or something like it, was the only motive, and deeply resented it. He also feared an ulterior motive, and confided in Lord Woolton. 'Macmillan wondered whether his departure from the Foreign Office at a time when things were not going very well – he described them as "Eden's chickens coming home to roost" – would not give the appearance of failure.'[18] He first demurred to the proposal, then after agreeing to the change in October laid down very tough conditions. He warned that he would make changes, bring in outside advisers, and attempt to reorganise the Bank of England; 'there is no point in my leaving the Foreign Office to be an orthodox Chancellor of the Exchequer. I must be, if not a revolutionary, something of a reformer.' His main condition, though, was that his position as 'undisputed head of the Home Front under you' should be protected by abandoning the practice of calling Butler the 'Deputy Prime Minister'.[19] Eden agreed to a form of words which established a convention that Butler 'in the absence of the Prime Minister...will continue as hitherto to preside over meetings of the Cabinet', and the deed was done.

Life at the top of the Conservative government in 1955 was anything but peaceful. The Cabinet reshuffle nearly caused a revolt in the House of Lords, and there was considerable discontent in the Tory press. Hugh Dalton, now a semi-retired opponent, had observed cheerfully in April that there was 'no friendship at the top here' between Eden, Butler and Macmillan,[20] and the manner of the reshuffle confirmed the very positive dislike which both ministers felt for their leader. Neither was to be at all reluctant to hasten his downfall when the government came under pressure a year later.

Like many new Chancellors, Macmillan soon discovered that 'The position is *much* worse than I had expected. Butler had let things drift, and the reserves are steadily falling. If and when they are all expended, we have total collapse, under Harold Macmillan!'[21] The problem at the end of 1955 was that the economy was growing too fast with too little structural change. Butler and his advisers had contributed to this situation by a succession of budgets which had reduced the burden of taxation from the heights at which Labour had left it, while relying on monetary policy – both interest rates and controls on credit – to stabilise the economy. Until 1955 this policy seemed to work, but after the April 1955 Budget, later condemned as an electioneering exercise because of its considerable income tax reductions, there was heavy pressure on sterling. A good deal of this was the result of Britain's move towards convertibility between sterling and the dollar: non-residents had been able to convert sterling into dollars since February 1955, and were by now busily engaged in selling the sterling holdings they had built up, in expectation of convertibility, since 1952. A full-scale crisis in the summer of 1955 was met by an emergency Budget in October which substantially reduced the government's capital spending and increased both purchase tax and taxation on distributed profits. Butler pointedly told an International Monetary Fund meeting in Istanbul that the pound would not become convertible, but on the other hand would not be allowed to 'float'. It was during Cabinet discussions over this Budget, in which Eden had interfered persistently without showing any sign that he understood the reasoning behind the Treasury's desire to reduce purchasing power in the economy, that the prime minister decided to move Macmillan to the Treasury.

The Treasury was not satisfied with the October measures, and at the turn of the year warned that it would be necessary to take further steps to protect the balance of payments, even though the Budget had apparently curbed inflation at least temporarily. Macmillan's advisers wanted to get rid of the bread and milk subsidies, the abolition of which Eden had vetoed in October, and to increase the Bank Rate from 4.5 per cent to 5.5 per cent. Macmillan himself also wanted to make severe cuts in defence spending and to increase income tax, in both cases with an eye first on the protection of sterling and second on the need to restrain inflation which was then running at 3 per cent per annum. Eden objected to all these proposals and demanded that all economic measures be gathered into a single budget in March or April 1956. Macmillan was almost openly contemptuous of this approach. He warned the prime minister that 'you would not be wise to attempt an essay in economics' in a forthcoming speech in January; he remarked that 'it would be nice if we could do everything in a single operation. But I am sure we can't...' at the end of that month; and in the same letter he threatened to resign if he was not allowed to announce the end of bread and milk subsidies in the middle of February.[22] He repeated the threat a fortnight later, and won a phased reduction in the subsidies and the increased Bank Rate he wanted, both of which were announced on 16 February. This pleased him and enabled him to claim credit for facing down the prime minister.

Nevertheless, the decision to stagger the announcements of economic measures worked against him. As soon as the February proposals were out of the way he suggested to Eden that the Budget in April should contain a thorough review of defence expenditure, on the grounds that 'it is defence expenditure which has broken our backs'.[23] This was refused point blank. On 5 April he demanded instead to be allowed to raise £100 million by increasing income tax, arguing that 'this demonstration of absolute determination to overcome inflation would have a great effect abroad. It would also have a large – perhaps decisive – psychological effect at home.'[24] Eden once more refused.

Historians have commented rather patronisingly on Macmillan's failure to get his own way on this issue when he had made such a fuss about the bread subsidy,[25] but in fact there are no grounds for surprise. The argument over the February measures had been conducted with great passion, and Macmillan had only been able to win partial concessions (even though he called them 'four fifths' of his demands) by using the heaviest artillery any Cabinet minister can command. Over income tax increases he would have had the additional difficulty that Butler would have objected to the direct and public reversal of his cuts of the previous year. Macmillan had no further leverage with which to force his colleagues to accept the strong budget proposals he would have liked to have made. This is all the more significant since it coloured the tone of his only Budget, and thus contributed mightily to his subsequent reputation. Without anything fundamental to offer, he made a witty speech in which the high point was the announcement of Premium Bonds. This was a sensible, even ingenious way of attracting small savers and thus fractionally reducing the pressure of demand in the economy: interest payments were to be rolled up into a fund from which a small number of savers would receive appreciable prizes. Harold Wilson, the Labour Party's economic spokesman, duly warned that 'They will be fighting the next election on "Honest Charlie always pays"'. In fact the Conservatives were to fight the next election on a position easily caricatured as 'You've never had it so good', which was not very different from Wilson's cruel prophecy; but the noteworthy point is that Macmillan had been forced by his colleagues to announce a bookmaker's budget which did his reputation no good. His own instinct had been to grasp the nettle of controlling an overstretched economy.

Officials were quick to contrast Macmillan's achievement as Chancellor with that of his predecessor. Robert Hall, the Chief Economic Adviser, had described Butler as 'a weak Chancellor who came in at a time when the tide was running in his favour and was clever enough to give it a chance'; in contrast, Macmillan seemed determined to be strict. Although he shocked his Adviser at a meeting with City journalists which 'went on too long and the Chancellor really got a little drunk which surprised and somewhat horrified me as I thought a man of his experience would not run any risks', Macmillan gave the impression of a man who knew his business much more than his predecessor, both in his first memorandum to the Cabinet entitled 'Thoughts from a Treasury Window' and his habit of drafting his own economic speeches. His dispatch of business also impressed.[26] He moved on too soon for his competence to take effect, and seems to have regretted the lost opportunity: as prime minister he was always ready to give pointed advice to his own Chancellors.

.   .   .

SUEZ

In the middle of 1956 Macmillan's main interest in foreign affairs was in the balance of payments and the defence of sterling. This led him into protracted negotiations over German contributions to the cost of the British Army on the Rhine, and for the longer term sustained his interest in Plan G, the proposal for closer association with Europe, described above. He had little direct contact with other aspects of foreign policy except as a Cabinet colleague of his successor, Selwyn Lloyd, who was himself a patient sufferer from prime ministerial interference. All this was changed by Nasser's seizure of the Suez Canal on 26 July, a decision taken in direct retaliation for the refusal by Britain and the United States to finance the massive Aswan High Dam project. Macmillan was a member of the Cabinet's 'Suez Committee', set up by Eden on 27 July, and took a full part from the decision to invade through to the decision to withdraw under American pressure. He then played a full part in the removal of Eden, co-operating with Butler and the Americans to bring pressure on the prime minister to resign. At the end of it all, he was prime minister, charged with repairing the enormous damage which he had helped to inflict on Britain's position in the world.[27]

An analysis of Macmillan's rôle must start with an outline of the crisis. Within days of the nationalisation the Cabinet had decided to regain the Canal Zone by force, in consort with the French, and to overthrow Nasser's regime. Almost immediately it became clear that world opinion was less offended by the nationalisation than were the British and French governments as owners of the Suez Canal Company. In particular, Eisenhower and his Secretary of State, John Foster Dulles, were unwilling to contemplate the use of force to regain control of the Canal, and Dulles came to London in August in search of a settlement. At his suggestion a conference met in London, attended by representatives of twenty-two nations closely concerned as users of the Canal. A majority of those present voted to send a committee to Cairo, led by Sir Robert Menzies, the Australian prime minister, to propose an international authority to Nasser. By 9 September it was quite clear, from the tone and contents of a letter from Nasser to Eden, that the Egyptian leader regarded an international authority as an unacceptable limitation of Egyptian control.

Meanwhile Dulles had thought of an alternative approach, the Suez Canal Users' Association (SCUA). This hypothetical body would collect canal dues from users, who would use their own pilots, and pass on a fair share to Egypt. This scheme was welcomed by Eden, and accepted by the Cabinet on 11 September after the failure of the Menzies mission was clear. As an alternative to military action, which was not yet possible, it seemed attractive, especially since when first presented it was presumed that if Egypt interfered with SCUA it would be a complete justification for the use of force. Britain and France pressed on with a formal case before the United Nations Security Council. Unfortunately Dulles and Eisenhower disapproved of this move, believing it to be a weak case in law, and in any case the American presidential elections forced them to protest at every opportunity that the United States would not support other countries who used force in the event of the breakdown of the SCUA arrangements. At the beginning of October, when asked in a press conference whether SCUA's teeth were not being pulled, Dulles made the memorable observation that 'there were no teeth in it, so far as I am aware'. This alone should have alerted the British government to the dangers of relying on American support, but by now there were two further complications.

The more threatening complication at the time was the alarming expression of interest by the Soviet Union. Bulganin warned Eden in late September that 'small wars can turn into big wars', and this stimulated Eden to renew his efforts to get American support for Britain as part of the defence of the free world against communism: 'I feel sure that anything which you can say or do to show firmness to Nasser at this time will help the peace by giving the Russians pause.'[28] Eisenhower's response, in the full flood of a presidential campaign in which he was representing himself as a man of peace, was completely unhelpful.

The other complication was in the military plan for invasion and seizure of the Canal Zone. In early September the French government approached Israel with an offer of exploratory talks about co-ordinated action against Egypt. Although some sort of co-operation with Israel had been suggested (by Macmillan) in the earliest stages of the crisis, the French did not at this stage tell the British government. Detailed military discussions between France and Israel took place at the end of the month, and at last, on 14 October, the French acting Foreign Minister, Gazier, and the deputy chief of the air force, General Challe, met Eden and proposed what has become known as the Challe Plan. This was that Israel would invade the Sinai Peninsula and move into Egypt, whereupon Britain and France would exercise their treaty rights to occupy the Canal Zone in order to keep the combatants apart and prevent damage to the Canal itself. Eden jumped at this, put it to the Egypt Committee on 16 October, and won its support, with Macmillan speaking strongly in favour. On the afternoon of that day Eden flew to France with Selwyn Lloyd to close the deal with the French and the Israelis. Without officials present, they met Guy Mollet and Christian Pineau, the French prime minister and Foreign Minister, and reached a preliminary agreement. On 22 October Selwyn Lloyd attended a conference at Sèvres at which the Israeli government was also represented. There is no evidence that the Plan was ever put to the full Cabinet for its approval.

After further discussion two British officials, Patrick Dean and Donald Logan, went to France on 24 October and signed an agreement now known as the Treaty of Sèvres, which provided for the Israelis to attack on 29 October with the objective of reaching the Canal the next day; for the British and French governments 'separately and simultaneously' to appeal to the combatants to withdraw 15 kilometres from the Canal; and, on receiving the expected rejection for an Anglo-French force to attack Egypt in the early hours of 31 October. When Eden was given his signed copy at 10.30 that evening, he ordered Dean and Logan to return to France the next day to retrieve all copies, but without success. All British copies of the document were then destroyed.[29]

Destroying the paper did not destroy the plan, which was put into operation almost precisely to timetable. On 30 October, after the Israeli invasion and the Anglo-French ultimatum, both the United States and the Soviet Union put resolutions to the United Nations Security Council calling for Israeli withdrawal. Both were vetoed by Great Britain. Air attacks began on 30–31 October, along with naval attacks on Egyptian vessels. Parachute troops landed at Port Said on 5 November and a seaborne invasion force arrived the next day. At midnight on 6 November, after a successful battle in Port Said and Port Fouad, a storm of international protest, and a run on the pound led by the United States, a cease-fire was ordered. Macmillan was at the head of those who demanded that American objections should be heeded. By 3 December the British and French governments had been forced to withdraw their forces, unconditionally, and cede control to a United Nations force. The Challe Plan had failed, utterly, and the principal reason was the determination of the United States to defeat the use of force by Britain and France. Within a few weeks of withdrawal from Suez, Eden had fallen and been replaced as prime minister by Macmillan.

Macmillan himself looked back on Suez as 'a very bad

episode'[30] and the most memorable comment on his rôle was Harold Wilson's 'First in, first out'. Nigel Birch, one of Eden's most loyal acolytes, thought he had done it all to bring about Eden's retirement and his own succession. Anthony Head, Minister of Defence during the critical period, merely found his behaviour puzzling; 'It wasn't naked ambition, though if you had a nasty mind you might have thought so. I didn't.' Whatever the motive, it is an unedifying story. From the news of Nasser's nationalisation of the Canal until the invasion of Suez on 5–6 November Macmillan was an ardent supporter of vigorous military action, not only to regain the Canal but also, by implication, to overthrow Nasser. On realising the consequences he was no less ardent in calling for a cease-fire, and during the month which followed he was also outspoken in his insistence on an early and unconditional withdrawal. The plainest thing to be said about his behaviour is that he had made a very bad mistake; but also that he had quickly realised its magnitude, and taken the only possible steps to correct it.

As a very senior Cabinet minister Macmillan was in the thick of decision-making from the beginning, and used his own international experience and contacts even though he was no longer Foreign Secretary. On 30 July he entertained Robert Murphy from the State Department (his old friend from Algiers) and warned him of the British view that 'Suez was a test which could be met only by the use of force.'[31] He took further opportunities to impress the point on Dulles when the American Secretary of State was in London in mid-August. His own convictions were apparently unassailable at this point and were based on a potent use of the Munich myth which often served him well. Even his *ex post facto* justification for expanding the operation beyond the mere reoccupation of the Canal Zone was based on Munich symbolism:

> If force was ever to be used, its purpose must be to contain or nullify the threat to the whole peace of the Middle East. We knew well – for we had all lived through those terrible years – that had we taken action against Mussolini in 1935 at the time of his attack on Abyssinia, or against Hitler in 1936, when he remilitarised the Rhineland, the world might have been spared the horrors of the Second War.[32]

This logic appealed to Eden, who had marked Nasser down as an 'Asiatic Mussolini', and also to Churchill, in whom Macmillan confided on 5 August. This was also the spirit in which Macmillan first thought of involving the Israelis. 'I said that unless we brought in Israel it couldn't be done. Surely if we landed, we must seek out the Egyptian forces, destroy them, and bring down Nasser's government. Churchill got out some maps and got quite excited.'[33] There was no doubt either about Macmillan's enthusiasm for the use of force, or about his conviction that force could succeed.

The Munich argument convinced Macmillan himself, and he seems to have been persuaded also, in the teeth of the evidence, that it could convince the Americans upon whom everything depended. In late September he used a visit to the International Monetary Fund to make a number of exhortatory speeches in the United States, using anti-appeasement language. He also spoke intimately to his old friend Eisenhower, and distilled from an amiable chat the conclusion that Eisenhower wanted to see Nasser overthrown and understood that Britain needed economic help if it was necessary to 'play it long'.[34] On the same day he spoke to Dulles and on the next day to the Secretary of the Treasury, George Humphrey, both of whom seemed to say that the United States realised Britain's needs and saw the need for American financial support. Here lay the seeds of error. Macmillan had misinterpreted Eisenhower's view, and his favourable report of Dulles' conversation, which included the distinct hint that Suez might play an important part in the presidential election, was almost certainly interpreted in London, and probably by himself as well, in the light of this misunderstanding.[35]

Macmillan returned to London on 1 October. While he was away Lloyd and Eden had been in Paris discussing military plans with the French government; the day after he returned, Lloyd went to New York to join the French Foreign Minister, Pineau, in presenting the Anglo-French case to the UN Security Council. The next fortnight saw active diplomatic efforts to resolve the Suez dispute without resort to force, accompanied by energetic preparations for an attack. Cabinet and Egypt Committee records from the beginning of October are missing or heavily weeded, and Macmillan's own diary was deliberately destroyed, so the events themselves, and Macmillan's part in them, have to be reconstructed from memoirs and, indirectly, from the Foreign Office telegrams. As a result the principal source in practice is Anthony Nutting, a confirmed

114

and passionate opponent of the Suez adventure, who was at this point Lloyd's Minister of State at the Foreign Office. Nutting has stated in his published account, and insisted in subsequent conversations with a number of historians, that between 2 October and 14 October Eden was willing to entertain a diplomatic settlement based on the so-called Six Principles. Between 11 and 13 October, with the Egyptian Foreign Minister, Mohamed Fawzi, making concessions at the UN, it appears that Eden actually preferred a diplomatic solution.

He was deflected by the opportunities offered by the Challe Plan, which was presented to him on Sunday 14 October. Eden promised the French emissaries that he would reply after consulting his colleagues. The only evidence for such a consultation comes from Nutting, who reports a meeting of the Egypt Committee on Tuesday 16 October, after which Eden and Lloyd went to Paris for highly secret conversations with the French. This Egypt Committee meeting does not appear in the numbered series in the Cabinet records, and it is therefore impossible to check Nutting's recollection that neither Macmillan nor Butler were present.

If Macmillan was absent, he took no part in the original decision to agree to the French proposal; but the minutes show that he was present at the meeting on 17 October which heard the results of the visit to Paris. He was also present at the Cabinet of 18 October, which heard a deliberately understated account of the proposed co-operation with the French and the Israelis. There is little doubt, though, that he was very hawkish indeed in the period up to the Cabinet meeting of 25 October, when the Cabinet was first informed of the intention of 'going in on the backs of the Israelis'.[36] During this period Lloyd went to Sèvres to settle details of the scheme with the French and the Israelis; before he did so, a conference on 21 October between Eden, Butler, Macmillan, Lloyd and the new Defence Minister, Anthony Head,[37] had blessed his going, and the same group debriefed him on his return. The group decided late in the evening of 24 October to recommend the scheme to the Cabinet, whose discussions on Egypt had begun earlier in the day and were adjourned until 25 October. The contents of the Cabinet discussions are recorded in reasonable detail, and confirm that Eden was disingenuous in explaining the degree of collusion which already existed between Britain, France and Israel. The other meetings are not minuted, and the vital information about Macmillan's contribution to the discussion is therefore lost. Eden's press secretary, William Clark, reports that Macmillan threatened to resign if the issue was not pressed to a military conclusion, and attributes the threat to this short period between 14 and 25 October; the official biographer reports Macmillan's own denial that he ever threatened to resign.[38] Even the extent of his knowledge is disputed, with Eden's biographer (echoed by Alistair Horne) remarking that 'Eden did not confide in him any more than he did in Butler.'[39] But it is very difficult to see how he could have been present at the small meetings with Eden and Lloyd and not known what Lloyd had been doing in France.

A divided Cabinet agreed, after long discussion on 25 October, to the proposals which Eden put before them: that if Israel attacked Egypt, as he expected, Britain and France should intervene. The Israeli attack took place, as arranged, on 29 October, and the British government, as arranged, sent Notes to Egypt and Israel informing them that in default of an immediate cease-fire there would be an invasion by British forces to protect the Canal Zone. The military plan, Operation Musketeer, required a bombardment on 30 October, which was postponed to the night of 30–31 October, and a parachute attack followed by a seaborne invasion on 7 October. The invasion fleet had been at sea since 28 October, leaving Malta on the 31st. Although the plan had been agreed with the French and the Israelis, ministers were under constant pressure to revise their plans in response to events, and this was a period of unremitting responsibility. The position taken by almost every senior minister, from Eden downwards, is a matter of some difficulty to ascertain. Of no one is this more true than Macmillan.

Macmillan's departmental role during the last week of the crisis was as important as his contribution to the Egypt Committee. In Cabinet on 30 October he warned that the gold and dollar reserves were still falling, after reductions of $57 million in September and $84 million in October; on the same day he discussed with the Governor of the Bank of England the likely prospect for the sterling balances.[40] As Chancellor he tried to stem the run on the pound, which originated mostly in New York, and eventually tried to get repayment of the British quota from the reserves of the International Monetary Fund. In this last effort he found himself blocked by the Americans, who according to the rules of the Fund had to approve the repayment; he had decided against applying before the first air attack, and found that American intransigence was insuperable once the fighting had begun. He also became aware that the Federal Reserve Bank was selling sterling very heavily. None of this seemed to deflect him from supporting the operation as it was developing. On 4 November, at the Egypt Committee, as Selwyn Lloyd reported 'Macmillan threw his arms in the air and said "Oil sanctions. That finishes it"', when warned that the Americans were considering this step in support of their UN cease-fire resolution, which had been introduced and passed in an enormous hurry the previous day.[41] For all that, he does not seem to have carried his point through to the logical conclusion when in the evening of 4 November, after two meetings of the Egypt Committee, the Cabinet decided to press home the assault.

The Cabinet decision was taken in the light of the UN cease-fire resolution, overt American hostility to the Anglo-French operation expressed by every important American statesmen from Eisenhower down, and a cease-fire between Israel and Egypt which both sides had now accepted. Most of the case for the Anglo-French intervention, carefully confected through the Sèvres Treaty, was in ruins, yet neither the military nor the political objectives had been achieved. General Keightley, commanding Musketeer, needed a decision that evening. After long discussion, Eden called for a vote. Twelve ministers voted to continue the operation; six, including Butler and perhaps Macmillan, voted for delay. Eden then adjourned the Cabinet and, by all accounts, warned Butler, Macmillan and Salisbury that without a united Cabinet he could not go on. Meanwhile Israel was persuaded to withdraw its consent to the cease-fire, thus resurrecting the ostensible justification for intervention to protect the Canal. The Cabinet reconvened, and agreed unanimously to order Keightley's forces forward.

The operation, which began on 5 November, was a military success. Both the military objectives, Port Said and Port Fouad, were captured, though with considerable loss of life among the civilian population. British and French forces penetrated over twenty miles south of Port Said, and were in a position, according to one of the local commanders, to reach Suez itself within forty-eight hours. While this was going on, however, the American government inspired heavy selling of sterling and tightened the noose on Britain by withholding consent to withdrawal of the British IMF balances, as described above. In the United Nations, Lester Pearson, the Canadian prime minister, had introduced a resolution calling for the establishment of a United Nations Force on 4 November, and during 5 November Israel had armed the Secretary-General, Dag Hammarskjöld, with further ammunition by accepting the cease-fire with Egypt about which they had been dickering for the previous three days.

At this point Macmillan, 'near panic',[42] intervened in a Cabinet meeting on the morning of 6 November. He warned that the reserves had fallen by an eighth since the beginning of the month, and that the lack of a cushion from the IMF made the situation intolerable. It is futile to try to decide whether Macmillan's intervention weighed more or less heavily with his colleagues than the collapse of the pretence that British troops were preventing damage to the Canal by standing between Israel and Egypt, or the cold calculation that the mission had been accomplished. One historian has even attributed the initiative to Eden, who after a personal communication from Eisenhower some time in the morning of 6 November 'allowed Macmillan to play the leading rôle in winning over his colleagues'.[43] The bare fact is that under all these pressures the Cabinet decided to order a cease-fire. The claim that it was done because the job was finished, and for no other reason, which is the basis of Macmillan's memoir account, is utterly unbelievable. What is more important is that Macmillan himself had reversed his position because the financial situation had deteriorated beyond control. Butler, whose cautious opposition to the whole scheme was only overborne by Eden's threat to resign if the Cabinet did not back him in the operation, was quite right to observe that Macmillan 'switched overnight from being the foremost protagonist of intervention to being the leading influence for disengagement'. After Macmillan's intervention, the case for carrying on was not pressed, the order for cease-fire was given, and Eden prepared to announce in the Commons that evening that the operation would now halt. No one could tell what further humiliations awaited the Cabinet which had so convincingly mishandled a major performance on the world stage.

Macmillan himself had gone into the Suez affair with his eyes open, warned repeatedly by his officials that pressure on the

pound would be difficult to resist.[44] As early as 8 August Sir Edward Bridges, the Joint Permanent Secretary at the Treasury,
had warned him that the Suez dispute was threatening the balance of payments, but Macmillan convinced himself that 'we
are pretty well armed for Suez'.[45] A month later Bridges urged
that unless American support was unequivocal any military action would jeopardise sterling; this time Macmillan minuted an
admission that 'this is just the trouble. U.S. is being very difficult.'[46] By late September the reserves were falling fast; by late
October, with the invasion force preparing in Malta, Macmillan was telling his Cabinet colleagues that he expected to lose
$300 million (out of something more than $2,000 million) in
November. He and the Cabinet knew that an important charge
on the reserves was the repayment due to the United States under the post-war Loan Agreement. They also knew that military
action would 'cause offence' to the United States.[47] Macmillan
advised that they should keep on using the reserves rather than
float the exchanges, and retain informal links with the United
States to help when it was necessary to borrow from the International Monetary Fund. On 30 October he told his officials
that the government's policy was to see the affair through.

On November 6 Macmillan was told by the Americans that
without a cease-fire they would not support his application to
the IMF, nor give any other assistance. Accordingly, he insisted that the Cabinet should order a cease-fire. This was bad,
but worse was to come since the Americans wanted withdrawal
and were prepared to wait for it before contemplating financial
aid. At the beginning of December the Cabinet bowed to pressure, with the reserves threatening to drop to the lowest level
since 1949. With American support the British government
was able to draw on international credits of $1800 million, re-
lieving short-term pressure on the exchanges at the cost of a
major burden of debt which, ironically, was to fall on Macmillan's shoulders in the New Year. Worse than that, international
confidence in sterling was gravely injured by the whole affair,
and sterling crises were thereafter to be a frequent accompaniment to economic and international strain. As one historian has pointed out, much of this could have been avoided if
Macmillan had passed the Treasury's advice on to his Cabinet
colleagues, instead of arguing for a firmness which the reserves
could not bear.[48] His judgement, much more than his courage,
was called into question by the reversal on 6 November.

THE RECKONING

The Suez crisis destroyed Eden's career and injured Butler's, but Macmillan survived triumphantly. Eden's physical health, never very secure, collapsed after the Suez débâcle; his doctor packed him off to Jamaica on 23 November, whence he returned on 14 December. In his absence Butler as Deputy Prime Minister, with Macmillan as his 'main confidant', dealt with the Americans, the United Nations, the French, the Cabinet and the Conservative Party. The prime minister, isolated in a beach-house, was denied detailed information and almost gagged by his colleagues when he wanted to make a firm statement to the press on his return. His political fate was sealed by the confusion of the Conservative Party in Parliament: his biographer, who was present as a House of Commons Clerk, records:

> Indeed it was a melancholy occasion. Eden slipped into the House virtually without any attention being paid to him. One Conservative MP, Godfrey Lagden, leaped to his feet and waved his order paper; he looked around him, was stunned by the pervasive silence on the Conservative benches, and subsided with a thunderstruck look on his face. The Opposition just laughed. Eden looked hard at his shoes, and his colleagues shuffled papers and looked at each other meaningfully. At that moment one knew that it was all over.[49]

Decisions taken by the Cabinet in Eden's absence, and the changed mood of the Conservative Party, had made inevitable the resignation which was to follow on 9 January. Macmillan's part in these transactions, in which he so convincingly triumphed over Butler, reminds one of the removal of Clifford Allen from the Next Five Years group twenty years earlier, but played for higher stakes on a larger stage: a brutal, self-seeking, but, in the last resort, very necessary manoeuvre to preserve the interests of the country, the government and the Tory Party.

Macmillan's first concern was to control the impact of the crisis on the position of sterling. American pressure on sterling had brought the Suez operation to a halt; but it was not certain that that pressure would be removed without even further concessions on Britain's part. Treasury officials told him on 7

November that the State Department was still likely to obstruct any IMF drawing, while the closing of the Suez Canal and of oil pipelines in the Middle East would force Britain to buy oil in the Western hemisphere at a cost of over $800 million in a full year. Losses to the reserves of this order were not sustainable if the sterling–dollar exchange rate was to be maintained, and contemporary wisdom held that resort to a floating rate would cost as much even in the short term, quite apart from its crippling effect on British prestige. Macmillan's view was therefore that Britain must immediately do anything necessary to regain American support. The main obstacle was Eden, who on 7 November refused the United Nations General Assembly's request for the immediate withdrawal of British troops.

The next two weeks were occupied in energetic but futile attempts to restore Britain's international prestige and reinvent the Anglo-American 'special relationship', a nexus which was now regarded with scepticism and contempt on both sides of the Atlantic. Selwyn Lloyd was sent to New York to stave off a vote of censure in the United Nations; arrange for a smooth transfer of control from Anglo-French forces to the UN peace-keeping force, rather than to Egyptian troops; negotiate with the Egyptians for better terms in the management of the Canal, using continued occupation of the Canal Zone as a bargaining counter; persuade the United Nations to allow British salvage vessels to begin work immediately to reopen the Canal; and persuade the State Department that continued Anglo-French occupation was in the best interests of the world community. This last, the most important point, was received singularly badly by the Americans.[50] American pressure continued, to the point that Macmillan asked the Cabinet on 21 November to authorise petrol rationing as an emergency measure to reduce the pressure on the exchanges. The Treasury continued to warn of the danger to sterling, until on 29 November the Cabinet ordered an unconditional withdrawal from Suez, expecting that this alone would persuade the Americans to prop up the pound.

American policy-makers were driven to their punitive attitude towards British needs by an acute distrust of Eden and ultimately of Selwyn Lloyd, and it was this which gave Butler and Macmillan, with some help from Salisbury, the opportunity to undermine the prime minister. Eisenhower, re-elected as president on 6 November, moved from geniality to suspicion in a matter of hours on the following day as Eden pressed him to receive a visit from the British and French prime ministers. Lloyd's activities in New York left him cold, and by 19 November the president and his closest colleagues were dealing directly with Macmillan and Butler through the American ambassador in London, Winthrop Aldrich. It has been shown that this dialogue was initiated by the Americans, and coexisted with a channel of communication through Butler to the Secretary of the Treasury, George Humphrey.[51] While there is no direct evidence that the Americans made Eden's departure a condition of support, their decision to deal directly with Eden's subordinates even before the prime minister had gone on holiday suggests that Eisenhower–Eden relations could never pick up again exactly where they had left off. Macmillan was keen to establish his own private communication with the White House, but this was deftly discouraged by Eisenhower, who asked Aldrich wherever possible to see Butler and Macmillan together.[52]

Thus Butler and Macmillan were left not only in charge of events but grappling directly with the central problem, of resurrecting the 'special relationship'. Macmillan, however, was getting no help from Eisenhower in any attempt to turn the situation to his personal advantage ('we don't want to be in a position of interfering between those two' remarked Eisenhower to Aldrich). This job he had to do alone. Butler's rôle as Deputy Prime Minister and understudy in Eden's absence gave him the odium of defending an indefensible policy to the country and the Conservative back bench, knowing that whether he lied or told the truth he could not possibly please everybody. This was to Macmillan's advantage. On 12 November, during the debate on the Address, he made liberal use of Munich analogies to persuade a sceptical House that the attack on Suez was justified.[53] After Butler's distinctly ambivalent defence of the government's position to the Commons on 22 November, the two men went together to address the back-bench 1922 Committee. Butler's biographer has called this joint appearance 'a highly expensive mistake', especially because Butler, the senior man, spoke first, leaving Macmillan to give a performance which Enoch Powell described as 'One of the most horrible things that I remember in politics... – seeing the way in which Harold Macmillan, with all the skill of the old actor-manager, succeeded in false-footing Rab. The sheer devilry of it verged upon the disgusting.'[54] Macmillan's speech played again on the Munich legend, which was soon to become the creation myth of Macmillanite Conservatism; his effect upon both wings of the party, but especially on the Left, was noticed immediately. While Butler was getting steadily more tired and less popular as the burden of defending the indefensible settled upon him, Macmillan spoke little in public and took care that when he spoke he was ebullient and uplifting.

His contribution to unscrambling the mess was not, however, an insignificant one. On 28 November, on Treasury advice which coincided with his direct understandings of American views, he told the Cabinet that American goodwill, which was essential to the defence of sterling, 'could not be obtained without an immediate and unconditional undertaking to withdraw the Anglo-French force from Port Said'.[55] He pressed this point home in the two subsequent meetings, and finally won the decision on 30 November. His colleagues had not agreed that the withdrawal had to be unconditional, fearing that the back bench would not accept such a humiliating climb-down. By the end they were convinced that it was necessary. This was, of course, a collective decision. As such, it was announced in the Commons by Selwyn Lloyd, who was humiliated by the gentle contempt of the opposition and the fierce contempt of the Suez Group. Unkind critics blamed Butler for not taking the job himself. No one blamed Macmillan.

It was clear soon after Eden's return that his health could not support the strain of office. His doctors told him that he would die if he did not resign; and although he did not wish to go, he was convinced (by a third and fourth medical opinion) that he must. He therefore resigned on 9 January 1957. Anticipatory mutterings have been documented.[56] Although these do not seem to have amounted to an attempt, by Butler or Macmillan or anyone else, to get rid of Eden at that moment, Macmillan told Butler in mid-December that younger members of the Cabinet, especially Peter Thorneycroft, 'did not think Eden could or would go on'. This observation was soon to be linked in Butler's mind with 'frequent talks & reunions . . . in the study at No. 11. Those present included those principally since elevated namely Peter Thorneycroft, David Eccles, Alan Lennox-Boyd and more distantly Sandys.'[57] Even so Macmillan at one point had tried to dissuade Eden from going on a Jamaican holiday from which he would return as a political casualty. The precise date of Eden's departure was evidently unexpected, even by his senior colleagues, who had to devise very swiftly the procedure for choosing a successor. In the event Salisbury and Kilmuir interviewed each of their colleagues individually. Kilmuir's account of the process –'To each Bobbetty said, "Well, which is it, Wab or Hawold?"' – is uncorroborated but immortal nonetheless. Patrick Buchan-Hepburn, and perhaps also Walter Monckton and James Stuart, favoured Butler; the rest chose Macmillan, as did the Chief Whip (Edward Heath), the chairman of the party (Oliver Poole) and the chairman of the 1922 Committee (John Morrison).[58] With no further consultation, the deed was done, and Macmillan was summoned to the Palace the next day.

• • •

NOTES AND REFERENCES

1. Robert Rhodes James, *Anthony Eden* (London: Weidenfeld and Nicolson, 1986), p. 409.

2. On this episode see John W. Young, ' "The Parting of the Ways"?: Britain, the Messina Conference and the Spaak Committee, June–December 1955', in Michael Dockrill and John W. Young, *British Foreign Policy 1945–1956* (Manchester: Manchester University Press, 1989), pp. 197–224.

3. FO 371/110635. The OEEC consisted of nineteen countries.

4. Sir Roger Makins to Macmillan, 22 Dec. 1955, FO 371/5999.

5. Untitled memorandum by H. Macmillan, 6 Feb. 1956, T 234/183.

6. 'United Kingdom Commercial Policy. Memorandum by the Chancellor of the Exchequer and the President of the Board of Trade', 28 July 1956, CAB 129/82.

7. Diary of Sir Raymond Streat, 17 Oct. 1956, in Marguerite Dupree (ed.), *Lancashire and Whitehall: the Diary of Sir Raymond Streat* (2 Vols, Manchester: Manchester University Press, 1987), II, 841–2. Streat was Chairman of the Cotton Board, and very anxious for protection of the textile industry.

8. Consequently the historiography is murky; but see Leontios Ierodiakonou, *The Cyprus Question* (Stockholm: Almqvist and Wiksell, 1971).

9. Harold Macmillan, *Tides of Fortune* (London: Macmillan, 1969), p. 670.

10. Memorandum by Armitage, 25 June 1955, PREM 11/834.

11. Macmillan to Eden, n.d., PREM 11/834.

12. Diary, 2 Sept. 1955, quoted in Alistair Horne, *Macmillan 1894–1956* (London: Macmillan, 1988), p. 365.

13. Minute, 9 June 1955, FO 371/115869.

14. Shuckburgh Diary, 31 August 1955, in Evelyn Shuckburgh *Descent to Suez: Diaries 1951–56*, ed. John Charmley (London: Weidenfeld, 1986), p. 277.

15. Simon Shamir, 'The Collapse of Project Alpha' in W.R. Louis and Roger Owen, *Suez 1956: the crisis and its consequences* (Oxford: Clarendon, 1989), pp. 73–100, especially p. 89.

16. Diary, 23 Sept. 1955, quoted in Horne, *Macmillan 1894–1956*, p. 368.

17. 'Dizzy with Success', 31 August 1955, CAB 129/77, CP(55)111.

18. Bodleian Library, Woolton Papers, Diary 24 Oct. 1955, ff. 170–2.

19. Macmillan to Eden, 24 Oct. 1955, quoted in Macmillan, *Tides of Fortune*, pp. 692–3.

20. Dalton Diary, 1 April 1955, in Pimlott (ed.), *The Political Diaries of Hugh Dalton*, p. 658. He also remarked that 'Macmillan shuffles along like an old man.'

21. Diary, 30 Dec. 1955, quoted in Horne, *Macmillan 1894–1956*, p. 378.

22. Macmillan to Eden, 12 Jan. 1956, quoted in Horne, *Macmillan 1894–1956* pp. 379–80; Macmillan to Eden, 29 Jan. 1956, PRO Treasury Papers, T273/312.

23. Macmillan to Eden, 23 March 1956, PREM 11/1326.

24. Macmillan to Eden, 5 April 1956, PREM 11/1326.

25. Richard Lamb, *The Failure of the Eden Government* (London: Sidgwick & Jackson, 1987), pp. 56, 58; Horne, *Macmillan 1894–1956* p. 381.

26. *The Robert Hall Diaries, 1954–1961*, ed. Alec Cairncross (London: Unwin Hyman, 1991), pp. 56, 58, 61.

27. The fullest recent account of British policy-making over Suez is in W. Scott Lucas, *Divided We Stand: Britain, the U.S. and the Suez crisis* (London: Hodder & Stoughton, 1991); but see also Keith Kyle, *Suez* (London: Weidenfeld, 1991).

28. Rhodes James, *Anthony Eden*, p. 525.

29. Ibid., p. 532.

30. Horne, *Macmillan 1894–1956*, p. 447.

31. Robert Murphy, *Diplomat among Warriors* (London: Collins, 1964), p. 463.

32. Macmillan, *Riding the Storm*, p. 111.

33. Martin Gilbert, *'Never Despair': Winston S. Churchill 1945–1965* (London: Heinemann, 1988), p. 1203.

34. Diary for 25 Sept., quoted in Macmillan, *Riding the Storm*, p. 134. Lord Sherfield (Sir Roger Makins), who was present, is convinced that Eisenhower neither gave nor implied any such assurances.(Interview).

35. Macmillan to Eden, 25 Sept. 1956, PREM 11/1102; Macmillan, *Riding the Storm*, pp. 135–8.

36. Nutting, *No End of a Lesson*, p. 104.

37. Walter Monckton, who disapproved of planning for an attack on Egypt, had by now resigned on 'health grounds'.

38. Clark was interviewed by Alistair Horne; Horne, *Macmillan 1894–1956*, p. 434.

39. Rhodes James, *Anthony Eden* p. 532, quoted (out of context) by Horne, p. 433.

40. Sir Leslie Rowan, 'Note for the Record', 31 Oct. 1956, T 236/4188.

41. Selwyn Lloyd, *Suez 1956* (London: Coronet, 1978), p. 206.

42. According to Selwyn Lloyd's recollection in *Suez 1956*, p. 209.
43. David Carlton, *Anthony Eden*, (London: Allen Lane, 1981) p. 452. This depends on Pineau's supposition of a message from Eisenhower in *1956. Suez* (Paris: R. Laffont, 1976). See also the account in Lucas, *Divided We Stand*, pp. 291–3.
44. On the financial question, see especially Diane B. Kunz, 'The Importance of Having Money: the economic diplomacy of the Suez crisis', in W.R. Louis and Roger Owen, *Suez 1956: the crisis and its consequences* (Oxford: Oxford University Press, 1989), pp. 215-32.
45. Bridges to Macmillan, 8 Aug. 1956, T236/4188; Minute by Macmillan, 12 August 1956, on 'Controls', a memorandum by Sir Bernard Gilbert, ibid.
46. Bridges to Macmillan, 7 Sept. 1956, ibid.
47. CAB 128/30, CC(56)85, 26 Oct. 1956; ibid., CC(56)84, 25 Oct. 1956.
48. Lewis Johnman, 'Defending the pound: the economics of the Suez crisis, 1956', in T. Gorst, L. Johnman and W.S. Lucas, *Postwar Britain, 1945–1964: themes and perspectives* (London: Pinter Publishers, 1989), pp. 166–81.
49. Rhodes James, *Anthony Eden*, p. 592.
50. Reported in an interview between Lloyd and Richard Lamb, cited in Lamb, *The Failure of the Eden Government*, p. 284.
51. Carlton, *Anthony Eden*, pp. 459–62; Howard, *RAB*, pp. 241–2.
52. Carlton, *Anthony Eden*, p. 460.
53. *H.C. Debs*, 1956–57, Vol. 560, 12 Nov. 1956, col. 688, part-quoted in Macmillan, *Riding the Storm*, pp. 171–2.
54. Howard, *RAB*, pp. 240–1, reporting an interview with Powell.
55. See Kunz, 'Importance of Having Money', in Louis and Owen, *Suez 1956*, pp. 230–1.
56. In a confidential memo from Heath to Butler, cited in Howard, *RAB*, p. 245.
57. Untitled, undated holograph note by Butler, apparently Feb. 1957, Trinity College Library, Butler Papers G31/70.
58. The Earl of Kilmuir, *Memoirs* (London, 1962), p. 285. Buchan-Hepburn's name was mentioned by Anthony Head to Alistair Horne, and Butler also named him; the others were named only by Butler, as noted by Howard, *RAB*, p. 247.

Chapter 6

FROM SUEZ TO THE PARIS SUMMIT

Macmillan reached the premiership in January 1957 because the Conservative Party, and above all his Cabinet colleagues, trusted him more than it trusted Butler, and respected his courage. The reasons for this preference are still not clear and may not have been clear to Macmillan himself. His contributions to policy in recent months had been erratic (though hardly more erratic than Eden's); though fertile in ideas he had never been at the centre of the party's policy-making as Butler had been; his periods of senior office as Foreign Secretary and Chancellor had not been as successful as his term as Housing Minister; and above all he was not the heir-apparent. Butler's jaundiced conclusion was that 'what I call affectionately the "Young Turks Movement" had decided in their own minds to rally round the European Free Trade system, a military onslaught on Nasser, the retirement of Anthony Eden and the eventual succession of Macmillan'.[1] This alone would not have given Macmillan the premiership without at least the acquiescence of a wider body of opinion in the Conservative party. Even so the new premier predicted that his ministry would only last six weeks; yet as soon as he had ridden past the aftermath of Suez, the party's acceptance of new leaders was enough to assure him two comfortable years in office. Moreover, his parliamentary style and the happy coincidence of a buoyant economy and a divided opposition tended to strengthen his personal position in his first eighteen months in 10 Downing Street.

But if he could rely on his Cabinet colleagues and in due course on his back bench for political support, he could not expect them to find new answers overnight to the problems of the second half of the 1950s. Britain was still living with the consequences of the Second World War. In office Macmillan had demonstrated a talent for improvisation, but he had occupied no office for long enough to grapple convincingly with the main issue: that Britain's commitments and aspirations far exceeded its resources, and that a 'solution' to one problem (whether in housing, defence, or foreign relations) was more likely than not to exacerbate problems elsewhere. Now he had to take responsibility for reconciling these conflicting demands, as well as the conflicts within his party which had grown up under Churchill and Eden.

In Macmillan's eyes the most important task was to restore Britain's relations with the United States, because he believed that America would help Britain preserve some international influence despite the manifest weakness of the British economy. To persuade the Americans of this simple proposition was a priority for his first year, which brought him first to the Bermuda Conference in March 1957 and then to Washington in the subsequent October to enunciate with Eisenhower what he rather grandly called 'the doctrine of interdependence'.[2] The essence of this was that the United States would continue to support NATO and provide Britain with warheads and the rockets to deliver them, which would enable it to remain a nuclear power. All this had been jeopardised by Suez, and the question of Anglo-American relations was raised in his first Cabinet meetings.

By that time, though, Macmillan and his Cabinet had already been confronted by other symptoms of Britain's retreat from power. Minor colonial policing matters illustrated a growing gap between Britain's responsibilities east of Suez and the military and economic resources available to discharge them. At the same time the Cabinet had to consider the cost of defence, and Duncan Sandys, the new Minister of Defence, had been ordered to draw up a new, cheaper defence policy. His proposals, including the reduction of British forces in Germany by nearly 40 per cent, were presented in a White Paper in April.[3] This could hardly be separated from the issue of Anglo-American relations, since the plausibility of Britain's defence and contribution to NATO were now to rest on its nuclear forces, which were in turn dependent on the United States.

Weakness abroad was a direct consequence of economic weakness at home. To his Cabinet colleagues, Macmillan was frank about Britain's economic dilemmas in the mid-1950s.

Although the 'austerity' of the immediate post-war period had given way to economic expansion throughout the industrial world, Britain's real growth in the early 1950s had been slower than that of any other industrialised country, and the twin problems of balance of payments stability (symbolised throughout this period by the question of whether to seek free convertibility between the pound and the dollar, and the perpetual anxiety about the sterling balances), and rising internal prices made every Chancellor's life fairly miserable. The financial crisis caused by Suez added further difficulties, and although these were largely overcome by the middle of 1957 the underlying inflationary trend seemed to remain. Macmillan's approach to foreign affairs during his premiership was always conditioned by worries about money.

For most of his premiership Macmillan behaved as though internal and external problems were separate. He gave less attention to domestic than to foreign affairs, and in foreign affairs often seemed to his critics to be trying to cut a figure as an international statesman rather than working for British interests. But one foreign problem was intimately related to Britain's domestic politics. Since the blunderings of British policy towards the Messina proposals, Macmillan's attitude to the economic integration of Europe had reflected his profound pessimism about the British economy. 'Europe' was a solution to the structural problems of the British economy, as well as a political move in defence of the Western alliance. Macmillan and his confidants believed that an exposure to European competition would achieve by micro-economic means what the macro-economic manipulations of Keynesian policy could not do for the decaying structure of British industry. He therefore pursued a closer association with Europe, partly by completing the stages of Plan G, but in the end by applying to join the Common Market. He failed; but he had the consolation that a majority of his party were eventually persuaded that the pursuit of economic modernity with Europe was not incompatible with sentimental attachment to the Empire or a preference for English-speaking Americans over any sort of foreigner.

By the end of Macmillan's first year of office an agenda of foreign policy problems had thus been set out. None of them went away before 1963, and although some of them acquired new twists the measure of Macmillan's premiership was that he had to run very hard to make even the slightest progress in any field. His efforts, and the deliberate cultivation of the *persona* of an unflappable wonder-working leader, can best be understood by examining each area of external policy in turn: relations with the superpowers, the problems of Empire, and the opportunities in Europe.

. . .

NOT QUITE A SUPERPOWER

Harold Evans, who served as Macmillan's press officer throughout his premiership, remarked in March 1960 that 'he tends eventually to say indiscreetly in public what he has been saying discreetly in private, e.g. the British as the Greeks in the Roman Empire of the Americans'.[4] This was indeed a major theme of the new prime minister's private and public ruminations even before he reached Downing Street. He was hardly alone in taking this view, but he was alone among post-war prime ministers in making it the fulcrum of his foreign policy. Others either distrusted the Americans too much (like Eden and Wilson), or retained a less pessimistic view of Britain's independent prospects (like Churchill). Macmillan had made his point to Richard Crossman in North Africa in 1942,[5] and continued to make it throughout his years in opposition and as a Cabinet minister. In his mind it was entirely compatible with a commitment to European unity, because its main purpose was to create a secure bulwark against Soviet expansion in Europe. A further aim was to support Britain's overseas presence, also threatened by indigenous nationalist movements which looked East for moral support and sometimes material aid.

To make this work it was essential to bring about a *rapprochement* with the United States. Macmillan admitted later that during the Suez crisis he had misjudged the American mood. He felt, in particular, that John Foster Dulles had been unexpectedly unhelpful to Britain and that the officials closest to President Eisenhower were unwilling to take the British government into their confidence. Macmillan intended to rely heavily on the memory of his successful wartime collaboration with Eisenhower, but to do this he would have to establish a personal contact. He had also to convince his Cabinet colleagues of the political wisdom of approaching the United States again; the 'Suez group' of angry right-wing back-benchers were not alone in nourishing a fierce resentment against all things American. There were, in addition, many potential differences between the two countries even after the end of the Suez episode, and these had to be resolved satisfactorily in Cabinet as well as with the Americans.

Macmillan's greatest ally in this mission was the Soviet Union. After Suez the Kremlin made no secret of its enthusiasm for intervening in the Middle East, where many regimes were vulnerable to popular uprisings, and where Western powers, all tarred with the 'imperialist' brush, were automatically suspect. To prevent trouble, Dulles and Eisenhower evolved at the end of 1956 the 'Eisenhower doctrine' which followed the pattern of the Monroe and Truman doctrines in defining an area of the world in which the President of the United States thought it his right and duty to intervene to maintain essential American interests. The Eisenhower doctrine gave the president permission to operate in the Middle East, and by March 1957 the Senate had voted him $200 million with which to support friendly countries.

This gave the Administration greater leverage to make demands, especially on Israel, and at first this upset British efforts to emerge with some shred of dignity from Suez. During the effort to reopen the Canal, the Egyptian government demanded that Israeli troops should withdraw from the Gaza Strip before French and British ships were once more allowed to pass, even though other nationalities were to be allowed through as soon as the waterway was clear. This demand Macmillan tried to resist, but the United States government urged Israel to withdraw, leaving the Gaza Strip under United Nations control. Macmillan observed that 'our honour and our interest are in conflict',[6] and made sure that Britain was not put in the position of having to vote at the United Nations in favour of sanctions against Israel.

American decisions also played a large part in the resolution of the central Canal controversy, which was whether, if British ships did start to use the Canal, the dues should be paid to the Egyptian government or into a special blocked account which Britain was maintaining as security for British claims against Egypt arising from nationalisation. Although the United States initially supported British and French demands that the dues should be paid to the United Nations, American diplomats were unable to persuade Nasser to reconcile his conditions for opening the Canal with the Six Principles agreed at the United Nations the previous October,[7] and in April Cabot Lodge, speaking on behalf of the United States at the United Nations, recommended that Nasser's proposals should be given a try. This in effect obliged Britain to capitulate, lest economic competitors should gain an advantage from readier access to oil supplies. The decision to allow British ships to use the canal and pay dues to Egypt was announced on 13 May and debated in the Commons on 15 and 16 May: the greatest parliamentary test yet faced by the new prime minister. Macmillan noted soon after he made his announcement that 'the Tory dissentients are beginning to organise themselves...'; and even before the debate 'Lord Salisbury has joined the rebels, with a rather bitter statement in the House of Lords about the Suez decision.... (What a blessing he went over Makarios!)'[8] Macmillan recorded the 'extreme degree of nervous strain involved' in preparing his speech, was disappointed in his performance, and fussed about press reactions; but he was exhilarated to win the division by forty-nine votes, with only fourteen Tory abstentions. In retrospect, he declared this a watershed for his new administration, which could now be assured of a full term in office.[9] Apart from a few doubters, he had apparently convinced the Conservative Party that American hegemony had to be accepted.[10]

Despite the lowering of tension after British withdrawal, American attitudes in the Middle East were still at odds with British interests. Nevertheless, the frustrations and humiliations surrounding Anglo-American dealings in the Mediterranean could be seen as the end of a chapter, the unavoidable denouement of the Suez drama. The fruits of the new beginning, in which Macmillan's policy and his personal prestige were much more closely involved, were first seen at the Bermuda Conference of March 1957. Here a select gathering, consisting of Eisenhower, Dulles, Macmillan, Selwyn Lloyd and supporting officials, went over the most important matters at issue between the two countries.

Over Suez, Egypt and Israel it was difficult to reach common ground, and the attempt was not pressed. On the closely related subject of the Baghdad Pact, Macmillan scored a significant success, using the analogy of the Eisenhower Doctrine to persuade the Americans to take part in the organisation's military planning committee, while getting American approval of Britain's position as protector of small states in the Persian Gulf. For the moment there was no likelihood of repeating the fiasco of 1951, in which American influence had been thrown on the side of anti-British forces in Iran and Iraq. The most important agreement reached at Bermuda, though, was the undertaking by the Americans to supply Britain with intermediate-range ballistic missiles with American warheads (the Thor missiles) to bridge the gap until British missiles and warheads had been developed as an independent nuclear deterrent. The British nuclear arsenal, such as it was, consisted of bombs to be dropped by long-range aircraft (the V-bombers); this was reckoned to be inadequate against newly developed anti-aircraft weapons, and the Defence White Paper which Duncan Sandys was perfecting in the spring of 1957 depended on an effective nuclear deterrent to justify very large reductions in conventional forces. The supply of American missiles was the only way to make Macmillan's defence policy work. He was duly grateful, though he later had reason to regret this dependence on American equipment. Compared with this very practical aid, Anglo-American agreement to co-operate in disarmament was of little more than metaphysical significance, at least until the middle of the year when the American negotiator at the regular disarmament conferences let his enthusiasm run away with him.

Macmillan's later estimate of the effect of Bermuda was guarded and ambivalent, though he made a successful defence of his achievement in Parliament by wrong-footing Gaitskell over Labour's attitude to nuclear weapons. Understandably, his later reflections put great emphasis on the advantages of a personal link between a British prime minister and an American president. His conversations with Eisenhower were 'just exactly as in the old days'; 'the atmosphere was very good';[11] his approach to Eisenhower at the beginning of the meeting was to 'receive as host; greet as old comrade; welcome as head of the greatest and most powerful nation in the world'.[12] The language Macmillan used to bring this about was unequivocal. On the first day he reminded Eisenhower that 'you cannot be neutral in a war between two principles, one of which – Communism – is evil', and hung upon this the rest of his argument for Anglo-American co-operation in which Britain was needed 'for ourselves; for Commonwealth; and as leaders of Europe'.[13]

The rest of the discussion, from the practical problems of

nuclear weaponry to the creation of a common attitude in the Middle East, was underpinned by this reasoning. It certainly persuaded Macmillan. It probably persuaded Eisenhower, at least for a time. Its effect on Dulles, whose position in the United States policy-making machine was unassailable, was far less positive. Macmillan thought that 'Dulles, who by temperament and conviction is a sort of Gladstonian Liberal, who dislikes the nakedness of facts, has also come a long way',[14] but there was a long way still to go. Macmillan's hope was that in the struggle against communism Britain would be recognised not only as an ally but as a necessary and special ally, and this, as he realised, was by no means assured at Bermuda.

But after the Bermuda Conference, rebounding from Suez, the Anglo-American relationship became stronger and more 'special' as it took the practical form of military co-operation outside Europe as well as in it, and an increasing intimacy in nuclear weapons deployment. Macmillan carefully plotted a course to build up British strength, avoiding a mounting pressure at home and abroad to slow down or halt British nuclear weapons development. On 15 May 1957 the first British hydrogen bomb was tested successfully. Three weeks beforehand, Macmillan had received from Bulganin a proposal, buried in a wide-ranging document about Anglo-Soviet relations, that the two countries should immediately suspend nuclear tests and work towards a general prohibition of nuclear testing, independently of the continuing disarmament talks. Macmillan was later to dismiss this as 'the beginning of a propaganda offensive that was subtle and seductive',[15] whose aim was to exploit the widespread fears of nuclear war to undermine British resolve. The Labour Party's response convinced him that public opinion in Britain was susceptible; he minuted to Charles Hill[16] that 'I wonder ... whether all this propaganda about the bomb has really gone deeper than we are apt to think.... It presents many features useful to the agitator. It has an appeal for the mother, the prospective mother, the grandmother, and all the rest, and every kind of exaggeration or mis-statement is permissible.'[17] He therefore decided to embark on a propaganda offensive of his own, 'partly in the hope of some genuine détente and partly to satisfy public opinion at home',[18] and stepped up efforts to ensure that British nuclear capacity was firmly established before any concessions were made.

As if to prove that there was still work to do on the Anglo-

American relationship, the American representative at the Disarmament Conference, Harold Stassen, proposed a scheme on 1 June which would end not only testing but also the production of nuclear weapons material by any power. 'Is this America's reply to our becoming a nuclear power – to sell us down the river *before* we have a stockpile sufficient for our needs?' wrote Macmillan.[19] He resorted to his personal relationship with Eisenhower, and since the proposal had not in fact been authorised either by the President or by the Secretary of State it was easy enough to persuade the American government to back away, even though it was impossible to prevent the Russians from taking advantage of the gaffe. This experience emphasised the urgency of Anglo-American technical co-operation, and Macmillan duly prepared to ask for a repeal of the McMahon Act, which since 1946 had prevented the release of information about nuclear weapons to America's allies. He visited Washington in October, after preparation by Selwyn Lloyd, and secured both a 'Declaration of Common Purpose', including the McMahon repeal, and a plan of action which would consolidate the NATO alliance by extending the deployment of American Intermediate Range Ballistic Missiles (IRBMs) in Europe. The other NATO countries agreed in principle, after some heartsearching, in December. This was achieved by linking the scheme with the offer to the Soviet Union of a conference of Foreign Ministers to resolve outstanding disputes.

In these transactions Macmillan showed that he had both a tactical skill in reconciling American and European sensitivities, and a fundamental commitment to making a single front against Russian expansion; he noted in his diary that:

> We have got the Americans to take a more realistic view of the psychological and political situation in Europe.... There is *no* division between NATO countries who approve the rockets and those who disapprove – at least on ethical grounds.... We are beginning to get the Europeans out of the 'Maginot Line' complex and begin to look to their flanks. Suez – although a tactical defeat for us – is in this sense beginning to be vindicated strategically.[20]

Britain's survival as a major power after Suez depended on such efforts of co-operation, and occasionally on bluff. For the time being Macmillan was able to provide them.

There was never any doubt, though, that his success depended on the United States, and Macmillan found himself in the uncertain position of a witch-doctor who retains his hold over an anxious flock by controlling the weather. Some knowledge of meteorology allows the shaman to make the right incantations at the right time, knowing that the storm is about to break; Macmillan's long acquaintance with Eisenhower and strengthening links with Dulles enabled him to predict, roughly, when something could be done. But there were always sceptics to the Left and Right who complained that his influence over the United States was imagined, and that the government therefore had no real control over Britain's fate. Nuclear weapons and nuclear testing, with their associated diplomacy, exposed the government to many attacks.

Labour's hostility was predictable but much more dangerous to the Labour movement than to the government. The Labour leadership –'some of whom are pro-Russian, others defeatist and others sound loyal supporters of NATO and the Bevin tradition'[21] – was so bitterly divided over nuclear disarmament, with Bevan always eager to embarrass Gaitskell, that most parliamentary exchanges on the subject did Macmillan, and the government, more good than harm. The greater threat was from the Conservative Right, led by the 'Suez group' who most resented American intervention in 1956 and who were inspired, and sometimes led, by Salisbury after his resignation in March 1957. This group found it difficult to recognise the degree of British dependence on the United States, resented the terms on which American missiles were based in Britain, blamed the United States for forcing Britain to abandon the colonial empire, and resented any concession on nuclear testing which seemed to qualify Britain's status as a great power. Their hostility weakened Macmillan's power base within the Conservative Party, and on occasions threatened to produce embarrassing results in parliamentary divisions. Caught between the complaining factions, Macmillan became slightly querulous, and like almost all Conservative prime ministers since the war used Munich metaphors promiscuously to justify his position; in December 1957, after the NATO agreement on missiles had met a tepid reception at home, with the press calling for urgent talks with the Russian leaders, he protested that 'all this is pure Chamberlainism. It is raining umbrellas.'[22]

Always tendentious, the Munich metaphor was in this case

also not apt. Macmillan was now fully committed to preserving British interests by acting as an intermediary between two more powerful nations, and taking what amounted to a broker's commission in diplomatic advantage. His conception of global politics recognised the immense military strength of the superpowers. He was determined to maintain a nuclear deterrent, on the grounds that it was the only convincing defensive system which the country could afford. Even so, nuclear weapons were never cheap, and his efforts to move towards a test-ban treaty, which began in response to correspondence with Bulganin at the end of 1958, were a prudent measure of economy as well as an opportunity to cut an international figure. His relations with the United States grew closer, and his efforts to bring Britain into a closer relationship with Europe were limited during his first administration to the sterile completion of discussions about the European Free Trade Area. Macmillan's realism about Britain's capacity to behave as a Great Power was tempered, especially during his first administration, by his huge enjoyment of diplomacy as a pastime. Talking to American, and later to Russian leaders was the most competitive, and therefore enjoyable, form of the sport.

. . .

TILTING THE BALANCE OF POWER

Macmillan's diplomatic calculations in 1957 embraced the test-ban proposals themselves, linked as they were to the continuing disarmament discussions in Geneva, the integration of West Germany into NATO, and the nursing of British public opinion about nuclear deterrence and the Cold War, which was now beginning to polarise alarmingly. While contemplating his reply to Bulganin in late 1957 he paid an official visit to Germany, to seek German support for the EFTA–Common Market arrangements and to persuade Adenauer's government that it was safe to reduce British conventional forces on the Rhine because the remaining troops would be 'trip-wire' for a devastating nuclear riposte. The Germans, in Macmillan's view, did not understand the strategic and economic logic of nuclear deterrence which underlay the Defence White Paper. On the other hand, he needed German support for Britain's attempt

137

to establish a constructive relationship with the Common Market, and he therefore had to devote a good deal of effort to persuading Adenauer that British policy attached due importance to Germany's survival. Even in 1957 a strong current in German thinking was fearful of the implications for Germany of a purely nuclear defence of the Western alliance, and moves towards a *rapprochement* with Russia which would include some measure of nuclear disarmament were therefore politically desirable; yet at the same time Adenauer's government was keen to argue that the reunification of Germany must be made a condition precedent to any disarmament agreement with the Russians.

None of this made the reply to Bulganin any easier, and Stassen's intervention at the disarmament talks made things worse. The formal Anglo-American response to Russian suggestions for a test-ban treaty was merely to observe that disarmament would only be possible after a reduction of political tension.[23] This was overtaken by a proposal from the Russian negotiator that there should be a two- or three-year moratorium on nuclear tests, monitored by an international agency, with inspection posts on Russian and American soil. The Allies proposed a ten-month suspension to allow the technicalities of inspection and monitoring to be studied. When developed and put into a 'package' with other proposals for a reduction of conventional arms and a plan for non-military use of space vehicles, these proved unacceptable to the Russians, upon whom the onus of rejecting a test ban could therefore be allowed to fall. This was a temporary and far from complete solution to what was fast becoming a major political problem for Macmillan.

His main difficulty was still with domestic opinion. On the central issue of nuclear disarmament he had little to worry about. His own party was not interested in unilateral nuclear disarmament, and only a very few Conservatives had any time for any policy of multilateral disarmament which would inhibit British progress towards the military security promised by the Defence White Paper. The Labour Party was thoroughly embroiled in controversy over unilateralism, with the Bevanite Left in full cry against Gaitskell and the Right, so every parliamentary debate on the subject evoked more bitterness between Labour's factions than between government and opposition. On the issue of a test ban, especially outside parliament, the government was much more vulnerable. A test ban seemed to the public less drastic than the repudiation of all nuclear weapons, and because of the reiteration of Russia's proposals it seemed to be an issue on which Russia and the West could realistically be expected to agree. Macmillan was much preoccupied by the domestic response to his carefully paced replies to Bulganin, fearing that the nuclear issue had 'drawn away from us that wavering vote with vague Liberal and nonconformist traditions which plays such an important rôle because it is still the no-man's land between the great entrenched Parties on either side'.[24] In October he was elated by Bevan's unexpected repudiation of unilateralism, which seemed to confirm his feeling that Russian rejection of the 'package' had not pleased the Left in Britain, and incidentally threw the Bevanites into a satisfying confusion. To take advantage of this shift in opinion, he suggested a British initiative, to be made public at the autumn meeting of the United Nations. He proposed to limit the number and potential radioactive fallout of tests, whether or not the Russians agreed, and to give advance warning of all tests. This would either advance international agreement, or rally British support for the government; either outcome, or both together, would be acceptable.

The corollary of this was that Britain needed access to American nuclear technology, for without tests the British nuclear programme could not develop enough information for itself. This would require the repeal of the MacMahon Act of 1946. Macmillan's main aim in going to Washington in October 1957 was to persuade Eisenhower and Dulles that the time had come to share nuclear information with Britain, and to his surprise they agreed. The practical importance of this dramatic step was much greater than the flowery 'Declaration of Common Purpose' in which it was embodied. On the one hand it allowed Britain to develop the nuclear weapons programme of the Defence White Paper without expensive duplication of basic research; on the other hand, as part of the Declaration, it gave Britain some leverage over American policy, which enabled Macmillan to persuade his most powerful ally that the deployment of nuclear weapons in NATO countries in Europe would only be accepted by the countries concerned if an offer of talks was made simultaneously to the Russians.[25]

The offer was a qualified political success. The meeting of NATO in December 1957 accepted the deployment of nuclear-armed IRBMs in Europe; and the next day the House of Commons, heavily whipped, accepted the result of the NATO meeting. Macmillan was displeased with his majority of thirty-nine, attributing the shortfall largely to the Suez group who resented the missile bases as the outward and visible signs of American hegemony within the alliance. He also found reason to complain at the press, which was urging him to get on the next plane for Moscow.[26] He responded with a party-political broadcast in early January, targetted on three heresies he had identified within the Conservative Party and the public. Anti-Americanism was a major problem, 'the English form of the great disease from which the French are suffering more than any other people – that is, looking backwards to the nineteenth century', compounded with a phobia of European connections and finally a susceptibility to 'the clever Russian propaganda for peace' which affected the public more than the party.[27] Part of this broadcast was a candid statement of the case for refusing to work for the total abolition of nuclear weapons; he also made the case for progressive negotiations between the West and the Russians, aimed first at a non-aggression pact and later at reductions in conventional and nuclear forces. A test-ban agreement was an essential part of this package.

The initiative still lay with Russia. On 11 December another note from Bulganin proposed an immediate ban on nuclear tests, and on 9 January 1958 a further note actually proposed a summit conference. Despite the broadcast, this threw Macmillan and indeed the whole of the leadership of the NATO alliance into a stew. There was considerable suspicion of Russian motives, resentment that the Russians were sending identical letters to the Allied governments and exploiting the differences in their replies, and a widespread fear that a summit would break down in such a way that the West would be blamed for its failure. The Russians declined to accept the argument for a preparatory meeting of Foreign Ministers. Macmillan did not want a summit without adequate diplomatic preparation, but wanted to get the credit for breaking the deadlock. He therefore tried unsuccessfully to get the Cabinet to agree to a letter to Bulganin in which he would offer to go to Moscow in person, but only to settle an agenda and to set out a procedure for future discussions. This idea was rejected, though Macmillan warned his colleagues that some initiative from Britain would be necessary sooner or later. His final, approved answer merely reiterated the suggestion of preparatory talks either by Foreign Ministers or through ordinary diplomatic channels. Tepid as it seems with hindsight, this was well received in the Press and in the Commons. Macmillan's stock went up when he defended the government's record successfully in a foreign affairs debate in February, and although he had to rescue Selwyn Lloyd, whose performance in the same debate had been wooden and ineffective, he was generally satisfied with the result.

Macmillan's concern now was that 'we should come forward as soon as possible with a constructive proposal that will put the burden firmly back on the Russians and be understood to do so'.[28] Until the formal repeal of the McMahon Act he did not want to take too many risks with a test ban, so he was anxious to make the Western initiative some sort of prolegomena to a summit meeting. In this he was only just in time. Khrushchev finally got rid of Bulganin on 27 March, and two days later an agreed three-power statement went to the now sole Russian leader from France, Britain and the United States, proposing a summit after preparation by ambassadors and Foreign Ministers. Two days later the Russians made their announcement of a unilateral suspension of nuclear tests – not an enormous sacrifice, since they had just completed a series of tests, but a significant gesture. Macmillan reckoned that the propaganda effect of the two announcements probably cancelled each other out, and this appears to have been his intention. The British tests of the new hydrogen bomb were accelerated, while the government resisted demands from the Labour Party for an immediate response to the Russian offer with some devastating debating points – 'This is as if in a football match, one side having scored two goals asked the opposing team not to play any more.'[29]

A developing crisis in the Lebanon[30] cut across international discussions about a summit, and it was not until August that Macmillan returned to the subject. In the meantime, although there had been some coolness between Britain and the United States over the detailed handling of events in the Middle East, and although the Americans, especially Dulles, expressed reluctance about appearing too closely associated with Great Britain,[31] the practice of close discussion between the two powers had been cemented. Macmillan was pressing the Americans to relax the restrictions on trade with China and the Soviet bloc and had succeeded so far as Russia was concerned.

Then, to his surprise, Dulles proposed the abandonment of nuclear tests by the West 'pending a workable agreement on inspection'. Macmillan was unenthusiastic, especially since the details of the exchange of nuclear information between Britain and the United States had not yet been worked out. Dulles, who won Eisenhower's support, was insistent, and Macmillan was forced to follow, announcing on 22 August that Britain would suspend testing after the current series was finished and enter talks on 31 October for an internationally agreed general suspension of tests. When the Russians agreed to talk, Macmillan was satisfied.

Having won political advantages from the planned negotiations, Macmillan was irritated when the Americans added a further condition, that suspension of their tests would depend upon upon progress towards general conventional disarmament: 'the Americans have suddenly and surprisingly turned round. Too weak in August, they are being too tough in October.'[32] While technical talks continued at Geneva, Macmillan pressed Eisenhower to be more flexible: 'the Russians are now in a better position to fool the world into believing that it is we who are preventing agreement by insisting that discontinuance of tests should be conditional on satisfactory progress towards real disarmament'.[33] Even though he was not keen to hurry the process unduly, he was determined to retain the political advantage.

Macmillan's belief that he was better than Eisenhower or Dulles at the game of high diplomacy was if anything reinforced by the crisis over Berlin, which blew up in November. Khrushchev, ostensibly alarmed by the signs of a *rapprochement* between France and Germany over European security, declared that Russia intended to abandon the four-power agreement under which Berlin was governed in sectors by representatives of Britain, France, America and the Soviet Union. The Soviet sector was to be handed over to East Germany, the implication being that the Western sectors should also be handed over. The official Soviet note promised that there would be 'no changes in the present procedure for military traffic from west Berlin to the Federal Republic of Germany for six months'. Macmillan correctly described this as 'an ultimatum with six months to run'; it threatened the tenuous lifeline which had held the population of West Berlin to the Federal Republic since the days of the Berlin airlift in 1949.[34] His reaction was to try to take the initiative in forming the Western response.

Accepting that it would be unreasonable to reply with aggression to a post-dated ultimatum, he threw British influence in NATO behind a statement of policy which rejected the Soviet plan, upheld the Western governments' rights (based on the Potsdam Agreement) and proclaimed their responsibilities to the citizens of West Berlin. At the same time he discouraged the Americans from planning a major military effort to rescue Berlin, warning Dulles in February that 'we must not slip into the 1914 position – mobilisation sliding into war'.[35] The NATO allies had, besides their declaration, no agreed plan to deal with the evolving situation, and Adenauer for the Federal Republic was urging a firm stand: 'he stands (officially) for absolute rigidity and a solid front against Soviet Russia. Behind the scenes, he wrings his hands and says that Russia and the West are like two express trains rushing to a head-on collision.'[36] The next Soviet suggestion was to recognise the two Germanys as separate states and demilitarise both of them; the British and their allies held that this would expose the NATO alliance to an intolerable military risk. Both at home and abroad Macmillan faced the problem that this exchange of notes could easily go on until the six-month ultimatum had expired, with Britain and the other Western governments exposed to increasing pressure from left wing and even centrist dissentients at home to make a settlement in accord with Soviet wishes. The Commons in early January 1959, in particular, was distinctly restless.

Amidst these troubles, Macmillan now revived the plan of visiting the Soviet Union. It was a risk even to suggest a visit, since a rebuff from the Kremlin would be a humiliating setback in itself. The attitude of Germany, France and the United States could not be assured in advance. In the event the Russians did agree; the French and American governments eventually approved, though with no great enthusiasm on the part of Eisenhower or Dulles; the German reaction was frosty and cynical, with a suggestion from Adenauer that it was no more than an election-year stunt. Macmillan went to Russia on 21 February, returning on 3 March, and extracted the maximum publicity and some diplomatic advantage from a strenuous and unpredictable tour. Wearing a succession of fur hats, including a white one from the Finnish war, Macmillan was photographed in Moscow, Leningrad and Kiev in the company of workers, students, milkmaids, nuclear scientists and many other ordinary citizens. He broadcast on Soviet television. He gave and received gifts, ranging from a stuffed elk's head to a two-volume history of Moscow University 'and a small plaque' from the Russians, and a considerable quantity of antiques from the British government to Khrushchev, his family and colleagues. Selwyn Lloyd, in attendance, was sent spinning across a frozen lake in a large basket in a party game with Kremlin leaders. Caviar and vodka were copiously consumed. There were visits to the ballet and the opera.

These diversions occupied a good deal of the ten-day visit, but the meat of the trip lay in three episodes. Khrushchev, while Macmillan and Lloyd were on a visit out of town, made a long speech in Moscow which attacked all the Western allies – often with personal comments directed at their leaders – but largely ignored Britain and concluded with the suggestion of an Anglo-Soviet non-aggression pact. To this blatant attempt to divide the alliance Macmillan felt obliged to reply in the formal meeting which took place the next day. In the course of the conversation both Khrushchev and Macmillan became heated. Eventually Macmillan remarked that 'if you try to threaten us in any way, you will create the Third World War' and Khrushchev lost his temper.[37] Thus ended a difficult day. The next morning, 26 February, Khrushchev renewed his attack on the Western powers' attitude to Berlin, blaming the West for the increase of tension and for having warlike intentions. Finally he brought out the 'toothache insult': a swiftly developed indisposition which prevented him from accompanying the British party to Kiev. Although the final discussions of the visit were much friendlier, the tangible outcome was hardly an advance upon the state of wariness which had been typical of Anglo-Soviet relations before the visit. The final communiqué produced no more than a reiteration of the need for an early agreement to stop nuclear tests and a reminder that the two sides were very far apart over Berlin.

With nothing practical done, the visit nevertheless acquired significance because of the mercurial shifts in the official Soviet temper from cordiality to bitter hostility and back again. Moreover, the Soviet offer of an early summit meeting was pointedly reiterated, and Macmillan was persuaded of its utility. Macmillan was thought by some to have held his own in the exchange because he had kept faith with the Western allies by tough talking; but he had done so only in response to a Soviet attack, without leading the heckling himself. This was his own optimistic view. Adenauer and de Gaulle both disagreed strongly, and said so when he visited Bonn and Paris to report the results of his trip. When he visited Washington, his suggestion of an early summit, prepared but not over-prepared by prior discussions at ambassador level, was greeted with suspicion by Dulles (who was, admittedly, terminally ill) and even by the normally benign Eisenhower. He was able to get the allies to agree to move towards a summit conference, but they would only do so very slowly 'as soon as developments in the Foreign Ministers' meeting warrant' such a step.[38] Dulles's resignation in April 1959 left the more pliable Christian Herter at the State Department, but Macmillan had perforce to 'assume at least the moral leadership of the West'[39] because no other country really wanted to move fast in his direction.

In effect Macmillan was at odds with the other Western allies both about Berlin and about the desirability of an early summit. The conference of Foreign Ministers at Geneva, assembled at Russia's suggestion, spent June and July working at the Berlin problem. Repeatedly Macmillan complained at the 'legalism' of his allies' demands over Berlin, and warned that the Soviet position, though always expressed offensively, was softening in practice. When a Russian proposal offered a long extension of the ultimatum of the previous year, he was aghast when the rest of the allies refused to make a corresponding concession. Since the Americans were also dragging their feet about a test-ban agreement, largely because new technological developments made verification more difficult, any hope of rapid progress seemed to be thwarted. The greatest frustrations for Macmillan were the repeated changes of plan in Washington. Herter suggested in mid-June that Macmillan should simply invite Eisenhower, Khrushchev and de Gaulle to London for an 'informal' summit. It transpired that Eisenhower and his advisers did not like the plan. Eisenhower believed that the Foreign Ministers must make progress to justify a summit; but then he suggested that an informal meeting between himself and Khrushchev could take place in New York 'without presenting the picture of a "Summit" meeting'.[40] A month later Eisenhower had once again changed his mind, accepting that a summit meeting should take place in August, whether or not there had been progress at Geneva over the

Berlin question; but Macmillan was soon cast down to discover that he had changed his mind back, and he fired off another appeal to the president. This appears to have had some effect, though Macmillan was at first unwilling to recognise the benefits. Eisenhower extended an open invitation to Khrushchev to visit the United States, which was accepted.

Interestingly, Macmillan was incensed.

> ... this foolish and incredibly naive piece of amateur diplomacy has the following results:
>
> (a) He has made any further 'progress' at Geneva less likely. The Russian position will harden.
>
> (b) He will have a very difficult task in explaining to the American people that there is *no* progress at Geneva and yet he has asked Khrushchev to have a jolly visit to America.
>
> (c) There will be no Summit.
>
> (d) The French and German Governments and people will be suspicious and angry.
>
> (e) My own position here will be greatly weakened. Everyone will assume that the two great Powers – Russia and U.S.A. – are going to fix up a deal over our heads and behind our backs. My whole policy – pursued for many years and especially during my Premiership – of close alliance and co-operation with America will be undermined.
>
> .... This shows that Gaitskell and Crossman and Co. are right. U.K. had better give up the struggle and accept, as gracefully as possible, the position of a second-rate power.
>
> .... Ministers were very angry indeed when I unfolded this story to them. I purposely did not try to underestimate the dangers or excuse the failure of my diplomacy.[41]

The panic of a man who thinks he has failed in his principal and overriding objective – not to allow himself and his country to take second place in the eyes of the world – is obvious enough here. Within a fortnight he had changed his view of the proposed Eisenhower– Khrushchev meeting, largely because the press was giving him part of the credit for it: 'this is said to be the result of the Macmillan initiative. The British broke the ice.... I am relieved that this is the interpretation of history which is universally accepted.'[42]

By the middle of 1959, in short, Macmillan's sense of diplomatic timing was closely attuned to the forthcoming General Election. He had been amusingly rude to a Labour MP who had taunted him with going to Russia to court domestic popularity. He had irritated Eisenhower and Dulles by his avidity for public exposure during his Washington visit in March.[43] He was now determined to have the best possible context for the poll. He urgently wanted a test-ban policy, before the election, because of 'the intense emotional preoccupation, especially among young people, with the fall-out effects from nuclear tests'.[44] On the other hand 'from the electioneering point of view [a summit] would be better as a prospect in the future than a modified success or even failure in the past'.[45] He made sure that Eisenhower's world tour in July began in London, and staged a televised 'discussion' of foreign affairs between president and prime minister. Finally, he expressed 'considerable relief' when, a few days before the election, Eisenhower announced that the Khrushchev visit, which took place in September, had removed most of the American objections to an early summit meeting.[46]

After winning the election Macmillan was nonetheless anxious to maintain the momentum which had steadily gathered in 1959. Eisenhower wanted a summit in December, with a preparatory meeting of Western heads of government. De Gaulle, on the other hand, saw no substantial change resulting from the Khrushchev visit and proposed a 'Western summit' rather later – perhaps in April. Macmillan, who by now was prepared to go anywhere at almost any time so long as he had a summit to go to, was predictably annoyed, and duly relieved when de Gaulle was brought round. At the preparatory meeting – in Paris on 19 December – there was a consistent effort by France, Britain and the United States to prevent Adenauer from making preconditions about Berlin which would frustrate the intentions of a summit. When Adenauer tried to get back to the *non possumus* position about Berlin which the Western allies had taken before the Geneva Conference began, Eisenhower was 'very firm and almost rude'. The Chancellor, only temporarily quelled, subsequently suggested to Macmillan that a proposal to hold a series of summits in different capitals would be 'helpful in winning elections', to which Macmillan replied 'that I was not thinking of elections but of our duty to God and to mankind'.[47]

The Paris discussions lasted for three days, during which Macmillan and Lloyd were able to get 'nearer to the French without losing the Americans'.[48] This was in part because de Gaulle seemed, temporarily, to accept the stately moves by Britain towards the Common Market, which the Americans were encouraging; in part because de Gaulle, for his own

147

reasons, was interested in tripartite discussions between Britain, France and the United States over defence, even though France had by now withdrawn from the NATO staff structure. The Paris meeting could therefore be counted as a considerable success for Macmillan in many areas. He got substantial agreement that the Western powers would make moderate demands about Berlin. He persuaded Eisenhower, at the last minute, to continue the moratorium on nuclear tests, so that negotiations for a treaty could go ahead. He brought France closer to an equal footing with Britain and the United States on defence matters, inside Europe and beyond; and in return for this mediation between de Gaulle and Eisenhower he hoped for support in Britain's efforts to enter Europe. Looking forward to 1960, he could expect a fruitful year in international relations.

Macmillan was too optimistic about the forthcoming summit, which was settled for 16 May in Paris. He had lengthy discussions with de Gaulle in March, which seemed to offer the prospect of continued friendly discussions and concerted action on defence and other matters. Out of the blue, the Russian representatives at the technical conference on the nuclear testing produced a proposal linking a ban on large tests (which could be monitored) with a moratorium on smaller tests. Macmillan leaped at the chance to persuade the Americans to make a further move in reply, and went to Washington at the end of March to hold talks, which resulted in a joint communiqué accepting the Russian proposals; this was achieved by bolstering Eisenhower against vested interests within the American defence establishment which wanted to continue testing indefinitely. All this confirmed his view of the merits of steady, incremental and piecemeal efforts to improve Great Power relations.

The early months of 1960 were filled for Macmillan with diplomatic activity. His trip to Africa, with the Winds of Change speech carefully prepared to be delivered in Cape Town, and the Commonwealth Conference which dealt with South Africa,[49] were taxing; the state visit of General de Gaulle, in April, was more of an opportunity to display Western solidarity and remind the public of the better aspects of wartime co-operation between Macmillan, de Gaulle and the Americans. Then, days before the Paris summit, an American U2 reconnaissance aircraft was shot down in Russian airspace, and the pilot, with his cameras, photographs and espionage equipment, captured and put on display by the Russian government. Macmillan's first reaction was an angry amazement that the pilot had omitted to kill himself and blow up his aircraft. He was further taken aback when the American government produced a series of implausible cover stories instead of refusing to discuss intelligence matters at all.

Since all the powers were spying on one another, and Britain's own series of photographic reconnaissance flights had only just finished, Macmillan found it easy to take a pragmatic view of what had happened. '[E]spionage was a fact of life', as he tried to tell Khrushchev when the leaders finally reached Paris, and it was not something for statesmen to become excited about. His main concern was for the summit. The first signs were that Khrushchev was not going to let the incident frustrate the conference, but the crescendo of American excuses and counter-denials culminated in Eisenhower's admission on 11 May that he had authorised the U2 mission. Hence Macmillan's second encounter at Paris, after a brief formal meeting of Western leaders, was with an angry Khrushchev, supported by his foreign affairs and defence ministers, demanding a full apology from Eisenhower, a promise to desist from any future aerial espionage, and punishment of those responsible in the United States government. Talking it over with Eisenhower and de Gaulle afterwards, Macmillan urged that the conference should continue, even though de Gaulle was convinced that Khrushchev intended a rupture of relations. There was not much he could do in the first plenary session the next day, where Khrushchev was bitingly critical of the American position; nor did he make much impact on the three heads of government when he visited them in turn that evening. Khrushchev was no more accommodating in private, refusing to attend the first formal session of the summit (planned for 10 a.m. the next day and postponed until 3 p.m.) unless Eisenhower met his conditions. Macmillan, in some desperation, prevailed on Eisenhower and de Gaulle to withhold their statement declaring that the summit was over until 10 in the evening, but 'So ended – before it had ever begun – the Summit Conference.'[50] At Khrushchev's press conference the next day 'it is possible that none of the experienced chroniclers of an antic world had ever before heard one leader of a great nation address the leader of another great nation in words of such abrasive and calculated bitterness and challenge'.[51]

Macmillan was naturally anxious that the conference should not be a complete loss. During the comings and goings of 17 May Gromyko, the Russian Foreign Minister, had made encouraging noises about the test-ban conference going on in Geneva. On the 18th de Gaulle and Eisenhower had opened up the possibility of strengthening the 'tripartite' arrangements if Khrushchev unilaterally signed a peace treaty with East Germany, as he was threatening to do. But the outcome devastated Macmillan's policy of being seen to be indispensable to the settlement of the world's problems. He was inseparably identified with the idea of a summit. Yet when the world's leaders were at last brought together, it was shown that at such an occasion a series of false steps, by any or all of the powers represented, could do more damage to world peace in a couple of days than in months or even years of diplomatic posturing. Macmillan was hit hard. Eleven years later he wrote in his memoirs of 'disappointment amounting almost to despair'; his private secretary later remembered that 'this was the moment he suddenly realised that Britain counted for nothing; he couldn't move Ike to make a gesture towards Khrushchev, and de Gaulle was simply not interested. I think this represented a real watershed in his life.'[52] Whatever Khrushchev's motives in refusing to be conciliated – and it is likely that he was under pressure from conservative voices among his own colleagues, and was also profoundly shaken by the tactlessness of the American reaction to the U2 incident – this was a major blow to Macmillan's prestige as a statesman. The immediate effect on British public opinion was slight, but it was a failure to be remembered when his domestic popularity began to wane.

. . .

NOTES AND REFERENCES

1. R.A. Butler, 'Diverse reminiscences ending with Suez', TS memorandum, 18 April 1957, Trinity College Library, Butler Papers G31/88. The reference to EFTA suggests that Butler had Thorneycroft especially in mind.

2. *H.C. Debs*, 1957, Vol 577., 5 Nov. 1957, col. 35.

3. Cd 124 *Defence: outline of future policy* (HMSO, 1957). This was in fact approved by the Cabinet before the Bermuda Conference.

4. Harold Evans, *Downing Street Diary* (London: Hodder & Stoughton, 1981), p. 112, entry of 26 March 1960.
5. Crossman in the *Sunday Telegraph*, 9 Feb. 1964, though since by this time the phrase was in the public domain the detail should perhaps not be relied upon.
6. Diary, 21 Feb. 1957, quoted in Harold Macmillan, *Riding the Storm* (London: Macmillan, 1971), p. 217.
7. See above, p. 115.
8. Diary, 13 and 14 May 1957, quoted Macmillan, *Riding the Storm*,p. 235.
9. Ibid., pp. 234–8.
10. See Max Beloff, 'The Crisis and the Consequences for the British Conservative Party' in W.R. Louis and Roger Owen, *Suez, 1956* (Oxford: Clarendon, 1989), p. 333. Beloff remarks that 'Macmillan himself was the conscious agent of this revolution.'
11. Diary 20 March 1957, quoted in Macmillan, *Riding the Storm*, p. 250.
12. Notes for opening statement, quoted ibid., pp. 251–4. He also circulated them as a Cabinet Paper.
13. Ibid.
14. Macmillan to Menzies, 26 March 1957, quoted in Horne, *Macmillan 1957– 1986*, p. 26.
15. Macmillan, *Riding the Storm*, p. 296.
16. Chancellor of the Duchy, in charge of news management for the Cabinet.
17. Ibid., pp. 298–9.
18. Ibid., p. 298.
19. Ibid., pp. 300-1.
20. Ibid., p. 338.
21. Ibid., p. 340.
22. Ibid., p. 341. Only Edward Heath seems to have been able to resist the oratorical temptations of the appeasement myth.
23. The correspondence was published in a White Paper, Cmd 380.
24. Macmillan to Charles Hill, 4 June 1957, quoted in Macmillan, *Riding the Storm*, pp. 298–9.
25. Ibid., p. 337; 'Declaration of Common Purpose', CAB 129/85, C(57)77.
26. Macmillan, *Riding the Storm*, p. 341. He was particularly concerned that the *Daily Express*, normally far to the Right, had joined the *Daily Herald* and the *News Chronicle* in calling for a grand gesture.
27. Macmillan to Chief Whip, December 1957, quoted ibid., p. 460.
28. Macmillan to Eisenhower, 17 March 1958, quoted ibid., pp. 477–8.
29. Speech to the Primrose League, 25 April 1958, quoted ibid., p. 488.
30. See below, pp. 205–7.
31. Harold Caccia (Ambassador in Washington) to Selwyn Lloyd, 3 June 1958, PREM 11/2689.
32. Diary, 18 October 1958, quoted in Macmillan, *Riding the Storm*, p. 568.
33. Macmillan to Eisenhower, 1 Jan. 1959, ibid., pp. 569–70.
34. Macmillan to Selwyn Lloyd, 28 Nov. 1958, quoted ibid., p. 573.
35. Diary 4 February 1959, ibid., p. 588.
36. Diary 16 January 1959, ibid., p. 581.
37. Macmillan in conversation with his biographer, reported in Horne, *Macmillan 1957–1986* (London: Macmillan, 1989), p. 125.

38. Diary, 31 March 1959, quoted ibid., p. 132.
39. These are the words of his biographer, ibid., p. 133.
40. Eisenhower to Macmillan, 17 June 1959, quoted in Macmillan, *Pointing the Way*, p. 70.
41. Diary 26 July 1959, quoted ibid., pp. 79–80.
42. Diary 6 August 1959, quoted ibid., p. 81.
43. Dulles (by telephone) to Herter, cited by Horne, *Macmillan 1957–1986*, p. 147.
44. Macmillan, *Pointing the Way*, p. 86.
45. Ibid., p. 80, discussing the state of affairs at the end of July.
46. Ibid., p. 92.
47. Ibid., pp. 104–5.
48. Diary, 20 December 1959, quoted ibid., p. 109.
49. See below, pp. 186–91.
50. Diary, 17 May 1960, quoted in Macmillan, *Pointing the Way*, p. 211.
51. James Cameron, *Point of Departure* (London: Panther, 1969), p. 245. Cameron has conflated two or more press conferences in his account; it was this second formal press conference which other correspondents described as 'reminiscent of Hitler at his worst' (Macmillan Diary, 18 May 1960, quoted in Macmillan, *Pointing the Way*, p. 212.)
52. Interviewed by Horne, quoted in Horne, *Macmillan 1957–1986*, p. 231.

Chapter 7

FROM THE PARIS SUMMIT
TO THE TEST-BAN TREATY

· · ·

THE NUCLEAR THREAT

The diplomatic sequel to the failure of the Paris Summit in 1960 was depressing. Khrushchev refused further personal dealings with Eisenhower, and any summit was thus postponed until the new president was in office. The Russians withdrew, abruptly, from the Geneva Disarmament Conference at the end of June. There was a minor incident when an American survey aircraft was shot down in international airspace in July. On the other hand the Russians made no further progress towards signing a peace treaty with East Germany, and although East–West relations did not markedly improve during 1960, they did not become catastrophically worse than they had been immediately after the Summit. Nonetheless, Macmillan's preoccupation was now with strengthening the military posture of the Western alliance, and strengthening Britain's position within it. He pressed ahead with 'tripartitism', the plan for regular meetings between the heads of the three Western nuclear powers to discuss problems of global politics and strategy which transcended NATO.[1] He also tried to exploit the doctrine of 'interdependency', which he had worked out with Eisenhower in 1957, to make Britain's nuclear deterrent effective. It was in these negotiations that it finally became clear, albeit two years later, that Great Power status in a nuclear world was more than Britain could afford; but while they lasted Macmillan was able

153

to persuade himself that he had solved the problem of being poor and powerful at the same time.

The 1957 Defence White Paper was, in its time, one of Macmillan's most substantial contributions to Britain's global stance. Its central concept, that of getting the maximum effectiveness at a reasonable cost, was the essence of his approach to the problems of government in his first year as prime minister. The idea had evidently been formed by his year at the Treasury and also his service at the Ministry of Defence, for although he had not had long in the Defence Ministry, and felt overshadowed by Eden when he was there, he had been given an excellent opportunity to think about the economics of modern warfare.[2] In 1957 the aspiration to maintain a military force based on conventional weapons, large forces under arms, and peacetime conscription had been abandoned. In its place came a smaller, all-volunteer force, with the planned abolition of National Service in 1962; a reduction of the regular army; a net reduction in the size of the Navy, especially in its contribution to NATO; and a reduction of Fighter Command, with the withdrawal of tactical air forces from Germany. All of these cuts were to be counterbalanced by reliance on the nuclear deterrent to prevent war in Europe, and major improvements in the mobility of the army to discourage trouble overseas.

Although the nuclear solution was expected to be cheaper than conventional forces, there were two paths to potentially uncontrollable expenditure. On the one hand, effective nuclear warheads had not been developed for large-scale production in Britain in 1957. The series of nuclear tests described above had been part of the development process of these new weapons. The difficulty, and indeed the cost, of such development was sharply reduced by the repeal of the MacMahon Act by the Americans in 1958; this gave Britain access to bomb-making technology which could readily be used in British factories. The problem of delivery systems was rather more complicated. The V-Bomber fleet, despite its hoped-for longevity,[3] could not be expected for very much longer to be able to drop nuclear bombs on towns protected by sophisticated anti-aircraft systems. The Blue Steel air-to-ground missile was developed to extend the V-Bombers' range and service life. The perceived vulnerability of piloted aircraft then led to the development of Blue Streak, a land-based surface-to-surface missile, which was extensively tested. Blue Streak was in turn abandoned in

February 1960, on the grounds that weapons launched from fixed sites on land were vulnerable to pre-emptive strikes. This left Britain with the capacity to make nuclear bombs, but no way to drop them on the enemy except the early version of Blue Steel. The Chiefs of Staff made the case for a submarine-launched missile as the most desirable delivery system for the future. This was accepted by the Cabinet Defence Committee, but this left a gap until the Polaris rocket, then being developed by the United States, was ready for service. Incidentally, it committed the Cabinet to an 'independent' deterrent which depended entirely on American supplies.

During Macmillan's visit to Washington in March 1960, he obtained a promise that until Polaris was ready the Americans would supply the Skybolt air-to-ground missile, now in a late stage of development, on which British-made warheads could be mounted. 'This allows us to abandon Blue Streak (rocket) without damage to our prospects of maintaining – in the late 60s and early 70s – our *independent* nuclear deterrent.'[4]

Macmillan effectively admitted in his memoirs that the government had mishandled Blue Steel and Blue Streak, and recorded with gratitude that the Labour Party's divisions over unilateral disarmament once more allowed an easy victory in the Commons against what might have been 'legitimate censure'. He had also committed himself, in advance of full discussion in Cabinet, to allowing the Americans to build a Polaris base on the Clyde as a *quid pro quo* for Skybolt, and had an uneasy moment in October when, after the Cabinet approved the submarine base, there were rumours that Skybolt would never be finished. Although the test-ban negotiations continued lackadaisically, Macmillan was now leading his Cabinet more and more closely into an interlocking military alliance with the United States. Confrontations over the Congo, and an amusing row with Khrushchev at the United Nations in November 1960, confirmed the impression that the new Russian leadership and the NATO alliance were drifting further apart, with the consequence that British policy was more and more bound up in the 'special relationship' with the United States.

This had two consequences. American pressure reinforced a tendency which was already established to strengthen Britain's political links with the EEC; this is discussed separately below. The other consequence was that Macmillan's relationship with the incoming president was of great significance. He had traded for many years on his intimacy with Eisenhower; now he had to make some connection with a new leader of the most powerful nation on earth. As soon as John Kennedy was elected he sent him a long and ruminative letter which emphasised four themes. He led with the need to reflate the Western economy by easing credit, with the corresponding need to restore Third World confidence in capitalism by increasing commodity prices; his other two themes were the test-ban talks at Geneva, and the need for a general disarmament agreement.[5] This was intended only as an introduction, for he was already preparing a paper on the future of the Western alliance, later known as the 'Grand Design', which met the new decade with a curious mixture of resignation and defiance.

1. The Free World cannot, on a realistic assessment, enter on 1961 with any great degree of satisfaction.

In the struggle against Communism, there have been few successes and some losses over the past decade.

In the military sphere, the overwhelming nuclear superiority of the West has been replaced by a balance of destructive power.

In the economic field, the strength and growth of Communist production and technology have been formidable. (Indeed, it ought to be, for that after all is what Communism is for.)

In the political and propaganda field, Russian ... subversion, blackmail, seduction and threats, as well as the glamour of what seems a growing and dynamic system, have impressed hesitant and neutral countries, and are proving especially dangerous among the newly independent nations of Africa and Asia. Against this background the long predominance of European culture, civilisation, wealth and power may be drawing to an end.

2. On the other hand, we have seen a pretty firm cohesion on our side, based on the readiness of the United States to reject 'isolationism' and play its full role, militarily and economically, as the leading nation of the Western coalition....

3. Britain – with all her experience – has neither the economic nor the military power to take the leading rôle. We are harassed with countless problems – the narrow knife-edge on which our own economy is balanced; the difficult task of changing an Empire into a Commonwealth ...; the uncertainty about our relations [with] the new economic, and perhaps political, state which is being created by the Six countries of continental Western Europe; and the uncertainty of American policies towards us – treated now as just another country, now as an ally in a special and unique category.

[Section omitted] 5. I am an unrepentant believer in 'interdependence'.

The Communist danger – in its various forms – is so great and so powerfully directed that it cannot be met without the maximum achievable unity of purpose and direction . . . . [6]

Like so much of Macmillan's writing, this document demonstrates an acute intelligence and a reasonable command of the great Churchillian sweep as a form of literary expression. It also highlights the gap between his understanding and his achievement, for although he was able in the short term, to a very remarkable degree, to call in the New World and its new president to redress the balance of the old, the exercise had shown few lasting results by the time he left office in 1963. The first omens were good. Kennedy confirmed all the nuclear weapons agreements which the Eisenhower administration had made. He was less forthcoming about Britain's relationship with Europe; in particular he did not like Macmillan's theme of tripartitism, because he distrusted de Gaulle's politics. But he was ready to meet Macmillan at the end of March and a visit to Washington was duly arranged. In the event the meeting was advanced in an atmosphere of emergency. Macmillan's visit to the West Indies was interrupted by an urgent message from Kennedy seeking talks about the developing crisis in Laos, and the two leaders met on 25 March 1961 at Key West. This was their first meeting, although Macmillan had naturally had full briefings about the president from the Washington ambassador, his old North Africa colleague Harold Caccia.

The Key West meeting launched a personal relationship between Macmillan and Kennedy which deepened and strengthened even as the 'special relationship' between their two countries came under pressure in the early 1960s. Indeed the relaxed intimacy which became apparent whenever the two men met may have shielded Macmillan from a full appreciation of the truth about the relative power of the two nations and the importance attached to the United Kingdom by policy-makers in Washington. Above all the disparity in age between the two men – Kennedy was forty, Macmillan sixty-seven when they first met – pandered to all Macmillan's romancing about British Greeks in the new Roman Empire. There is no doubt that Macmillan felt unexpectedly at ease in Kennedy's company and developed an affection for him which scarcely waned even when, many years after Kennedy's assassination, the more unsavoury aspects of his life and character were made public.[7]

This first meeting was an occasion to match Macmillan's concerns. Kennedy had summoned him early for advice and help. In the late 1950s the United States was deeply involved in Laos, propping up the government of Prince Souvannha Phouma against the communist Pathet Lao, who were supported by their neighbours in China and North Vietnam. Macmillan had counselled Eisenhower against military intervention, but 'advisers' were sent covertly in 1960, and the outgoing administration left Kennedy with a plan to intervene in strength in association with the other SEATO powers. Britain, the chief of these, believed that this would fail militarily, whatever its political effect. By now the anti-communist government in Laos was divided, with Phouma in exile and the former Defence Minister, General Phoumi, in control. Phouma, much more conciliatory towards the Pathet Lao, was recognised by the Soviet Union, which caused more anxiety in Washington. 'They back a certain Phoumi', recorded Macmillan of Eisenhower and his advisers, 'we, I do not know why, prefer Phouma.'[8] Although Macmillan was concerned to keep communism out of South-East Asia, his principal worry was that the British Chiefs of Staff, mindful of the difficulties experienced by Templer in suppressing the communist revolt in Malaya, had decided that this was a war which could not be won by conventional forces. He arrived at Key West and went almost directly into a presentation of the military options by the American staffs, who at this point proposed an all-American invasion. Only then were Kennedy and Macmillan left alone, and they agreed rapidly that the huge expedition just described to them was 'not on'.[9] Macmillan went on to warn that the SEATO operation, which was the alternative, was no more likely to succeed, and that the British Chiefs of Staff were warning against even symbolic commitment of British troops to the operation. His best offer, which Kennedy reluctantly accepted as final, was that Britain would 'join in the *appearance* of resistance' but would not be committed to *doing* anything.[10]

Surprisingly this cautious note did not sour relations between the two leaders; partly no doubt because of Macmillan's charm but partly because events overtook it between the Key West meeting and the planned visit to Washington which took place in April. Kennedy did not immediately countermand the Pentagon's plans. A SEATO meeting in Bangkok accepted the full plan – alarming the Foreign Secretary, who was present – but meanwhile the Russians agreed to a British proposal for a cease-fire and a conference. Macmillan credited this as 'a great triumph for British diplomacy';[11] Khrushchev merely observed that Laos would in any case 'fall into our laps like a ripe apple'.[12] Whatever the reason, the improvement in Laos seemed to justify Macmillan's stance, and the Washington talks were more productive for it. However, the gap between British and American expectations soon became clear, especially in regard to Russia and the bomb.

The 'Grand Design' document was built upon the assumption that the United States would support her allies economically and militarily, in return for which Western solidarity would inhibit communist expansion wherever that expansion seemed to be a threat. Advice, both from Britain and to a lesser extent from France, would help the United States to the correct policies throughout the world. Macmillan was busy developing the 'Grand Design' argument to show that the two 'major dangers' to the cohesion of the Atlantic Community were the development of the Common Market 'as a political entity which may deviate from the concept of the Atlantic Community and develop into something like a "third force"', and 'the aspiration of France to develop an independent nuclear capacity'. His preferred solution was to bring Britain closer to the Common Market and engage the French in tripartite consultations.[13] Kennedy's response to this, in Washington, was open in principle but reserved in detail. He surprised Macmillan by accepting the spirit of Tripartitism with a proposal to meet Macmillan and de Gaulle every six months outside the aegis of NATO; on the other hand, he was unwilling to give the French very much nuclear information, as Macmillan had wanted. He reiterated the American desire that Britain should join the Common Market, to make the economic revival of the West more likely.[14] He pointedly did not take Macmillan into his confidence about the 'Bay of Pigs' operation in Cuba, which the United States was about to undertake, nor did he suggest that the forthcoming talks with Khrushchev (set for June, in Vienna) should be anything but a bilateral private meeting between the two leaders of the Great Powers. Perhaps because he resented Macmillan's tepid attitude to anti-communist operations in Asia, his inclination at this stage was, if anything, to consider Britain mainly as a potentially important actor on the European stage, whose global influence was distinctly patchy and likely to diminish. He was also inclined to distrust the cautious British line on Berlin. The personal 'special relationship' was even at this point more comprehensive than the diplomatic relationship between the two powers.

Macmillan's standing with Kennedy improved somewhat after the president's first official visit to Europe in May and June. First, having decided that 'it would be undesirable to assist France's efforts to create a nuclear weapons capacity',[15] Kennedy was exposed to the full force of French displeasure. Second, he had a catastrophic meeting with Khrushchev in Vienna, in which the Soviet leader refused to concede anything on nuclear tests, abused the president about his readiness to consider nuclear war, and reiterated his threat to Berlin. Kennedy, not expecting such a robust, confident and aggressive performance, lost his temper but later regretted that there was no subject on which he could find agreement with Khrushchev. He returned from Vienna via London, and in private talks with Macmillan seemed glad to relax and be consoled and advised. The immediate consequences of the London visit were small – Macmillan tried to impress on Kennedy the foolishness of sabre-rattling over Berlin, but this advice did not long survive exposure to the hawkish influence of the State Department when Kennedy got home – nevertheless, it improved personal relations. Kennedy later said touchingly of Macmillan that 'I can share my loneliness with him', even though he did not necessarily accept all the advice he was given.[16]

The real test of the 'relationship' came in the Berlin crisis which began with the sudden erection of the Berlin Wall in August 1961. Kennedy's European visit had been accompanied by a definite hardening of military preparations on both side of the Iron Curtain in Europe, and a loss of momentum in any progress towards disarmament. The test-ban talks were foundering (with Macmillan ruminating about 'how are we to throw the blame on the Soviet Government. Or (more hopefully) is there any chance, if we keep the Conference alive, of some change for the better?')[17] When on 15 June Khrushchev, not for the first time, announced the imminence of a peace treaty between Russia and East Germany, the Americans responded with military contingency planning and a supplementary defence budget which included provisions for more air-raid shelters and an increase in the selective service draft. Macmillan, dismayed by the air-raid shelters and what they implied, was even more dismayed by the impact of international uncertainty on sterling, which was already in some discomfort because of the trade cycle. He urged Kennedy to be more circumspect and to emphasise negotiation more strongly; and in the resulting diplomatic excitement had to accept that the American press, under inspiration, were once more criticising him for being 'soft' on Berlin. Macmillan believed that the Americans were in fact softening themselves when the crisis was brought to a head by the East German government, which sealed its borders with West Berlin on 13 August, in part to stop the efflux of refugees whose departure threatened the viability of the crumbling East German economy.

This took place in the midst of the West German elections which added further tension. The Americans were inclined to make demonstrations by sending troops and tanks to Berlin; the French, as Macmillan remarked, 'seem to contemplate war with equanimity', but, as he also observed, had neither the resources, nor ultimately the determination to resist the Russians by force. Macmillan's preference was to negotiate, on the straightforward grounds that if the Western allies threatened to go to war over Berlin and then, inevitably, backed down, they would lose very much more than they could ever hope to gain. Intense telephonic discussion with Kennedy, and more leisurely and formal interchanges with de Gaulle, only enabled him to control events intermittently. Exchanges of notes, and troop movements in Berlin, took place against the background of tiresome negotiations about nuclear testing, in which both America and the Soviet Union resumed tests while talking about banning them altogether. Macmillan was always in favour of negotiation over Berlin and as much restraint as possible in resuming nuclear tests, but throughout 1961 he was rarely able to prevent hawkishness in Washington or in Europe. Only towards the end of the year did he succeed in getting Kennedy and his advisers to accept the prudence of negotiation, while de Gaulle was still loftily opposed and the new German government, in which Adenauer was now only the head of a coalition, still hankered in public after a reunified Germany. There was no sign that 1961 had healed the damage caused by the abortive summit of May 1960.

A further meeting at Bermuda in December 1961 was intended to restore some cohesion to the Western alliance. Once again, it had a wonderfully restorative effect on the personal relationship between Macmillan and Kennedy, but left a great deal still to be done to harmonise the policies of Britain and America. The British Cabinet was politically committed to a moratorium on atmospheric testing; the American defence establishment wanted to resume atmospheric tests to keep up with developments made by the Russians in their recent tests, and wanted to carry them out on Christmas Island, a remote British possession in the Pacific; the British defence establishment, with the Cabinet's support, wanted to test the Skybolt's warhead underground in Nevada. At Bermuda the Americans wanted to trade the Nevada tests, which they had earlier blocked, for access to Christmas Island, and Macmillan was forced to agree, despite some energetic pleading. On the other hand, he found Kennedy prepared to negotiate over Berlin, and impatient with Adenauer and de Gaulle. This was the one area in which British and American policy had converged since their last meeting, and contrasted with the other matters under discussion which included Laos, the Congo and the European Common Market. The failure to make any real progress at Bermuda inspired Macmillan to write a long letter to Kennedy in January 1962, urging 'a supreme effort to make progress in the field of disarmament and nuclear tests, in which we at present have not worked out an effective plan of campaign'.[18] This persuaded some officials in Washington, but not all. Kennedy finally agreed to answer his letter positively, but the impression was abroad in Washington that the British were soft, and given to emotional blackmail. As a result the Anglo-American position on relations with Russia was distinctly blurred in the first part of 1962, with Khrushchev's unpredictable temper adding further to the uncertainty. The 'effective plan of campaign' proved all too elusive.

The most tangible, but perhaps least effective moves came through the disarmament talks, opened once again in Geneva in March. It was preceded by some ill-tempered Notes between Khrushchev and the Western leaders, and by the American announcement at the beginning of March of a new series of atmospheric nuclear tests. All Macmillan could do was to get Kennedy to postpone this announcement by two days, so that the other Western powers would know about it before the newspapers. Russian objections to on-site inspection to monitor nuclear testing remained the main obstacle to a test-ban agreement, and Macmillan urged the British negotiators to persuade their American counterparts that on-site inspection was unnecessary, but to no avail. Kennedy refused a request to make a direct and personal appeal to Khrushchev over verification, and Macmillan was reduced to the observation that 'it may well be that both Mr. Ks are similarly placed and that both have to deal with military and political pressure'.[19] He did not add that neither Mr K was very much inclined to listen to British advice. The talks came to nothing.

. . .

CUBA

The state of superpower politics in the early autumn of 1962 was therefore not good. Macmillan was perhaps presumptuous to feel a great responsibility for this himself, but there is no doubt that British external policy, for example towards Africa and the Middle East, and British domestic economic policy were both frustrated by the apparent paralysis of detente. Yet there was no reason to think that because things were bad they could only get better. In the third week of October American photographic reconnaissance aircraft discovered 'a major build up of medium-range missiles in Cuba'.[20] By the time this was conveyed to Macmillan the president's National Security Council had taken the fundamental decisions which determined the course of the first part of what became the 'Cuban Missile Crisis'. Rather than attacking the bases by air and then invading Cuba to destroy the missile sites, the American policy-makers decided to establish a naval blockade to prevent Soviet or neutral ships carrying any further arms to Cuba. The decision was very narrowly taken, with strong pressure from groups within the Pentagon to foreclose with a military decision, and countervailing pressure for restraint from the Secretary of Defense himself (Robert McNamara), from the State Department and from Kennedy's brother Robert, the Attorney-General.[21] As a result there was rather little that Macmillan could do to influence the course of events. He spoke to Kennedy on a secure telephone link at 11.30 p.m. on 22 October, the first of many conversations during the crisis days. By this time, after some changes of mind, he had decided not to advise an immediate invasion. His estimate of the European situation suggested to him that Khrushchev might use Cuba as a bargaining counter to get the West out of Berlin, and he wished to avoid that;

he had not yet thought of the alternative bargain, which was a Soviet offer to remove missiles from Cuba in return for the removal of intermediate-range Jupiter missiles from bases in Turkey. He was therefore ready to say, when asked by Kennedy, that he would prefer a blockade to an air-strike, and was apparently pleased to be told that this had already been decided. For the next two days he was kept informed of American decisions as they developed.

The blockade was formally imposed on Wednesday 24 October. Soviet ships known to be carrying missiles were still some distance outside the quarantine area, and there was time for the Secretary-General of the United Nations, U Thant, to appeal to Kennedy to call off the blockade and to Khrushchev to call off the shipments. Both Kennedy and Macmillan recognised this message as dangerous to Western interests: 'it looks sensible and yet it's rather bad'.[22] During the next two days fourteen ships turned back, apparently because the Russians did not want missile-carrying vessels to fall into American hands, and others steadily approached the quarantine line, which was now drawn at 500 miles from Cuba. The Americans continued military preparations for an invasion. On the evening of the 24th Kennedy sought Macmillan's advice on whether to invade, and Macmillan replied the next day counselling against it, but this was a problem for the future. For the present, the state of play between the superpowers depended on Soviet decisions, and for two days no attempt was made to run the blockade. On 26 October the Soviet Union proposed to bargain the Cuban missiles against the Jupiters in Turkey. Macmillan suggested instead that the Thor missiles based in Britain be immobilised, at least temporarily, as part of a deal, but events moved on.

On Saturday 27 October an American U-2 plane was shot down over Cuba, and Kennedy threatened to invade the next Tuesday (30 October) if the missiles were not removed. On the same day Khrushchev sent two messages. The first offered to send no more missiles into Cuba, and remove those already there, if Kennedy withdrew his invasion threat and abandoned the blockade; the second made a formal, and of course much less accommodating, proposal to undertake reciprocal withdrawal of missiles in Cuba and Turkey. The president's advisers, constituted into a small group known as ExComm, spent a difficult day in which they 'felt nuclear war to be closer on that day than at any time in the nuclear age',[23] but finally decided to answer the first note and ignore the second. The Russians replied by agreeing to dismantle the missiles, and the crisis was over.

The significance of the Cuban Missile Crisis remains controversial. The simplest explanation was that on the Soviet side it was an attempt to alter the status quo in nuclear deterrence, which favoured the Americans as long as the prevailing delivery method for nuclear bombs was the intermediate-range ballistic missile; American weapons could be stationed in Europe (or Turkey) and attack the Soviet heartland, while the Soviet Union had no secure bases from which to threaten the United States. American leaders, quite naturally, preferred to retain the asymmetry until the intercontinental ballistic missiles, then under development, came into service. Alternatively Khrushchev might merely have been attempting to increase his bargaining strength over Berlin. Whatever the cause, Britain, and Macmillan, had no difficulty in taking the American side, and during the crisis British diplomacy was mobilised to urge the reasonableness of the American case on Europe and the Commonwealth. Another controversy arises over why, or indeed if, Kennedy and Khrushchev were prepared to risk nuclear war at this point in order to change or maintain the balance of power. Quite possibly neither leader wanted to move 'to the brink', but on both sides the management of the crisis seemed to leave both of them with too few options. Ignorance of one another's intentions was one problem; another was the infighting between interests in the decision-making structure. Historians are very well informed about crisis-management on the American side, but of course hardly informed at all about Russian problems.

Both these controversies add emphasis to the point that this was a crisis between the superpowers. No other nation had much to contribute to the vital decisions which might have led to a nuclear war. Macmillan's contribution, as a statesman on the world stage, is therefore very much in question. Observers best placed to judge, such as the ambassador in Washington, David Ormsby-Gore, were sceptical: 'I can't honestly think of anything said from London that changed the US action – it was chiefly reassurance to JFK.'[24] This is confirmed by the full record of conversations published in Macmillan's memoirs, and even more so by Macmillan's own observation that he 'played the cards above their face value' when describing his consultations with Kennedy to a sceptical House of Commons after the event.[25] His own description of the crisis as 'one of the great turning-points in history' is distinctly double-edged. It suggests, above all, that the immediacy of the crisis cut out the lesser powers, even as brokers, to be replaced by the telephone 'hot-line' between Washington and Moscow. However much the crisis 'brought the intimacy, and trust, between Macmillan and Kennedy to a new peak',[26] it confirmed that this was not a relationship in which Britain under Macmillan was genuinely playing the rôle of Greece to the American Rome.

. . .

SKYBOLT AND THE TEST-BAN TREATY

It should not have been a surprise to Macmillan or anyone else that in December 1962 Dean Acheson, formerly Eisenhower's Secretary of State, should have made a widely quoted speech to cadets at West Point, remarking that Britain's preferred rôle outside Europe, as head of the Commonwealth and with a special relationship with the United States was 'about played out'.[27] This fairly accurately represented opinion in the American foreign policy establishment, and it corresponded to consistent American pressures to bring Britain into the Common Market, a process of negotiation which was indeed then at its peak. Unhappily for Macmillan it coincided with the revelation that the Skybolt missile, upon which Britain's immediate plans for a nuclear deterrent had been based since the Washington Conference of March 1960, was likely to be cancelled by the American government. There is now no doubt that Skybolt ('a pile of junk' according to Robert McNamara)[28] would never have met NATO's needs, and was not worth developing. This was probably known to technical staffs in Britain in 1961, but was not appreciated by ministers. On 8 November 1962 Ormsby-Gore in Washington was told that the project was going to be cancelled, but the response of Peter Thorneycroft, then Minister of Defence, was to do nothing, in the hope that political considerations would lead the Americans to change their minds. In this he was doubly mistaken: firstly because political considerations in the US Department of Defense under McNamara were more likely to bias the decision in favour of cancellation than away from it, because they felt no enthusiasm for the independent British deterrent, and secondly because it was hard fact, not a political fiction, that the missile did not work.[29] On 6 December the information that Skybolt was to be cancelled had been leaked to the press. At a NATO meeting in Paris on 11 December Thorneycroft asked McNamara point-blank if the American government would 'be prepared to state publicly that it would do everything possible to help Britain preserve its independent nuclear role', but got no reassurance.[30] This was apparently the result of poor communications within the American administration: McNamara did not know that Macmillan had in November obtained Kennedy's agreement to the proposition that there would be no publicity before the decision was made and no decision about cancellation without consultation with the British.

Macmillan and his government were violently attacked in the press and the House of Commons for what many thought was fresh evidence that the 'special relationship' was a snare and a delusion. In this atmosphere Macmillan went to Rambouillet to meet de Gaulle and learn that there was little prospect of French help in admitting Britain to the Common Market, and then to Nassau to meet Kennedy for what had been planned as a discussion of world issues. Instead the whole conference was taken up with Skybolt and the question of its replacement by Polaris. In discussions, with advisers present, which Macmillan recorded as 'protracted and fiercely contested' the Americans agreed to supply Polaris missiles on which the British would put their own warheads. The British Polaris fleet would be 'assigned' to NATO except in the event of 'supreme national interests' being at stake, and the British government was to determine when that was. If there was ever a moment when Macmillan had been able to apply the leverage of the 'special relationship', this was it; and he did not do so only in the intimate private chats which had characterised his earlier private meetings with the president. On the American side many of the Defense Department representatives dismissed the independent British nuclear deterrent as a military absurdity, and among the president's foreign policy advisers there were some who argued that to give Britain special treatment over Polaris would offend the French and thus jeopardise British entry into Europe, which was now an important object of American policy. Against all this Kennedy himself appears to have argued that Macmillan needed Polaris for domestic political reasons, and was inclined therefore to give it. This was the final decision, and Macmillan was even able, after direct appeals to Kennedy, to get the weapon without paying a substantial contribution to development costs.

The Nassau Agreement underlined how much Macmillan in his international diplomacy was committed to the idea of Britain's independent nuclear deterrent, which was his ticket to the inner circle of power. It may well have caused trouble for the Common Market negotiations – though these were in great difficulty anyway – but it confirmed him in his own eyes as a fully paid-up international statesman. What he had done was to succeed in making Britain a technological client of the United States as the only means of maintaining Great Power status. This was a contradiction, as his political opponents at home were quick to point out. Even his Cabinet colleagues were perturbed, resolving while he was still in Nassau 'to emphasise their view that the Government were being asked to pay a heavy price and that for this reason the independent role of Her Majesty's Government in the use of nuclear force must be clearly and unambiguously expressed'.[31]

In contrast, Macmillan's contribution to the Test-Ban Treaty, signed in July 1963, was to make a success of the rôle of broker between the superpowers. His own commitment to the idea of banning nuclear tests had waxed and waned rather more than his memoirs admit. To seize the opportunity, even for a partial ban, in 1963 was a recognition that Britain's interest coincided with the world's interest in retarding a nuclear arms race.

In a sense the possibility of a ban on nuclear tests had never left the international agenda. Like the standing disarmament talks at Geneva, which were often paralysed if not actually adjourned, it often appeared as a point for argument in the diplomatic interchanges between Russian and American leaders. During the periods when leaders on either side were not actively hostile to it because their own armaments programmes were at a testing stage, the main obstacle was the question of verification. Atmospheric tests could be monitored fairly easily. They had been the norm when the nuclear powers had wanted to study the effects of nuclear explosions upon troops and armaments; but once the effects were known it was comparatively painless to abstain from them. Both superpowers undertook atmospheric tests in the early 1960s to check the effects of the new hydrogen bombs. Underground tests were more appropriate for testing and refining the mechanism of new warheads, and were much more difficult to detect. The art of seismic measurement had to develop rapidly to keep up with the problem of distinguishing small underground nuclear explosions from natural earth tremors. Until 1963, and indeed beyond, it was assumed by Western scientists that the indications from seismology would have to be checked by on-site inspections. The Russians, especially after the U2 affair, saw this as espionage, and at that point, usually, discussions broke down.

Macmillan's interest in a test ban, as shown by his early encounters with the problem described above,[32] was twofold. On the one hand it promised to be his own personal contribution to détente and thus to history; on the other hand it was an important part of his domestic political strategy to contain the opposition to nuclear armaments. Macmillan was shaken by the success of the Campaign for Nuclear Disarmament among the Christian middle classes and the groups whom he continued to identify as former Liberal voters whose true loyalty should be attached to the Conservatives. In his dealings with the Labour Party in Parliament the nuclear issue was almost an unalloyed advantage to him; divisions within the party were so acute that Gaitskell was regularly humiliated in public by his own followers. The advantage did not extend out of doors, where for long periods it seemed to turn public opinion against the British independent deterrent. Since the independent deterrent was the pivot upon which Macmillan's defence and foreign policy hinged, he needed any help he could get in justifying it. The possibility of a test ban, negotiated from strength and offering the prospect at least of a slowing down of the arms race, could give him the political lever he needed.[33]

He was therefore particularly eager to listen to suggestions emanating from Russia, especially after the Cuban Missile Crisis, that there was some hope of a limited agreement on testing. At the end of November 1962 Khrushchev proposed a total ban on tests, arguing that there was a *de facto* agreement not to test weapons under water, in the atmosphere or in space and this needed only to be made formal and extended to underground tests. The sting in the tail was his suggestion that inspection was unnecessary because seismic equipment could be devised to do the same job. This letter, to Macmillan, was soon followed by a letter to Kennedy repeating the proposal but offering to permit a limited number of inspections. The American reaction was that the three inspections per year, as proposed, would not be enough; and although Macmillan put some pressure on Kennedy at Nassau it became clear that disagreements within the decision-making establishment in Washington were once again limiting the President's freedom of action. Early in 1963 it could be seen that the military simply wanted to continue testing to build up American strength, and that they had powerful support in Congress. Kennedy himself appears to have favoured a test ban in principle, but counted the domestic political costs and found them daunting. Macmillan's most important initiative came after the Geneva disarmament talks had reached yet another impasse in early March, and on 16 March he sent a huge essay to Kennedy suggesting that Khrushchev's change of mind on inspection, though illogical, was a real opening.[34] He also emphasised the possibility of a non-proliferation agreement, since a formal test-ban treaty would encourage powers now on the brink of exploding nuclear weapons to halt their programmes.[35] One of the key issues in non-proliferation was to prevent German access to nuclear weapons, while making it impossible for the agreements which maintained Germany's status in the NATO alliance to be 'represented by a bad German in the future as the modern counterpart of Versailles'. Macmillan linked this with the understandable Russian hatred and fear of Germany, and saw a test ban treaty associated with a non-proliferation agreement as another means of containing Germany without rancour. He concluded with the suggestion of another summit conference, this time to be held at Geneva with some diplomatic preparation, to take advantage of Khrushchev's apparent flexibility.

Washington's response was distinctly cool. The summit idea was seen as an attempt to commandeer the president as part of Macmillan's forthcoming election campaign, and a project which might unsettle the other European allies. The Pentagon and the State Department were predictably opposed to further concessions over the substance of a test ban. Macmillan's efforts eventually bore fruit only in a joint letter from Kennedy and Macmillan to Khrushchev on 15 April, proposing a discussion between special emissaries. To get this Macmillan had had to fall in with the American suggestion that NATO's nu-

clear defences should be organised in a 'multi-manned' nuclear strike force; this being a development of a clause in
the Nassau agreement which had provided for a multilateral
force.[36] Macmillan had to run even harder after Khrushchev's
reply came in early May, complaining that Western leaders were
haggling about the number of inspections and remarking that
'Our people would be quite right to take their Government
very severely to account if it entered into negotiations about
how many spies we will admit on to our territory per year, and
what sort of conditions we will create for these spies.'[37] This
was the sort of thing which appealed to Macmillan's sense of
humour but not to that of the State Department. In the event a
fairly calm reply was sent, acknowledging Khrushchev's agreement to exchange emissaries, and after another rude letter
from Khrushchev about the multi-manned force and the threat
from a 'revanchist' Germany the meeting was settled.

Even so there remained considerable doubt about what
could be agreed. The two emissaries – Averell Harriman for
the United States and the surprising choice of the impetuous
and inexperienced Lord Hailsham for Britain – were selected
and briefed. On 2 July Khrushchev altered his longstanding
commitment to negotiating an absolute ban on tests, and accepted a limited ban which would enshrine in a treaty the
current (but transient) *de facto* agreement not to test in the
atmosphere, under water or in outer space. This effectively
brushed aside the argument about inspections by proposing to
allow underground tests. Macmillan, desperate for an agreement for domestic political reasons, urged the Americans on:
'The situation is dramatic and vital for me. If there is any
chance of our agreement and a Summit Meeting afterwards, I
will fight on in home politics. If not, I shall feel inclined to
throw in my hand.'[38] Up to the end he was bargaining with
Kennedy and his advisers about the symbolic importance of a
ban, even if it were partial.

There were, indeed, quite stark transatlantic differences in
policy. Kennedy made a triumphant tour of Europe in late
June, trying above all to emphasise the American commitment
to the defence of Western Europe against communism. He
spoke in Berlin (*Ich bin ein Berliner*); he inaugurated a presidential rite by visiting Ireland in search of his ancestors; and
he made a personal call on Macmillan at Birch Grove. The
Birch Grove meeting, the last personal encounter between the

two men, has been hugely romanticised by Macmillan, in his memoirs[39] and in a particularly heartrending television broadcast. The visit lasted twenty-four hours, and consisted largely of private talks between the two leaders. The agenda was dominated by the test-ban talks and the American proposal for a multi-manned force. On both issues the president yielded to Macmillan's preferences, agreeing to go fast on the test ban and slowly on the multi-manned force. Significantly, the two men agreed that 'the main object is not to provide more nuclear weapons for NATO (which already has too many) but to solve the German problem, now and in the future'.[40] Macmillan concluded that 'We got all we wanted'; the Americans got rather less, and resented the fact. The special relationship seemed to be creaking. A further source of friction was an unexpected proposal from Washington, in early July, that if France could be induced to sign the Test-Ban Treaty the Americans would release a good deal of the nuclear information which had once been withheld even from the British under the Macmahon Act. Macmillan, rather crossly, saw this as an opportunity to win the French over to a new British application to join the Common Market, but felt aggrieved that the offer had not been available in time to support the application which had failed. Even as the Moscow talks began he feared that American stubbornness would frustrate them.

In the event all was well. In ten days the negotiators prepared an agreement for signature. There was some disagreement between Harriman and Hailsham, particularly when the British negotiator seemed too keen to take Khrushchev's bait of a non-aggression pact. The treaty was definitely a partial ban, leaving underground tests unhindered. Technical wrangling delayed, but did not in the end prevent, a provision allowing any country which wanted to accede to the treaty to sign it: a provision which marked the beginning of a move towards non-proliferation. The treaty was signed on 25 July, after a number of minor American objections had been withdrawn. Macmillan, on hearing this over the telephone from Kennedy 'went to tell D. and burst into tears. I had prayed hard for this, night after night', and then visited the House of Commons where he found 'everyone very happy'. The reception of his announcement was 'like the greatest of my Parliamentary successes'.[41] For once there is little doubt that this was Macmillan's achievement. His voice had been persistent in advising

Kennedy to go ahead, when neither the president's own advisers nor indeed the rest of the British government had been convinced that either the opportunity or necessity for a partial treaty existed. It was the culmination of six years of diplomatic effort to keep Britain at the 'top table' in international diplomacy, and unlike the summit conferences for which Macmillan yearned it did some positive good and no apparent harm.

. . .

NOTES AND REFERENCES

1. Macmillan's note to Eisenhower and de Gaulle is reprinted in Harold Macmillan, *Pointing the Way* (London: Macmillan, 1971), pp. 241–3.
2. See above, pp. 84–90.
3. Vulcan bombers were used in 1982, without conspicuous success, to attack runways in the Falklands.
4. Diary, 29 March 1960, quoted in Macmillan, *Pointing the Way*, p. 252.
5. The full text is ibid., pp. 309–12.
6. Extracts entitled 'the Grand Design', are reprinted in Macmillan, *Pointing the Way*, pp. 321–6. The full untitled text, dated '29 December 1960 to 3 January 1961' is in PREM 11/3325.
7. Clearly Macmillan neither shared nor approved of Kennedy's thirst for women; and there was an element of theatre in his emotional discussion of his last meeting with Kennedy in his well-known television interview with Robert Mackenzie – a moment too long spent fighting back the tears. But the 'relief', amounting to gratitude, which Macmillan felt when Kennedy renewed the mutual confidence which had existed between Macmillan and Eisenhower, and the reassuring feeling that even the most powerful politician in the free world had intellectual weaknesses, seems to have endeared the president to the prime minister in a way which no subsequent disillusionment could efface. Even so there were early reservations, partly because Kennedy's youth and vigour contrasted with the stolidity of the Conservative leadership during the economic difficulties of the early 1960s. For the first time, Macmillan saw the disadvantages of his pose as an ageing grandee.
8. Diary, 8 December 1960, quoted in Macmillan, *Pointing the Way*, p. 331.
9. Diary, 26 March 1961, quoted ibid., p. 336.
10. Ibid.
11. Diary, 1 April 1961, quoted in Macmillan, *Pointing the Way*, p. 345.
12. To the US ambassador, quoted in Arthur Schlesinger, *A Thousand Days: John F. Kennedy in the White House* (London: André Deutsch, 1965), p. 312.
13. Untitled paper, at least partly drafted by Norman Brook, the Cabinet Secretary, 15 April 1961, PREM 11/3311.
14. 'Note by the Prime Minister', 6 April 1961, ibid.
15. Kennedy to Macmillan, 8 May 1961, PREM 11/3311.

16. To Henry Brandon, reported in H. Brandon, *Special Relationships: a foreign correspondent's memoirs from Roosevelt to Reagan* (London: Macmillan, 1989), p. 160.

17. Diary, 14 June 1961, quoted in Macmillan, *Pointing the Way*, p. 388.

18. Macmillan to Kennedy, 5 January 1962, quoted in Harold Macmillan, *At the End of the Day* (London: Macmillan, 1973), p. 160.

19. Diary, 7 April 1962, quoted ibid., p. 175.

20. Kennedy to Macmillan, 21 October 1962, quoted ibid., p. 182.

21. Graham T. Allison, *Essence of Decision: Explaining the Cuban Missile Crisis* (Boston: Little, Brown and Co., 1971).

22. Alistair Horne, *Macmillan 1957– 1986* (London: Macmillan, 1989), p. 372, quoting apparently from transcripts in the John F. Kennedy Library.

23. Theodore C. Sorensen, *Kennedy* (London: Hodder & Stoughton, 1965), p. 714.

24. Interview with Alistair Horne quoted in Horne, *Macmillan 1957–1986*, p. 382.

25. Ibid.

26. Ibid., p. 385. Horne himself, it should be said, makes clear his own view that Macmillan did very little to influence events.

27. Douglas Brinkley, 'Dean Acheson and the "Special Relationship": the West Point speech of December 1962', *Historical Journal*, XXXIII (1990), 599–608.

28. Interview with Alistair Horne, quoted in Horne, *Macmillan 1957–1986*, p. 435.

29. Macmillan's memoirs record that the Cabinet in December 'had clearly formed the view that the Americans had made up their minds to kill the project, *but whether on political or military grounds was still obscure*'. Macmillan, *At the End of the Day*, p. 345 (my italics).

30. Horne, *Macmillan 1957–1986*, p. 436.

31. Cabinet Conclusions, 21 Dec. 1962, CAB 128/36 CC(62)71.

32. See above, pp. 137–42.

33. Macmillan never had to face the problem, first brought into sharp public focus by the Skybolt question, that the arms race was in future not to be so much in warheads as in delivery systems and anti-missile defences. See, in general, J. Simpson, *The Independent Nuclear State: The United States, Britain and the Military Atom* (London: Macmillan, 1983); Martin S. Navias, *Nuclear Weapons and British Strategic Planning, 1955–1958* (Oxford: Oxford University Press, 1991).

34. Reprinted in Macmillan, *At the End of the Day*, pp. 456–64.

35. Sweden, India and Israel were mentioned.

36. It was never clear what had been intended by a multi-manned force: was it to be a union of existing forces or a force made up of submarines with multinational crews? See Collette Barbier, 'La Force Multilatérale', *Relations Internationales*, 69 (1992), 3–18; and 'M.L.F.', a particularly scathing satirical verse composed and sung by Tom Lehrer.

37. Quoted in Macmillan, *At the End of the Day*, p. 468.

38. Diary 12 July 1963, quoted Horne, *Macmillan 1957–1968*, p. 518.

39. Macmillan, *At the End of the Day*, pp. 471–5.

40. Macmillan to the Queen, 5 July 1963, quoted in Horne, *Macmillan 1957–1986*, p. 516.
41. Diary, 25 July 1963, quoted ibid., p. 522.

Chapter 8

IMPERIAL RETREAT

In January 1957 Britain had a fairly large and very turbulent colonial empire. Macmillan's anxiety to give at least some of it back to the indigenous inhabitants in part reflected his own estimate of the cost of keeping it on, but much of his policy was an attempt to channel the development of policies which had been under discussion since the Conservatives' return to office in 1951, or even before. Within the Conservative Party the Empire/Commonwealth was a potent symbol for the right wing. Protecting the interests of the old white dominions was uppermost in the minds of many opponents of closer integration with Europe, while the interests of white settlers had constrained the policies of the Churchill and Eden governments in both East and West Africa. In Britain's miscellaneous possessions east of Suez and in Cyprus, the desire to retain military or naval bases (or, in the case of Singapore particularly, airbases to help complete the encirclement of Russia) made both politicians and Whitehall uneasy about local political developments which tended to loosen ties between the colonies and the imperial power.

Macmillan's personal views on the Empire were not completely formed when he entered on his premiership. At the Colonial Office during the war he had been interested in land reform and economic reconstruction, especially in West Africa; in opposition he had paid a visit to India and spoken in the Second Reading of the India Independence Bill, accepting, on his party's behalf, that independence was inevitable. In his memoirs he was careful to assure his readers that 'The "wind of change" did not sound the "bugle of retreat" under my Premiership as a sudden and discordant note',[1] but he had played little part himself in the accommodation between Conservative instincts and local political necessity during the Churchill and Eden years. The immediate problems he inherited in 1957 were in Cyprus, Central Africa and the Persian Gulf. Cyprus was solved largely by negotiation, the Persian Gulf problem by sheer military force; the problems of the Central African Federation accumulated during his first administration and survived to deepen the gloom of his second.

By far the most important of Macmillan's initiatives, though, was the projection of an idea, for domestic as well as imperial attention. The 'Winds of Change' speech, delivered in Cape Town in February 1960, was addressed to audiences in Britain and East Africa as much as to the South African parliamentarians who heard it. By committing the British government to a rapid process of decolonisation, coupled with full political rights for native populations, he made a shining virtue out of unwelcome necessity. According to colleagues,[2] he did not find the leaders of the 'New Commonwealth' particularly congenial, and would probably have preferred the Commonwealth as a collection of white-run dominions, but that did not seem possible and he did not seriously attempt to hold back the advance to self-determination. In the short term, his policy antagonised no one who was not thoroughly disaffected already, and won the enthusiastic support of reformers; in the long term it gave his own government and later Conservative administrations a position from which to deal with African states emerging from colonialism into independence.

His policy towards other countries' ex-colonies, and towards the states on the periphery of Britain's present and former possessions which were part of the 'informal empire', was less clear cut. Since the bonds were not formal, it was not so obviously necessary to loosen them, and many anxious hours were spent attempting to maintain spheres of influence for Britain in the Middle East and Africa. In most cases this was expensive and futile. In Iraq and the Persian Gulf Britain simply could not influence the political process which produced General Qassim in Iraq and a number of violently anti-Western regimes in the Arabian Peninsula. In Africa, the collapse of the Belgian colonial empire embarrassed not only Belgium, but also the major Western powers, including Britain, which tried to intervene to maintain a pro-Western stability. Macmillan's opinions were influenced both by his belief in the dangers of Soviet expansion and by his reluctance to abandon a position of hegemony.

177

. . .

WINDING DOWN THE EMPIRE

On 28 January 1957 Macmillan fired a warning shot across the bows of Lord Salisbury, the Lord President, who was the leading opponent of imperial retreat in the Cabinet.

> It would be good if Ministers could know more clearly which territories are likely to become ripe for independence over the next few years – or, even if they are not really ready for it, will demand it so insistently that their claims cannot be denied – and at what date that stage is likely to be reached in each case.
>
> .... I should also like to see something like a profit and loss account for each of our colonial possessions, so that we may be better able to gauge whether, from the financial and economic point of view, we are likely to gain or to lose by its departure. This would need, of course, to be weighed against the political and strategic considerations involved in each case.[3]

This cold and unhurried calculation, rather than a policy of scuttle, underpinned even the contorted negotiations over Cyprus and the Central African Federation which so exhausted the Cabinet's patience under Macmillan. In relation to the Empire, his policy initiatives do not seem especially original: he decided to prostrate himself before the inevitable, but did little either to advance or to retard the decolonisation process except by choosing efficient and reform-minded Colonial Secretaries. At home, though, he was remarkably successful in reconciling his followers to his policy. Above all, he tried to handle relations with the dependent and recently independent Empire so that British interests, somewhat fuzzily defined, were preserved. Commonly this meant a continuing rôle for Britain's former dependencies in resisting the expansion of communist power either from Russia or from China. This was not always easy and sometimes proved impossible. When it failed, his reputation suffered accordingly.

Cyprus

Macmillan's comparative inexperience and rather obvious lack of interest in the colonial empire helps to explain why his handling of colonial questions was at first a matter of crisis management, only later becoming a fairly coherent programme of withdrawal from Africa and possessions east of Suez. The Cyprus question, for example, had taxed him while he was Foreign Secretary. After his departure to the Exchequer the guerrilla campaign run by the Greek-Cypriot EOKA movement had continued. Its immediate aims included the release of Archbishop Makarios, leader of the Orthodox community, from exile in the Seychelles; its relationship with Greek-Cypriot society had become more complex, as the right-wing antecedents of its leader, General Grivas, were balanced by the entry of left-wingers into the organisation. In an attempt to renew the movement towards a civil settlement, Macmillan persuaded his Cabinet in March 1957 to release Makarios, who was allowed to return to Athens but not to Cyprus itself. This caused Lord Salisbury, who had a resigning cast of mind, to leave the government. The government's subsequent policy moved from partition through 'Tridominium' – a scheme of shared suzerainty – to independence with a guarantee for British sovereign bases and a constitution drafted to preserve the rights of the Turkish minority. Agreement was finally reached in February 1959. It was an entertaining vignette of prime ministerial diplomacy, closely resembling the patient and exacting work Macmillan had faced in the Eastern Mediterranean during the war.

The main difficulties on the way were the unpredictability of the Greek and Turkish governments and the hesitation of Macmillan's Cabinet colleagues, who were concerned (with their back bench) about the possible blow to Britain's prestige in the apparent loss of empire, and were more practically troubled by the future of the British bases on the island. The governor of Cyprus, Sir Hugh Foot, was the instrument of policy. During 1958 he built on earlier constitutional proposals[4] to devise a power-sharing constitution which he proceeded to put into practice in readiness for elections in 1959, regardless of the unrelenting hostility of EOKA. Macmillan's contribution was to visit Ankara and Athens in July 1958, where he was able to write up his diary with the same verve and sardonic observation of Greek politics which he had demonstrated in 1944, and incidentally to move the Greek government a few inches towards a settlement. His response to the two governments' reception of British proposals was characteristic: he was 'relieved that both the Greeks and the Turks objected in the first instance. It would have been fatal if one had accepted and the other refused.'[5] He won the backing of the Cabinet and the

Opposition, but the Greek population of Cyprus reacted with a full-blown guerrilla war. Fortunately this did not sway the United Nations General Assembly, which was as co-operative over Cyprus as it had been outraged over Suez.

In December 1958 the Turkish and Greek governments decided to attempt their own solution. Macmillan and Lennox-Boyd, the Colonial Secretary, looked on with suspicion and ordered Foot to make no concessions directly to General Grivas, the EOKA leader. Macmillan's concerns were mainly for the domestic political complications, but also for the position of British bases. Fortunately the two governments were prepared to concede the status of the sovereign bases, and also to put pressure on Archbishop Makarios to accept a 'balanced' constitution. The settlement, negotiated between Greece, Turkey and Britain after earlier bilateral talks between the Greek and Turkish governments, was signed on 19 February 1959. Cyprus became an independent republic in 1960, with a Greek president, a Turkish vice-president, a legislative assembly with quotas from each community, and devolution of certain functions to communal assemblies. The new constitution gave the Greeks, as Macmillan reminded them, less than the Radcliffe Report or the Foot–Macmillan plan of 1958 would have done. British strategic interests were preserved, and indeed the British presence in Cyprus was to last longer than the 1960 constitution, whose collapse precipitated the Turkish invasion of Cyprus in 1974.

The Cyprus settlement was a success for Macmillan, for Selwyn Lloyd, for Lennox-Boyd, and for Sir Hugh Foot. It had been achieved by patience as much as by flamboyant gesture, and the final settlement reflected Macmillan's instinct for matching commitments to resources. Quite apart from the conflict between Greek and Turk, Macmillan had had to carry his party with him. The early departure of Salisbury had made this easier: without a focus for discontent, the Cabinet was able to accept the logic of the concessions to the Cypriots without revolt. A minority on the back benches was still disaffected, and made its position clear during the final discussion in February 1959. 'In a struggle about this, we shall have been very hard-pressed here – by the Socialists, by the Liberals, by all the wet-fish Press.... If we stood firm on sovereignty against leases, we would have been accused of being the wreckers. If we had given in, we should have had a Parliamentary crisis with the Party.'[6] In the event Macmillan's command of the House allowed him to deflect trouble by attacking Gaitskell, who was by then very unpopular among Conservative MPs, and preserve his own position.

The Central African Federation

The Central African Federation was another colonial issue which threatened Conservative harmony at home as well as Britain's position abroad. The unhappy history of the Federation dated back to 1939, when the Bledisloe Commission recommended that the three British possessions in Central Africa – Southern Rhodesia, Northern Rhodesia and Nyasaland – should form a closer association. The post-war Labour government had proceeded very slowly with the idea, aware that African opinion suspected it as a means to entrench white rule in the three territories. The white settlers, led by Sir Godfrey Huggins, the prime minister of the self-governing colony of Southern Rhodesia, pressed ahead; conferences were held in 1951 in London (March) and at Victoria Falls (September) which set out the principle that a federation was desirable for economic reasons, but that the political development of the two protectorates – Northern Rhodesia and Nyasaland – would be in the hands of the British government and the territorial governments rather than the Federation, as would the land rights of the African populations of those territories. The incoming Conservative government embraced the federation eagerly, and it was established in October 1953. Huggins became federal prime minister; he retired in 1956 and was succeeded by his protégé, Roy Welensky.

The CAF was partly an economic experiment, uniting Northern Rhodesia's mineral wealth with Nyasaland's labour surplus and the industrial and agricultural wealth of Southern Rhodesia. To reassure investors, the 1953 discussions had contained an explicit promise that the Federation would not be dissolved without the consent of all the territorial governments, although this was not written into the Federal constitution. This was the source of a major conflict for Macmillan's government. The African political parties in all the territories were opposed to the Federation, and politicians from the two northern territories had boycotted the 1953 discussions. The African parties also announced their intention to boycott the 1958 Federation elections, preferring to demand self-government outright. The early development of the Federation was dogged by arguments between the Colonial Office, responsible for the northern territories, and the Commonwealth Office, responsible for Southern Rhodesia. In Southern Rhodesia a Dominion Party sprang up, demanding full independence with Dominion status, and threatening a unilateral declaration of independence both from Britain and from the Federation. Centrifugal forces seemed almost irresistible, but to preserve the Federation the British government was party to a further extension of the powers of the Federal government in 1957, giving it more responsibility for external relations.

Helped by the African boycott, Sir Roy Welensky's Federal Party won the federal elections in November 1958, and relations between Britain and the Federation began to deteriorate rapidly. Welensky himself, a former engine-driver and boxing champion who had first come to Macmillan's attention as Director of Manpower in Southern Rhodesia during the war, imposed his own combative personality on the discussions, but he undoubtedly had the support of the majority of the white settlers throughout the Federation. His first contact with Macmillan after the election was in conferences to draw up a new constitution for Northern Rhodesia, in which he stood up for the interest of the white minority against Macmillan's rather languid attempts to take steps towards a multi-racial polity. Political discontent, especially in the northern territories, mounted steadily. In February and March 1959 riots broke out across the Federation, leading to a state of emergency in each of the territories. Mr Justice Devlin was sent out to investigate them, and returned in July with a report declaring that Nyasaland was 'no doubt temporarily – a police state, where it is not safe for anyone to express approval of the policies of the Congress Party'.[7] This prompted Macmillan to describe him as a 'Fenian'.[8] Although this episode temporarily found Macmillan and Welensky on the same side, the accord was not to last. Macmillan ordered the Governor of Nyasaland, Sir Robert Armitage,[9] to write an alternative report. This he did, in two days at Chequers, and the government officially preferred his view. The Cabinet discouraged the Colonial Office ministers from resigning, and Macmillan appeared to be a stout defender of the survival of the Federation.

For all this, the government was actively reviewing the future of the Federation, to Welensky's despair. In March a Royal Commission was set up under Lord Monckton, and the Commonwealth Secretary, Lord Home, persuaded Welensky to accept it. Macmillan saw his government's purpose as to 'get in again and influence the European settlers'.[10] Technically the commission was to take evidence and prepare materials for the review of the Federation's constitution which was due in 1960, but in practice it was expected to be the opportunity to air views and prepare positions, so its composition and terms of reference were tendentious. After much wrangling the Labour opposition refused to nominate members. The final constitution of the Commission called for five African members, but, as Macmillan noted, all the leading African politicians were in prison, so it could be said that those nominated would not be representative. There was considerable debate with Welensky about whether the Commission was to be allowed to entertain the possibility of breaking up the Federation by permitting secession. Welensky insisted on a strict interpretation of undertakings given in 1953; Macmillan had to be more flexible, at least in private, to get any non-Conservative representative on to the Commission. At the end of October Welensky changed his mind about the Commission and tried to get it called off. Macmillan refused, and the venture went ahead.

He tried to give it some impetus during his tour of Africa, which began on 5 January 1960. During his visits to the Federation territories he was confronted with two problems. A remark made in Lagos was either misquoted or misrepresented to mean that the African populations of the northern territories would have some choice about whether to stay in the Federation,[11] and the settlers were correspondingly incensed. In Nyasaland Macmillan concluded that 'the cause of the Federation was almost desperate because of the strength of African opinion against it,'[12] and had to bring about the release of Dr Hastings Banda, the leader of the Malawi Congress Party, to give evidence to the Monckton Commission. This caused further trouble with Welensky, who later claimed that Macmillan had misled him about British intentions towards Banda. At best Macmillan's visit to the Federation territories was a useful holding action which persuaded some of the white settlers in Southern Rhodesia that the British government was not going to abandon them immediately; at worst, it further eroded confidence between Welensky and the Cabinet ministers responsible for the affairs of Africa.

The speed and even the direction of policy towards the Federation was changed by the 1959 election and consequent Cabinet reshuffle. Lennox-Boyd, who was a slow decoloniser and enjoyed the confidence of much of the Conservative back bench on colonial issues, resigned for personal reasons. He was replaced by Ian Macleod. Even before the election there had been friction within the Cabinet over the pace of change in the colonial possessions, aggravated by the Cyprus affair, and the new Colonial Secretary was firmly at one pole in a newly polarised situation. Welensky immediately detested him, and tried to play him off against Home, who remained Commonwealth Secretary and who was by his own account much less eager to give up the colonial empire. After Macmillan's return from Africa, Macleod demanded that Banda be released from prison to give evidence to the Monckton Commission.[13] Home and the Commonwealth Office supported Welensky's demand that he should be kept in detention. Macmillan wanted to support Macleod, but found the Cabinet divided; after Home had visited Rhodesia it was decided that Banda should be released on the day Monckton left the Federation. At this Macleod threatened to resign, causing Macmillan to suspect a plot 'à la Thorneycroft'.[14] Fearful of the political consequences of resignation, Macmillan then resolved to let Banda out three days before Monckton's departure, and commissioned Home to bring Welensky round – which he did. Although this resolved the immediate Cabinet crisis, it was the first sign that Macmillan might have difficulty with his party if the process of decolonisation moved ahead too rapidly.

The Monckton Commission duly went to the Federation in February 1960, and duly reported in October. Within a month of its arrival Monckton, on the first of a number of regular visits home to consult the Cabinet, persuaded Macmillan in a private discussion that secession should be admitted as a possibility.[15] The Commission's enquiries revealed a profound suspicion of the Federation, especially among Africans in Nyasaland, and the final report[16] suggested that the right to secede should be acknowledged, even if only as a safety valve to encourage the northern protectorates to accept the Federation and its many economic advantages. Welensky exploded, accused Macmillan of a breach of faith in allowing secession to be mentioned, and demanded that the British government repudiate the report. Macmillan refused. Welensky was eventually persuaded to soften his position, but Macmillan thought he himself had had a difficult press,[17] and the omens for the Review Conference were not good.

The first attempt at reviewing the Federation was a conference in London in December 1960, but this came to nothing after both Banda and Joshua Nkomo (of Southern Rhodesia) walked out of the talks. In the subsequent February two separate conferences were held: for Southern Rhodesia in Salisbury and for Northern Rhodesia in London. Discomfort within the Cabinet, fuelled by Macleod's passion for early and generous transfers of power in Africa, was threatening Macmillan's position. Macmillan suggested that African representatives should have something close to parity with Europeans in the Legislative Assembly for Northern Rhodesia, but found some of his Cabinet shocked and Macleod once more talking of resignation because the proposed pace was too slow. Welensky's Federal Party boycotted the Northern Rhodesia talks, and Welensky warned that he would mobilise troops to prevent disturbance in the territory. Macmillan started to prepare for 'open rebellion' in Southern Rhodesia.[18]

By now Welensky's open dealings with the Tory Right were causing concern to the prime minister. Lord Salisbury was always ready to hear Welensky's views and amplify them, and there was a deep suspicion of Macleod on the back bench. The replacement of Home at the Commonwealth Office by Duncan Sandys did little to change the relationship between the Commonwealth and Colonial Offices, and the Cabinet was kept in a permanent state of tension. A White Paper was published, to the great displeasure of Welensky, and a protracted and emotional haggling ensued over the precise numbers of reserved seats to be given to European and African members in the two houses of the Assembly. Macleod's resignation threats became 'a daily event'.[19] No sooner was an agreement reached than riots in Northern Rhodesia led to a further postponement, and further tension between Macleod and Sandys. Finally Macmillan tried to solve the political problem by moving Macleod to be Chairman of the Party and making Reginald Maudling Colonial Secretary. It was the first move in an attempt to limit the domestic political damage of a colonial problem which had no obvious solution.

Maudling soon proved himself '*plus noir que les nègres*',[20] and held the job for only five months. His first effort was to re-open the question of further increasing African numbers in the Northern Rhodesia Assembly, which Macmillan described with some irritation as 'quite impossible'.[21] Resignations were once more in the air. On 27 February 1962 the Cabinet finally accepted Maudling's proposals for Northern Rhodesia, which would in effect give it the right to secede. The personal tension was so great, however, that Macmillan shortly afterwards appointed Butler as Secretary of State with responsibility for Central Africa, relieving both Maudling and Sandys of their respective rôles in the area. It is hard to resist the conclusion that this was a carefully poisoned chalice for Butler. Until the spring of 1962 it had been the government's policy to preserve the Central African Federation. By the end, the British government was probably the Federation's only friend, as the secessionist mood took root among the white settlers in Southern Rhodesia. Now this policy was to be reversed and Butler was to lead the retreat. Everyone understood that he was to wind the Federation down; the final act was brought about at the end of 1963, when the Federation was formally dissolved, but he had been prominent in arranging the successive conferences which had hammered out the details. Macmillan remarked at the end of 1962 that 'The Federation *was* a good idea', but his memoirs also make the point that 'It was an enormous relief to me to be spared the almost daily flow of telegrams...and the continual and divergent pressures which had operated under the old system.[22] For Macmillan, March 1962 marked the end of his direct interest in the affairs of the Central African Federation.

Black and White in Africa

Imperial problems in Africa did not at first seem to extend beyond the wretched Central African Federation. West Africa, which Macmillan knew from his war service in the Colonial Office, was moving rapidly towards self-government. At his first Commonwealth Conference, held in London in June 1957, Kwame Nkrumah of Ghana attended as the first African prime minister to be present at such an occasion. By then it was already decided that Nigeria would be represented at a future Commonwealth Conference, and expected that the Central African Federation would also receive its independence and join the Commonwealth. The Union of South Africa, even after the victory of the Afrikaner National Party in the 1947 elections, was a full member of the Commonwealth. Macmillan's optimistic policy was to use the idea of the Commonwealth to hold together the complex of strategic and economic interests which engaged Britain in Africa.

The difficulties of this course soon became apparent. On the one hand the newly independent African states, which were set up with Western-educated political leaders and parliamentary governments, were at risk of losing one or both of these assets under pressure from economic difficulties or inter-tribal and inter-regional friction which the post-colonial regimes were unable to contain. Their continued interest in Britain and the Commonwealth could not therefore be guaranteed. On the other hand, the African states were hostile to any political arrangements which seemed to perpetuate colonial domination. The Central African Federation, led by the strident Welensky, was one of these suspect arrangements; the other was the internal policy of South Africa, where the Nationalists were tightening apartheid and preparing to declare a republic.

In the first part of Macmillan's premiership, the African Empire outside the Central African Federation caused few problems, as policy already laid down saw the independence of Nigeria and apparently steady progress towards further self-government in Kenya after a lull in the Mau-Mau guerrilla campaign, which throughout the 1950s had threatened the lives and livelihoods of white settlers. In early 1959 two passing episodes suggested that the existing rate of change was politically unacceptable. A riot at the Hola internment camp in Kenya was forcibly suppressed, with eleven inmates beaten to death by their guards. Quite apart from the effect in Kenya, this affair gave the Labour Party an opportunity to pillory the government before a General Election, calling for an enquiry and for the resignations of Lennox-Boyd and the Governor, Sir Evelyn Baring. The Conservative Party was also up in arms. Macmillan feared a Cabinet split, and set up an 'African Committee' to avert it. The precise details are obscure, but it appears that the Attorney-General, among others, was by July anxious to see Lennox-Boyd resign, while Macmillan desperately wanted him to stay on until the election.[23] This affair undermined Conservative confidence in the long-term survival of an Empire which depended on such vigorous repression.[24]

The Hola massacre coincided with the second disturbing episode, the Nyasaland riots which led to the declaration of a State of Emergency in the territory, and also in the Rhodesias, and to a large number of arrests including that of Hastings Banda. The Devlin Report and the reaction in the Central African Federation, described above, further complicated the moves towards a political settlement in East Africa; the uprising itself confirmed that African opinion throughout the continent was not content to accept the timetable being imposed by the colonial power.

As a test for Macmillan's policy the tension in East Africa was augmented by developments within South Africa, which threatened both the Commonwealth as a potential international bloc, and Britain's control over the process of decolonisation in its remaining possessions. By the end of 1959, even after a successful General Election, Macmillan was faced with African challenges which unsettled his government and threatened to undermine his global policy. At the beginning of 1960, in what he described as 'a few weeks of comparative calm in our external and internal affairs',[25] Macmillan went on a grand tour of Commonwealth countries in Africa. This complemented a similar extended tour of the Commonwealth in Asia and Australasia which he had undertaken in 1958, but, as he admitted, was more testing because the relationship between Britain and the African countries was much more uncertain. In the short term his main concern in policy was to improve the situation in the Rhodesias, but he went with a longer term aim of defining in public the relationship between the Commonwealth and African nationalism. He went, in fact, to meet people and make speeches, and at the age of sixty-six this put considerable strain on his health. In Accra he engaged in a debate with Nkrumah, in which one phrase was a reference to 'the wind of change [which] is blowing right through Africa'.[26] He then went to Nigeria, where he found that tribal and regional tensions were scarcely being contained in the parliamentary structure set up in the 1947 Constitution. He could hardly have been expected to do anything about this on the spot, but it is significant that direct contact with the leading Nigerian politicians does not seem to have inspired him to any alteration in the thrust of British policy, which was to wait until some semblance of harmony broke out before granting full independence to a Nigerian federation. Moving on to Salisbury,

he confronted the problems of another doomed federation before going on to South Africa, where his main purpose was to
be consummated.

Macmillan had brought from England a speech written for
the most part by Sir John Maud, the British High Commis-
sioner to South Africa, and refined by the Cabinet Secretary and the Commonwealth Office ministers, Alec Home and
Macmillan's son-in-law Julian Amery. The press were warned
to wait for something especially significant at Cape Town, and
were obliged by a speech which directly criticised the internal policies of the South African government. Partly from the
need to soften the blow to an audience made up largely of solid
Afrikaners, but also because there was more than one message
to deliver, it was a complicated text whose subsequent reputation has over-simplified it. Undoubtedly the recommendation
of 'a society which respects the right of individuals, a society
in which men are given the opportunity to grow to their full
stature – and that must in our view include the opportunity
to have an increasing share in political power and responsibility' was a direct snub to the policy of apartheid and 'separate
development'. It was recognised as such by the world's press,
and therefore taken up with enthusiasm all over the Commonwealth, including the white Dominions. But it also contained
other strands of argument. There was a good deal of flattery
for the Afrikaner community as 'the first of the African nation-
alisms'. More to the point, Macmillan urged his listeners to accept the need to keep the communist bloc out of Africa, and to
tune policy so that the newly independent countries were not
tempted by Russian influence. He repeated his view that de-
laying the full recognition of political rights for Africans would
create both uncontrollable internal unrest, and the conditions
for the spread of communism. This was a definition both of
British policy, and of Macmillan's fears. Maud reported to
London that the speech and the visit had 'set South Africa in
a ferment'.[27]

The hypothetical problem became real within the year. The
Sharpeville massacre in March and the outbreak of civil war in
the Congo in July raised the stakes dramatically. South African
leaders had already decided to turn their country into a republic, and had the support of a referendum of the white population. They also wished to remain in the Commonwealth, but
even those Commonwealth countries which were inclined to let

189

them do so despite their internal policies could not stomach the regime's behaviour at Sharpeville. At the Commonwealth Conference in May, Macmillan strained every nerve to prevent the Commonwealth itself from breaking up. In April he had feared that if Britain vetoed a UN resolution critical of apartheid 'the new Commonwealth . . . will never forgive us',[28] but noted that Australia and New Zealand wanted it vetoed. Britain abstained, but the tension remained to be resolved, or not, by the conference. Although the plenary sessions on world problems went smoothly, informal discussion of South Africa's internal policies was emotional and dangerous. Macmillan's one aim was to keep the Commonwealth together, and he engineered a bland agreed communiqué which made matters no worse, but made them no better either.[29]

There is no doubt that Macmillan's aim was to keep South Africa within the Commonwealth. In this endeavour he failed completely, not because of any obvious mistake or misjudgement, but simply because every other party to the problem was stubbornly determined to maintain positions which would make South Africa's continued membership impossible. In July the South African government decided to hold a referendum on the question of establishing a republic. Macmillan, who had only weeks before warned Verwoerd that he thought it unlikely that the Commonwealth would accept an application for readmission if South Africa did become a republic, asked him to postpone it. He also looked for support from the other Commonwealth prime ministers, in effect asking them to say as little as possible in the hope that South African intransigence would not be increased by public pressure. For the moment Nkrumah, the principal African objector to apartheid, agreed not to object to readmission; Tunku Abdul Rahman, of Malaya, was much more forthright, making it clear that his country's boycott of South African goods was part of a consistent policy to resist apartheid which it would take as far as was necessary. The South African referendum, in October, produced a tiny majority in favour of the republic. Verwoerd promptly wrote to Macmillan asking his advice on how to manage an application for continued membership of the Commonwealth, and making it clear that South Africa would not amend its racial policies for the sake of gaining admission. Verwoerd's determination to avoid making any concession of any sort on apartheid very nearly succeeded in keeping South Africa in the

Commonwealth. Macmillan energetically urged Nehru and Diefenbaker of Canada, who both had great potential influence over the objectors, to remain uncommitted on the subject until the Commonwealth prime ministers met in March. His plan, repeatedly described, was to allow South Africa to remain so that Commonwealth influence could be exerted on behalf of black South Africans, and both Nehru and most of the sceptical African and Asian leaders were prepared to negotiate on this basis. The main difficulty before the conference was that Diefenbaker would not drop his objections. When the prime ministers gathered, the combination of Canadian determination and the characteristically offensive deportment of the South African delegation towards black Commonwealth leaders and their concerns left no room for manoeuvre. Macmillan recognised after two days of discussion that there was no hope of compromise, and he decided to avoid a vote which might have split the Commonwealth by aligning Australia, Britain and New Zealand on the side of readmission against all the rest. Verwoerd was persuaded to withdraw his application, and the prime ministers got on with other business.

There is no doubt that this was a major setback for Macmillan. He despaired for the future of British influence in Africa, and for the Commonwealth, and found himself heavily criticised by the usual opponents for his readiness to countenance Commonwealth interest in the domestic policies of a member state. Lord Salisbury was characteristically critical, with support from the Rhodesia lobby, and the argument made it more difficult to find a resolution of the problems of the Central African Federation. But by this time the government's position was so uncomfortable in so many respects that an extra setback hardly affected Macmillan's determination to continue.

．．．

THE CONGO AND THE LIMITS OF POWER

A sudden emergency in the Congo focused Britain's African concerns. The decolonisation of the Belgian Congo in 1960 showed that Britain's preferred course of procrastination and finesse was not the only road to disaster. The handover of power was agreed in January 1960, with Belgian withdrawal to be completed within six months. Optimistically, the agreement provided for a democratically elected constituent assembly, which would have to make fundamental decisions about whether the independent Congo would be a federal or a unitary state, and concomitantly to decide on the relationships between the central government and the disparate regions of Belgium's immense colonial empire in Central Africa. By July, as Macmillan noted, the result was 'murder, rape, intertribal warfare, mass flights of Europeans, etc. The Prime Minister (Congolese) called Lumumba...is [said to be] a communist and probably a Russian agent; the Premier of Katanga (where the mineral wealth is) is a moderate, and wants to be independent. Sir Roy Welensky wants Katanga to be independent and would like to send in troops.'[30] In short order, the Belgian government sent troops back to the Congo to protect Belgian civilians; Lumumba appealed first to the United Nations and then directly to Ghana and the Soviet Union for protection against the Belgians; and Tshombe, the prime minister of Katanga, who was on good terms with Belgium and the largely Belgian-owned mining companies in his province, declared his independence. Katanga shared a border with the Rhodesias, and Welensky wanted Tshombe's independent government supported as a buffer-state against communism or chaos in the Central African Federation. This conundrum tested Macmillan's tactical sense. In July, when Welensky asked him to keep the United Nations out of Katanga, he consulted Home, who had just become Foreign Secretary, and refused. His reasoning was that the presence of the United Nations would keep the Russians out. Nevertheless the United Nations contingent which began to arrive on 18 July was forbidden by Tshombe to enter Katanga, and did not force the issue. This heightened the pressure on Macmillan, who knew that his own right-wingers as well as business interests with connections in the rich Katanga mining belt wanted him to recognise Katanga as an independent state.

In early August he defined the 'chief objects of British policy' as:

(1) To prevent Congo turning into Korea. Therefore, however attractive in some ways the separation of Katanga may seem, the result may be a Korean-type war, following on Russian support to the rest of the Congo.

(2) To support, through U.N., some kind of *federalist* solution....
(3) To stop foolish but dangerous movements by *African* countries *alone*....
(4) To work as closely as we can with French and other Europeans in NATO, including Belgians.
(5) To get Americans to be temperate and intelligent.[31]

In practice this meant voting in favour of a United Nations resolution requiring the Belgians to withdraw from Katanga in favour of United Nations troops, but simultaneously forbidding the United Nations contingent to interfere in internal conflicts within the Congo. Fortunately Tshombe now accepted a United Nations force in Katanga, and the policy could be defended plausibly to a suspicious House of Commons.

The behaviour of Nkrumah confirmed Macmillan's fear of the ramifications of any Pan-African intervention, for the Ghanaian leader was reported to have imported Soviet aeroplanes with Soviet advisers to form the basis of an army of intervention. So long as this came to nothing, Macmillan could reassure himself that 'we seem to have avoided a direct or indirect intervention by the Great Powers'[32] but he kept getting news of further Soviet supplies to Ghana and to Lumumba's forces. Then on 5 September Lumumba and the President of the Congo, Joseph Kasavubu, dismissed one another, and in the subsequent chaos Colonel Joseph Mobutu, with American support, seized Leopoldville, declared Lumumba deposed and expelled his Russian advisers. In November the United Nations recognised Kasavubu as head of state in the Congo, and Lumumba was captured by Mobutu's forces at the beginning of December, but the escape of Lumumba's deputy, Gizenga, left the Congo divided in three. Tshombe remained in control in Katanga; Mobutu held Leopoldville; Gizenga maintained a pro-Soviet government in Stanleyville.

The fact that this tragi-comedy of errors represented something of a vindication of Macmillan's policy reveals what the essence of that policy was. His main concern was to prevent a communist hegemony in Central Africa by supporting the United Nations. While it was in theory desirable that the United Nations should finish the job of pacifying the Congo, it was far more important that they should be doing the job at all. Macmillan therefore makes much in his memoirs of the United Nations Assembly discussion of the Congo in October, attended by many national leaders, at which Khrushchev famously banged the table with his shoe by way of heckling Macmillan's speech.[33] His point was not that anything particular had been done about the unhappy Congo, but that Khrushchev had been tripped up by the Congo issue, and failed to take advantage of it as part of a general propaganda thrust against the West.

But the price of this success was an eternal vigilance. In January 1961, at Casablanca, the Conference of African States declared its support for Lumumba; some of the member countries withdrew their contingents from the United Nations force, and the Commonwealth members, led in this instance by Nehru and Nkrumah, denounced Tshombe and Kasavubu. Lumumba was murdered by the Katangan authorities into whose care he had been transferred, and both the Russians and the 'Casablanca powers' recognised Gizenga's government in Stanleyville as the legitimate Congolese government. In Leopoldville, Kasavubu replaced Mobutu with Joseph Ileo. In Katanga and the areas governed by Leopoldville, increasing use was made of European mercenaries, some British, to gain military advantage. The Russians stepped up their campaign against United Nations intervention, but on 21 February 1961 failed to get the Security Council to abandon the Congo operation. A brief outbreak of progress in February saw an agreement between Kasavubu, Tshombe and others which prefigured a federal system for the country, but this broke down when Kasavubu tried to bring Gizenga into the deal. Tshombe took this as a sign to repudiate the previous agreement, and was thereupon arrested. This episode provoked a reaction from Macmillan's right. Welensky, with backing from the Conservative right wing, reopened his attack on British support for the United Nations. Macmillan responded by repeating his plea that 'an independent Katanga, and its friends, would have to face the hostility, both on the ground and in the UN, of most of the rest of Africa. This would provide the Russians with just the kind of opportunity they are looking for.... '.[34] But Welensky and his Conservative sympathisers quite enjoyed the hostility of the rest of Africa, and Macmillan's position was further weakened.

In June Tshombe was freed, and signed but immediately repudiated an agreement to incorporate Katanga into a federal Congo. Nevertheless a Congolese parliament finally met in

July, without Katangan representatives, and Cyrille Adoula, a trade unionist who was supported by the CIA, was elected premier, with Gizenga as his deputy. When the United Nations contingent moved in force to invade Katanga in August, the pressure on Macmillan was stepped up. The Katanga government had employed large numbers of white mercenaries to strengthen their ground and air forces, and fighting was heavy. Remarkable atrocities were reported, carried out by all parties including the United Nations contingent, and the Conservative Right denounced British collusion in the attempt to destroy the independence of Katanga. Macmillan, privately, became nervous that Gizenga's influence in the Congolese government was growing too fast.

> Unless we and the Americans act quickly and resolutely, we shall have undone in a week all we have done – at huge expense – in a year. Congo will be handed to Russia on a plate. The Union Minière properties will be 'nationalised' and run by Russian communists, and a most dangerous situation created in Africa – as well as [a] great financial and moral blow to the West and especially to European civilisation.

Macmillan therefore sought help from President Kennedy to rein in the United Nations force. Dag Hammarskjöld, the Secretary-General, was persuaded to bring about a cease-fire, and was on the way to meet Tshombe when his aircraft crashed in Northern Rhodesia. In the event, this tragedy hardly deflected the processes of diplomacy, and a cease-fire was duly agreed in late September, but Macmillan was still impaled on the horns of his own political dilemma. In his view, only United Nations action would keep Russia out of Central Africa, but if United Nations action backfired he faced a dangerous rebellion from his right wing.

His difficulties extended from the 1922 Committee to the Cabinet. A decision was taken in early December to supply heavy bombs to the Indian airforce detachment serving in the Congo, to neutralise Katangan airfields from which white mercenary pilots were flying missions against the United Nations troops. This divided the Cabinet – the Foreign Secretary had been very reluctant to accede to the request and other ministers were also opposed – and enraged the 1922 Committee. It is striking that Macmillan was surprised by the vigour of the reaction. He remarked that 'for some reason (I suppose, age and infirmity) I have felt this "crisis" far more than I should have done – have worried and slept badly and so on'.[35] He was so anxious that he persuaded Kennedy to overrule his United Nations representative, Adlai Stevenson, and press for an immediate cease-fire, and also got Kennedy to promise financial support for a large hydro-electric project in Ghana. These rabbits were duly pulled out of the hat in the Commons on 14 December, helping the government to a majority of ninety-four. Only ten Conservatives abstained, including those whom Macmillan described as 'the small group of people who really hate me – Lords Hinchingbrooke and Lambton; Nigel Birch; Mr Turton...'.[36] The centre of the party remained loyal, in spite of Macmillan's fears.

The episode of the bombs indicates how haphazard Macmillan's policy towards the Congo had become. Because of his fears, perhaps exaggerated, for his own political safety, he had given United Nations policy a further, probably salutary, jolt towards a settlement. This led to the Kitona agreement of 20 December between Tshombe and Adoula, which like all previous agreements was soon repudiated by Tshombe. Macmillan optimistically reflected that the parliamentary crisis had come about because 'Members (who have up to now shut their eyes to the realities of the modern world) have been rudely awakened. Britain (or France, or Germany, or any European Power) can no longer exert a decisive influence on these world events.'[37] It is not clear, though, that his own estimate of the limits of British power was accurate, nor that he had an unambiguous policy towards the Congo. In late December, conferring with Kennedy at Bermuda, he complained that the United States was too eager to urge on the United Nations contingent and told the President that Tshombe was among the West's best friends in Central Africa. In return, Kennedy wanted Macmillan to discourage Welensky from supplying arms to Katanga, but found the British representatives immovable.[38] Macmillan was in the peculiar position of being more sympathetic to Adoula and the United Nations in public (and in his memoirs) than he was in private, and attracting criticism from his own right wing for adopting a position which did not really represent his policy. This was perhaps a greater misjudgement than the transient panic over the bombs episode, for it led him into more and more contradictions.

Although the principles which supposedly underlay Macmillan's policy towards the Congo remained constant, they interacted strangely with the march of events to produce a policy which for the rest of his premiership grew more, rather than less, inconsistent. After the parliamentary crisis of December 1961 he continued to insist that the best hope for the Congo was to leave Katanga with considerable autonomy in a federal system, so that it could contribute its mineral wealth to the paralysed Congolese economy. He condemned any attempt to impose a unitary state, and resisted United Nations action which might tend in that direction. He was encouraged in this attitude by the arrest of Gizenga, and corresponding reduction in the fear of Russian influence, in January 1962. In practice his principles now led him to defend Katanga against the authority of Adoula's government, and to resist the sort of military action by the United Nations which Britain had supported in 1961 – a position closer to Welensky's, but too late, of course, to please Welensky himself.

In March 1962 Macmillan made a lot of trouble before bowing to American pressure to contribute to the cost of United Nations operations in the Congo; in April he told the Americans that Tshombe's position had to be maintained so long as Britain was involved in the Central African Federation. The Americans concluded that Macmillan was encouraging Tshombe to obstruct the reintegration of the Congo, and protested. Without any progress in talks between Adoula and Tshombe, Adoula warned that he would have to resort again to force, and was only deflected by an American initiative to impose economic sanctions on Katanga. This threat had a small effect: the Katanga government agreed to a federal constitution, but no sooner was it inaugurated in October than Tshombe repudiated it, leaving the United Nations to carry out its sanction of using military force again. Macmillan, complaining that 'before the Communist danger had been happily overcome, we had worked in harmony; now that it had been removed, we seemed to be drifting apart',[39] continued to resist American pressure to support the United Nations. This led to a bruising confrontation at the Nassau conference in December 1962, in which the Americans pointed out that Tshombe seemed incapable of keeping agreements, and that any policy which depended on his agreement was therefore doomed to failure. Macmillan, as part of the price for the Polaris missiles, agreed to United Nations action; operations began almost immediately and Tshombe was finally forced out of the country in January 1963. He took refuge in Northern Rhodesia, but this implied no practical support and he fled to Europe in June 1963. Adoula's unitary state took over, and at the end of the year expelled all Russian diplomats from the Congo.

The best Macmillan could say about his Congo policy in retrospect was that 'through this somewhat painful journey we managed to avoid the main dangers, both internally and in the Commonwealth', though he later told a rightly sceptical biographer 'Kennedy and I, we drove the Russians out ... '.[40] In fact even the main dangers were hardly avoided, and the evolution of policy demonstrates with uncomfortable clarity the limits on Macmillan's power both internally and externally. His policy towards the Congo was predicated on keeping Russia out of Central Africa and protecting British interests, which were specifically British business interests in the mineral wealth of Katanga. He could only work indirectly, and none of the available instruments were really under British control. Welensky would not do what he was told, and enjoyed the support of the Conservative right wing in his disobedience. The Commonwealth, far from being a source of diplomatic strength, was prone to division, and represented a brake on British power. The United States had its own preferred solutions, and in extreme situations simply enforced them on a reluctant ally. The elimination of Russian influence was finally brought about by means precisely opposite to those favoured by Macmillan. At home, the dissatisfaction of the Conservative right wing seemed increasingly to frighten him, and his fumblings over support for Katanga in 1961 and the bombs episode at the end of that year contributed to the loathing which was felt for him by his party opponents, and even to discontent within the Cabinet. The sureness of touch which was his main claim to power was rarely in evidence over the Congo.

.   .   .

IMPERIAL OVERSTRETCH IN AFRICA?

The Congo affair, interlocked so closely in time and space with the demise of the Central African Federation, underlined the continuity between Macmillan's problems in the African empire, caused by the developments which prompted his Wind of

Change speeches, and his dilemmas as a Great Power diplomatist. It hardly mattered that one tract of African territory was
part of Britain's colonial empire, the other the residue of another country's defunct imperium. The pitfalls for Macmillan
had much in common. Local nationalism, intersected by tribal
and regional differences in countries whose borders were the
artificial product of nineteenth-century imperialism, was too
powerful to be contained permanently by colonial authority.
Self-government, followed sooner or later by independence,
was an outcome accepted by all parties. Disagreement was assured, though, over the rate of political change, over the best
means to ensure that decolonisation was not accompanied by
an increase of Russian influence in Africa, and over the best
way to secure the preservation of white interests in the independent African states.

The principles underlying Macmillan's policy were, in broad
outline, consistent. In every African territory he wanted Britain
to emerge with as much residual influence as was compatible with the consent of the emerging African political forces,
and he wanted the successor governments to be friendlier to
Britain than to Russia. Usually this meant moving faster than
at least half of his Cabinet would have liked, and there is no
doubt that Lennox-Boyd as Colonial Secretary, and Home, first
at the Commonwealth Office and later at the Foreign Office,
were more determined to hang on to the colonial empire than
Macmillan would have wished. The magnitude of Macmillan's
political problems, especially after the implicit warning broadcast in his Wind of Change speech in Cape Town, was pro-
portionate to the strength of the links between local white
interests in Africa and the Conservative Party. Bits of the
Empire could be given back to the inhabitants without attracting much attention if no powerful vested interests had
a foothold in British politics. Thus Tanganyika and Uganda,
with small European populations and insignificant economic
assets, gained their independence by 1963 with little fuss. The
Central African Federation was difficult to unravel because it
had been knitted together so carefully by an alliance between
the white settlers of Southern Rhodesia and the Conservative
governments of Churchill and Eden. Welensky's undoubted
political talents, working in harness with Salisbury and disaffected back-benchers such as Lambton, created parliamentary
difficulties which continually threatened to ambush the gov-

ernment. Even within the Federation there was less resistance to withdrawal from Nyasaland, which had few assets besides a surplus population, than to a settlement in Northern Rhodesia which contained some of the richest copper mines in the world. Parliamentary trouble reflected the anxiety of the proprietors. On the other hand the Conservative Party machine, which was loyal to the leadership, was used to make direct contact with tractable political movements among the settlers.[41]

A contrasting problem was presented by Kenya, where moves towards independence for an African-dominated polity had been rather faster after the end of the Mau Mau troubles. Instead of the mining wealth of Northern Rhodesia, Kenya had an efficient capitalist agriculture in the White Highlands, and a settler class with close connections at home. Macmillan summarised the position in conversation with Kilmuir in 1961:

> We both feel anxious about Kenya. In some ways this is more difficult *at home* even than Central Africa. People are not yet accustomed to the idea that, sooner or later, we shall have to accept independence in Kenya.... 'Sooner or later' – the Colonial Office are thinking in terms of 1964, which seems to many of us *too* soon. From the Party point of view, Kenya is going to create a big problem. We might even split on it. Lord Salisbury and Lord Lambton could easily rally a 'settler' lobby here of considerable power. The Kenyan settlement has been aristocratic and upper middle class (much more than Rhodesia) and has strong links with the City and the Clubs.[42]

In the event the settlers in Kenya struck a different bargain with African nationalism than had been attempted in Rhodesia. An adequate, if not generous, land settlement reduced the anxieties of the settlers, and no Welensky emerged to link settler anxieties with a Conservative lobby. There were in any case fewer whites in Kenya than in Rhodesia (about 50,000 against more than 200,000 in Southern Rhodesia). Macmillan noted in April 1961 that 'the Party here are very suspicious'[43] of moves to release the principal African leader, Jomo Kenyatta, but political conditions did not encourage the spread of this suspicion to the centre of the Party, and there was nothing approaching the panic which seized Macmillan in December about the Congo bombs episode. Internal self-government, with Kenyatta as prime minister, was inaugurated in June 1963 and independence in December. Kenyan independence was not painless, but its political fallout was less poisonous to Macmillan than the affairs of the Central African Federation.

In these transactions, Macmillan and his successive Colonial Secretaries took the view that a die-hard resistance would ultimately let in the Soviet Union, which would be even worse for trade and for British interests than early independence. Their position, and that of the interests, was fundamentally the same over the Congo. Pressed by business interests and the Welensky lobby to support Katanga at the expense of the economic viability of the Congolese federation, Macmillan and Home decided that keeping the Russians out took priority. As soon as the Soviet problem was eased by Adoula's success, Macmillan's sympathy for Tshombe was renewed, but he now found himself outflanked by the United States, whose policy-makers wanted to maintain support for the Congolese government after Macmillan had lost interest in it. It was a confusing and indeed rather confused policy, but it was largely consistent with what was going on at the same time elsewhere in Africa.

Did the Wind of Change blow Macmillan any good? It is evident from his memoirs that he was proud of the Cape Town speech, and that he credited it with some impact on the subsequent decolonisation of Africa. His enemies, if anything, thought it was even more influential than he did. Even so, it is difficult to resist the impression that Macmillan was not an enthusiast for colonial affairs. He was happy to delegate whenever possible, taking direct control only when Anglo-American or Anglo-Russian relations were at stake, or when the domestic political impact of some colonial issue was damaging the government's standing with the Conservative Party. Perhaps as a result of this detachment, his judgement on colonial and African matters was uncertain, and his achievements, even taking into account the intractable problems which he faced, were rather less than his aspirations.

.   .   .

THE END OF INFORMAL EMPIRE

The futility of Britain's diplomatic efforts in much of Africa was matched by frustration in the exercise of power on the periphery of British possessions in the Middle East and in Asia. For Macmillan and his immediate predecessors, one of the most uncomfortable legacies of the Second World War was the loss of Britain's rôle as a global prefect, keeping small and unruly nations in order wherever their behaviour threatened British or European interests. The Cold War sharpened the definition of British interests abroad, and of course brought in the United States as the principal military power in the West. Much of Macmillan's time and effort was spent in harmonising British and American policies towards political change outside Europe. He thought he was bringing the Americans in to support British policy under British guidance; the Americans, understandably, thought of Britain as a useful ally rather than as a mentor. The results were sometimes comic, sometimes tragic. In the early years of his premiership the major incidents were in Iraq, the Lebanon, and over the unhappy islands of Quemoy and Matsu; during his second government, he tried to offer advice and support to the United States about Laos and Vietnam. While British and American policies were undoubtedly closer together at the end of his premiership than at the beginning, contemporaries recognised that this had come about because the alliance was no longer being operated as a partnership between equals. America led; Britain followed, sometimes at a distance, sometimes with dignity.

The Middle East

Developments in the Middle East, besides Suez, neatly illustrate the logical progression from Great Power behaviour through partnership to very unequal partnership. In 1955, as Foreign Secretary, Macmillan had defended the position of one of Britain's clients in the Persian Gulf, the Sultan of Muscat and Oman, by sending troops to occupy the Buraimi Oasis. The occasion was a territorial claim by Saudi Arabia, which the Sultan disputed. Neither the United States nor the Commonwealth was consulted, and on one occasion armed conflict nearly broke out between British troops and American civilians working for the ARAMCO oil company, which had the support of the US government.[44] The same troops were conveniently available to help suppress a rebellion against the Sultan which began later in the year under the Imam of Oman, and was supported by Saudi Arabia and Egypt. The Imam and his brother, Talib, were persistent and energetic, and by the middle of 1957 central Oman was controlled by the rebels. The Sultan appealed for British help, and in July the Cabinet agreed to provide 'unprovocative' support, such as military supplies by airlift and the presence of a second frigate to patrol the coast. In addition the Cabinet decided to send RAF units to attack rebel positions with leaflets followed by rocket fire, it being too hot to send infantry.[45] On this occasion, Macmillan immediately informed Eisenhower and received a tentative message of support. But after the attacks had begun, Dulles turned up in London and it took some effort of public relations to link his visit to disarmament rather than to American concern about British excesses.

The initial operation against the Omani rebels was a qualified success, in that the towns were restored to the Sultan. Operations in the hills, conducted by the Sultan's army with British reinforcements, continued for some time. This was done without active co-operation from the United States, and in August 1957 Macmillan was irritated by American refusal to support Britain at the United Nations when a number of Arab countries tried to call a Security Council meeting to protest against British aggression.

At the same time, in Syria, an internal political struggle between left-wing officers and the old regime was being won by the left, with considerable support from the Russians. Dulles was duly alarmed, and proposed to invoke the new Eisenhower Doctrine to intervene. Macmillan, concerned at the growth of Russian influence but equally concerned that the Syrians might cut oil supplies to the West if provoked, tried at first to restrain him. 'The real problem is *not to discourage* the Americans, if they are really serious and will see through any action to the end; at the same time *not to stimulate* them to do something which (if it goes off at half-cock) will be fatal.'[46] On the same day he wrote to Dulles with a lucid exposition of the domino theory of communist subversion which was later to be the logical spine of American policy throughout the Middle and Far East:

> ...we seem to be unable to deal with this method of infiltration, which brings about Communism by an internal coup.
>
> The next stage, then, may be an attempt to subvert Lebanon and Jordan by the same methods. If we do nothing, both of these countries might easily fall. Then I suppose the pressure will turn against Iraq.... [47]

Macmillan was looking for a 'reasonable *casus belli*' to justify a military operation against Syria, but he was also afraid that Dulles might back out at the last minute. His old friend Harold Caccia – now ambassador in Washington – warned him that 'If anything goes wrong, you may be sure that Mr Dulles will place the blame elsewhere.'[48] Macmillan sent his private secretary to Washington to advance the discussions, and decided to stop consulting the Cabinet about the details of his exchanges with Dulles. In early September the Americans appeared to be getting ready to use force, and Macmillan asked Duncan Sandys, the Defence Minister, to find out what military action Britain could take in support of Iraq if war broke out between Iraq on the one side and Syria and Egypt on the other.

Although the United States began to step up its action with a well-publicised delivery of arms to Jordan, the Syrian affair went off the boil in September, causing Macmillan to complain that 'the Americans may be learning, but they are playing their hand abominably and allowing the Russians to take trick after trick'.[49] A further opportunity was provided by a border dispute between Syria and Turkey, which led to direct threats by Russia against Turkey and concomitantly by the Americans against Russia. At this point Khrushchev very pointedly backed off, telling the Turkish ambassador that the border incident posed no threat to peace. 'Thus', as Macmillan recalled in his memoirs, 'to all appearances the whole matter came to an end'.[50]

What, though, was 'the matter' which was now ended? Macmillan's very private communication with Dulles, and his contemplation of military action, both suggest that he was trying to lead the Americans towards an attack on Syria which would have had the effect of strengthening Western influence in the Middle East. If this was the intention, rather than the mere defence of an admittedly unsatisfactory status quo, it was clearly a failure, and Khrushchev's sudden affability towards Turkey was a significant and successful gesture to advance Russian interests. In that case, it could be said that Macmillan and Dulles had actually failed; and even if their intentions were more modestly to hold the ring in the Middle East, they had had no conspicuous success. As at Bermuda, there was now some evidence of close Anglo-American co-operation, but not much sign that it did either party any good.

In the first part of 1958 Britain was still exercising an unapologetic suzerainty around the Persian Gulf, and trying to retain its powerful influence in Iraq, whose economy and indeed political life was dominated by the Iraq Petroleum Company, a British concern with strong official links. In February Syria and Egypt announced their union in the United Arab Republic; the Yemen, though still a monarchy, joined in a federation with the new body in early March. The response by pro-Western Arab governments was to form the Arab Federation, consisting of Iraq and Jordan. Nuri Said, who returned to the premiership in Iraq in February, tried to get Britain and the United States to support the Iraqi economy if during a conflict with Syria the vital oil pipelines were cut. To this Macmillan agreed, but with some reservations that Nuri's schemes were too grandiose and that he was telling different stories to his British and American friends. Macmillan and Lloyd were also unhappy about Nuri's proposal that Britain should abandon her protectorate over Kuwait so that Kuwait could join the Arab Federation. The determination to hold on to control wherever possible was well illustrated by Aden, which was in political turmoil and vulnerable to direct attack from the Yemen. In July, after a couple of months of trouble in Lahej, one of the Aden protectorates, Macmillan recorded in his diary that 'the young Sultan has gone over to Nasser.... He will have to be deposed.'[51] He was. This was the exercise of colonial power.

The exercise of indirect influence, by comparison, was much more difficult. On 14 July the Iraqi monarchy was overthrown, taking with it Britain's closest friend in the Middle East, Nuri Said, who was lynched enthusiastically by an angry mob. The Iraqi revolt precipitated a crisis in Middle Eastern politics which threatened to exceed Suez in its range and severity. The pro-Western government of the Lebanon under President Chamoun had already warned Britain and the United States that it might at any moment ask for military assistance against Egyptian 'infiltration' and military threats from Syria,[52] and the Cabinet had agreed in May to take action if asked. Faced with the resurgence of pan-Arabism in Iraq, Chamoun now called in his promise, and Macmillan learned that the Americans intended to respond. His reaction, after making understandably arch comparisons with Suez, was to reflect on the wider problem. In the Cabinet:

The general feeling was uncertainty as to what the American policy really would be. Nothing could be more fatal than for the Americans to go to the Lebanon and rest content with that or soon retire in favour of a U.N. force. *We* had to carry, on our economy, all the evil effects that might follow – in Iraq, Syria and the Gulf. Our sterling oil might dry up and what real guarantee had we from U.S.?[53]

Macmillan soon learned, by telephoning Eisenhower, that the United States had already taken the decision to send troops to the Lebanon, and tried to persuade him that an action confined to the Lebanon 'entailed much greater risk to us than to the Americans'. This estimate was confirmed two days later when King Hussein of Jordan, whose cousin Feisal had just lost his kingdom in Iraq, appealed for British and American assistance against presumed military threats from Egypt, Syria and possibly Iraq. The Cabinet's reaction was a fascinating study in the effect of the Suez trauma. Macmillan's own view of the desirability of sending troops is heavily disguised both in his own memoir account and in the Cabinet records. The closest one comes to candour is his advice, to a Cabinet which already seemed very determined to go ahead, that it would be 'quixotic but honourable', and even this is delphic.[54] His greatest anxiety seems to have been to ensure that, in contrast to the Suez operation, all members of the Cabinet should have been fully informed of the political and military context, including discussions with allies, before taking a decision. In the small hours of 17 July he telephoned Dulles twice, only to discover that he thought it 'rash but praiseworthy' to intervene and would provide logistical and moral support but no troops. Macmillan then 'went with Butler and Norman Brook [the Cabinet Secretary] into another room' and in a private discussion concluded that the Cabinet were determined to press on. Even then, his summing up covered all the difficulties in some detail, including the point that the political risks in Britain were finely balanced. After all this, the Cabinet was unanimous. 'So I said "So be it." '.[55]

After all this trouble to avoid recriminations from disaffected colleagues, Macmillan went peacefully to bed, but woke up to a dreadful blow from the Foreign Office, which had forgotten to get permission to fly through Israeli airspace to deliver troops to Amman. This crisis in turn was averted, while the House of Commons gave the government a comfortable majority. With the troops in Jordan, Macmillan became anxious that they could not defend the monarchy without reinforcements and logistical support from the Americans. In the event this was unnecessary since the threat from other Arab powers evaporated and the troops were withdrawn in November, to the tune of mutual congratulation between Macmillan and Eisenhower. Although Britain had in part led the Americans into action, there was now no doubt that only the United States was actually capable of mounting a successful operation in the Middle East.

Quemoy and Matsu

Quemoy and Matsu were two very small islands off the coast of mainland China, which were occupied by the defeated army of Chiang Kai-Shek in 1949 when the body of his Kuomintang forces were withdrawn to Taiwan. Since 1954 the United States had been formally committed to defending the islands by force against territorial claims by the communist regime. For some reason still unknown Chinese forces began an artillery bombardment of the islands, which by now held a garrison of 80,000 men, on 23 August 1958. Britain had declared in 1955 that the mainland regime had a good claim to the islands. Macmillan was in a dilemma: should he support the Americans and risk his relations with India and the Afro-Asian group, or stick to the established British position and jeopardise 'the friendship and alliance which I have done so much to rebuild and strengthen'?[56] The Americans themselves were in difficulties because Dulles clearly believed that the loss of the islands would be the first stage in the collapse of the 'anti-Communist barrier'. The American response was to warn the mainland regime that they would use force to defend the islands and that this force would necessarily include the use of nuclear weapons against airbases.

Macmillan, alarmed, urged Dulles and Eisenhower to put together a movement at the United Nations to call for demilitarisation of the islands and the maintenance of the territorial status quo. Macmillan's initiative was in effect ignored by Washington, largely because Chiang Kai-Shek refused absolutely to withdraw from the islands. Eisenhower and Khrushchev were soon trading threats, but on 11 September Eisenhower declared on television that the United States would not yield to force but was ready for negotiation. In Britain a badly-handled article by Randolph Churchill gave *Evening Standard* readers the impression that Macmillan was prepared to back the Americans with force. This had to be deflected, but the House was not sitting and Macmillan was not unduly disturbed by the state of British public opinion. By 19 September Khrushchev and Eisenhower had reached the stage of exchanging written insults, but Eisenhower told Selwyn Lloyd on 21 September that he was against the use of atomic weapons in any operations to defend the islands.[57] At this point the crisis seemed to reach a plateau: the bombardment was temporarily suspended on 6 October, resumed on 20 October, then scaled down to alternate days from 25 October, and finally abandoned in March 1959. Nobody knew why it had started or why it had ended.

Although Macmillan himself wondered pointedly what was 'the moral to be drawn' from this affair, it is not too difficult to supply one. British policy over a matter which clearly threatened the global interests of the Western alliance was different in tone from that of the Americans. Although Macmillan himself had expounded versions of the 'domino theory' in his analyses of many international incidents, and had congratulated himself on the superior wisdom of British diplomacy, the reality of global power was that on the Western side the United States decided what would be done.[58]

. . .

STILL AT THE TOP TABLE?

While trying to exercise power outside Europe, Macmillan was concerned to maintain as much as possible of the *pax Brittanica* with which he had grown up. He believed himself to be a realist, compared with some of his Cabinet and many of his back-bench followers, and proposed to maintain British influence by co-operation with the United States. In the end Britain's withdrawal from Africa was conducted quickly, with more dignity in some countries than in others, and always with discomfort. While trading on Britain's experience and wisdom, in the 'Greeks and Romans' analogy which so readily came to his lips, he often criticised the Americans for diplomatic ineptitude. It was painful for him, no less painful for others, to recognise that the United States alone possessed the military force to police the world. His particular error was to assume that his relationship with American presidents, backed up by the British diplomatic machine, was enough to channel that power in the appropriate direction.

. . .

NOTES AND REFERENCES

1. Harold Macmillan, *Tides of Fortune* (London: Macmillan, 1969), p. 277.
2. Private information.
3. Prime Minister to Lord President of the Council, 28 Jan. 1957, CAB 134/1555. I am obliged to my colleague Dr A.J. Stockwell for drawing my attention to this memorandum.
4. From the Radcliffe Report, 'Constitutional Proposals for Cyprus', 12 Nov. 1956, Cmd. 42.
5. To Diefenbaker, 1 July 1958, quoted in Harold Macmillan, *Riding the Storm* (London: Macmillan, 1971, p. 671.
6. Diary 18 Feb. 1959, quoted in Macmillan, *Riding the Storm*, p. 695.
7. *Report of the Nyasaland Commission of Inquiry*, 16 July 1959, Cd 814.
8. Diary, 13 July 1959, quoted in Horne, *Macmillan 1957–1986* (London: Macmillan, 1988), p. 181.
9. Whom he had sacked from the Governorship of Cyprus in 1955.
10. Diary, 24 May 1959, quoted Harold Macmillan, *Pointing the Way* (London: Macmillan, 1972), p. 136.
11. Macmillan, *Pointing the Way*, pp. 145–6; see Harold Evans, *Downing Street Diary* (London: Hodder and Stoughton, 1981), p. 98, which suggests that Macmillan was having to cover up a genuine error.
12. Macmillan, *Pointing the Way*, p. 148.
13. Macleod had already discussed this with Banda's lawyer, Dingle Foot, whose report of the conversation to his client was 'bugged' by the Rhodesian secret service and passed directly to Welensky, thus giving the Federation prime minister plenty of time to get angry.
14. Diary, 24 Feb. 1960, quoted in Horne, *Macmillan 1957–1986*, p. 201.
15. Lord Birkenhead, *Walter Monckton* (London: Weidenfeld and Nicolson, 1969), p. 347, citing Lord Molson's authority for the conversation.
16. *Report of the Advisory Commission on the Review of the Constitution of Rhodesia and Nyasaland*, Cd 1148–50; also in CAB 129/101, C(60)149, 12 Oct. 1960.
17. Diary for 8 Nov. 1960, quoted in Horne, *Macmillan 1957–1986*, p. 210. His press secretary, Harold Evans, made no mention of the reception of the Report in October and November, though he refers elsewhere to embarrassments over the Federation. This suggests that Macmillan was becoming over-sensitive to the press.
18. Diary, 24 Feb. 1961, quoted in Horne, *Macmillan 1957–1986*, p. 389.
19. Diary, June 1961, quoted ibid., p. 397.
20. Diary, 10 Jan. 1962, quoted ibid., p. 408.
21. Diary, 2 Jan. 1962, quoted ibid.
22. Diary, 10 Dec. 1962, quoted in Macmillan, *At the End of the Day*, p. 323.

23. Horne, *Macmillan 1957–1986*, p. 175, citing the diaries.
24. The effect can be contrasted with that of the Amritsar massacre in 1919, when the Lloyd George Coalition government disciplined General Dyer, the officer responsible, and thereby divided the Conservative Party by crystallising right-wing opposition to the government.
25. Macmillan, *Pointing the Way*, p. 119.
26. Ibid., p. 124.
27. Memorandum by Maud, 18 Feb. 1960, in 'Prime Minister's African Tour. Note by the Secretary of the Cabinet', C(60)66, CAB 129/101. The text of the speech is reproduced in Macmillan, *Pointing the Way*, pp. 473–82.
28. Diary, 1 April 1960, quoted in Macmillan, *Pointing the Way*, p. 169.
29. The Commonwealth's jurisdiction over the constitutions of its member countries resembled that of Oxford women's colleges over the marriage of undergraduates in the 1960s: permission to marry, or to become a republic, was not required, but either action implied withdrawal from the institution. Permission to re-enter was at the discretion of the institution, and was only granted after a strict examination of the circumstances.
30. Diary, 10 July 1960, quoted in Macmillan, *Pointing the Way*, p. 260.
31. Diary, 8 Aug. 1960, quoted ibid., p. 266.
32. Diary, 27 Aug. 1960, quoted in Macmillan, *Pointing the Way*, p. 268.
33. It was this occasion, much beloved of Macmillan's admirers, which produced the deadly riposte 'perhaps we could have a translation, I could not quite follow'.
34. Macmillan to Welensky, 9 May 1961, quoted in Macmillan, *Pointing the Way*, p. 440.
35. Diary, 18 Dec. 1961, quoted in Macmillan, *Pointing the Way*, p. 451.
36. Diary, 18 Dec. 1961, quoted in Horne, *Macmillan 1957–1986*, p. 402.
37. Diary, 20 Dec. 1961, quoted in Macmillan, *Pointing the Way*, p. 456.
38. Richard D. Mahoney, *JFK: Ordeal in Africa* (New York: Oxford University Press, 1983), p. 141.
39. Macmillan, *At the End of the Day*, p. 282.
40. Ibid., p. 286; Horne, *Macmillan 1957–1986*, p. 406.
41. S.R. Murphy, 'The Conservative Party and decolonisation, 1953–1964', Paper read at the Institute of Historical Research, Feb. 1992.
42. Diary, 20 Jan. 1961, quoted in Macmillan, *At the End of the Day*, p. 290.
43. Diary, 18 April 1961, quoted ibid., p. 290.
44. Tove Tingvold Petersen, 'Anglo-American rivalry in the Middle East: the struggle for the Buraimi Oasis 1952–1957', *International History Review*, XIV (1992), 71–97.
45. Macmillan, *Riding the Storm*, p. 271.
46. Diary, 28 Aug. 1957, quoted in Macmillan, *Riding the Storm*, p. 280.
47. Macmillan to Dulles, 28 Aug. 1957, quoted in Horne, *Macmillan 1957–1986*, p. 41.
48. Caccia to prime minister, 29 Aug. 1957, quoted ibid. p. 42.
49. Macmillan to Eden, 2 Oct. 1957, quoted Horne, *Macmillan 1957–1986* p. 44.
50. Macmillan, *Riding the Storm*, p. 286.
51. Diary, 6 July 1958, quoted in Macmillan, *Riding the Storm*, p. 505.

52. Lebanon's troubles arose from divisions between a dominant Maronite Christian group, from which Chamoun and his many of his Cabinet were drawn, and the Muslim communities who were influenced by pan-Arabism. External threats were only part of the problem.

53. Diary, 14 July 1958, quoted in Macmilan, *Riding the Storm*, p. 512. The need to replace Middle Eastern oil, bought for pounds, with Western Hemisphere oil, bought for dollars, had arisen during and after the Suez crisis, with dire effects on the reserves.

54. Macmillan, *Riding the Storm*, p. 519.

55. Ibid., pp. 517–19, including diary entries for 16/17 July.

56. Diary, 28 Aug. 1958, quoted in Horne, *Macmillan 1957–1986*, p. 105.

57. Diary, 28 Sept. 1958, quoted in Macmillan, *Riding the Storm*, p. 555.

58. See Tracy Lee Steele, 'Allied and interdependent: British policy during the Chinese offshore islands crisis, 1958' in Anthony Gorst, Lewis Johnman and Scott W. Lucas (eds), *Contemporary British History, 1931–1961: politics and the limits of policy* (London: Frances Pinter, 1991), pp. 230–47.

Chapter 9

TOWARDS EUROPE

For almost the whole of Macmillan's premiership Britain's relations with Western Europe were contentious and important. At the beginning, he was determined to complete the edifice of the European Free Trade Area, the incarnation of 'Plan G'. Next he had to overcome the prejudices of his party and persuade them that full British membership of the Common Market would be desirable. Finally he launched Britain's application to join, with strong support from the United States. His commitment to closer association with Europe was consistent and enduring. The conventional wisdom is that his reasons for this were 'political' rather than 'economic'; in other words that he did not closely calculate the financial or economic implications of joining the Common Market, because he saw overriding diplomatic reasons for strengthening Western Europe against Russia. Moreover, it is said, he saw Britain as the effective leader of the new Europe, cementing the Western Alliance with its close connections both to the United States and to the Commonwealth. Largely for that reason the British application was thwarted by de Gaulle, and Macmillan's policy came crashing to the ground, the victim of his inability to understand the European perspective on European integration.

It would be hard to deny that Macmillan and his Cabinet were preoccupied by the strength of the Western Alliance, or that, especially after the 1959 election, they saw Britain's entry into Europe as part of a Grand Design for the West which did not happen to appeal to de Gaulle. Pressure from the United States was also based on the hope that Britain in Europe would help to curb the Germans and the French. Yet the history of Macmillan's own commitment to Europe belies any purely *politique* explanation. As we have seen,[1] he began his European enthusiasm in the late 1940s as a Cold Warrior who also saw domestic political advantages for his party in pressing for greater integration with Europe. During his brief encounter with the European Defence Community, as Minister of Defence and as Foreign Secretary, he supported closer integration but backed 'confederal' rather than 'federal' solutions to defence problems. But as Chancellor, responding after the event to the Messina proposals of 1955, he had co-operated with Thorneycroft to introduce a wholly different note into the discussion. With the six Messina powers obviously determined to build upon the functional institutions of the European Coal and Steel Community, he began to see European economic integration as a way to shock the British economy into life. Taking the view that it would be impossible to integrate Britain into the Common Market which the Messina powers were devising, because of Britain's trading links with the Commonwealth, he elicited 'Plan G' from officials and backed it strongly in Cabinet from the middle of 1956.[2] Henceforward the 'political' and the 'economic' motives for the closer integration of Europe were inseparable in his mind. As he put it, with supreme ambiguity, in his memoirs: 'Our purpose was to consolidate the political and economic resources of all Europe in the common stand of the free world against Communism and disruption'.[3]

Suez overshadowed all other foreign policy problems for Britain between the autumn of 1956 and the Bermuda conference, when the process of mending fences with the United States began in earnest. Although official Whitehall monitored the development of the Messina plans up to the signature of the Treaty of Rome on 25 March 1957, there was no serious discussion by ministers. Plan G was accepted by the Commons in November 1956, and a White Paper appeared in January. After this, British attempts to 'enter Europe' took the form of two campaigns. From April 1957 until the end of 1958 ministers pressed ahead with Plan G. Reginald Maudling, eventually with a seat in the Cabinet, was given the job of co-ordinating departmental activity and negotiating with European governments, while a ministerial committee oversaw policy and tried with some success to inspire the Conservative Party in support of the idea. This effort collapsed when the French, at an OEEC meeting in December 1958, declared flatly against any co-operation between the Common Market countries and the proposed European Free Trade Area. There was then a long pause. In July 1961 the Cabinet decided to make a formal application to join the Common Market as a full member. In January 1963 these negotiations in turn collapsed in the face of a French veto. Macmillan, who had spent a great deal of political capital in persuading the country and reluctant members of his party that entry was a good idea, was deeply shaken.[4]

What was Macmillan's contribution to these negotiations, and his attitude to them as they developed? For the most part he was concerned with high policy, squaring de Gaulle and Adenauer and trying to reconcile British interests in economic co-operation with political tensions which were very often caused by developments in defence policy and superpower relations. Macmillan paid visits to Paris and Bonn (respectively in March and May 1957) which at least made the difficulties clear. In both capitals he was attacked for the defence cuts and met resistance over his EFTA proposals. From the beginning the French were less helpful than the Germans. They had pressed successfully for their colonial empire to be included within the Common Market tariff wall, a move which was bound to make it more difficult to negotiate an amicable settlement with the Commonwealth countries. The German position was more promising, in that Adenauer seemed simply to want to delay discussions until the Treaty of Rome was not only signed but ratified by the six signatories. Macmillan, impatient at the delay, was struck by the strength of mutual suspicion between France and Germany which was likely to make any negotiation difficult; more immediately difficult was that he did not warm to Adenauer, and that the French republic was about to enter a period of political turmoil, inaugurated by the fall of the Mollet government in May. 'What I chiefly fear', he wrote in April, 'and what we must at all costs avoid, is the Common Market coming into being and the Free Trade area never following . . . . '[5]

To prevent this, he tried to launch a political initiative, on the grounds that

> I feel sure that the pressure for European integration, though expressed in economic terms, really derives from the strong desire of many European countries for some form of closer *political* association. We should take advantage of this, since, while we are in something of a straitjacket as regards economic integration, we may well be able to show Europe that we are prepared for a closer political association . . . .

...we must take positive action in this field, to ensure that the wider Free Trade Area is more attractive than the narrow Common Market of the Six. We must take the lead, either in widening their project, or, if they will not co-operate with us, in opposing it.[6]

Reginald Maudling was appointed as an 'Apostolic figure' to negotiate both with the Messina powers and with the larger group who were to make up the Free Trade Area. His main problem, it then seemed, was the interest of many of the potential EFTA nations, and also of the Commonwealth, in the arrangements to be made for foodstuffs. The British plan was to exclude foodstuffs altogether from the arrangement between the Six and the Eleven (EFTA countries). The Six let it be known that they wanted a system of managed markets. Although they were not much concerned to export food to Britain, this would imply that tariff barriers would eventually be raised against the import of Commonwealth foodstuffs into Britain. This was a sticking point for the Empire interest in the Conservative Party, and provided ammunition for the Beaverbrook press, which was consistently opposed to any sort of co-operation with Europe throughout Macmillan's premiership.

While Maudling carried on his negotiations in the second half of 1958, Macmillan's rôle was merely avuncular. The OEEC decided firmly to go ahead with a Free Trade Area in October, and Maudling set about negotiating its terms and the terms of its relationship to the Six. Macmillan was able to tell Commonwealth countries, on his 1958 tour, that the agricultural problem could probably be settled, but in fact the suspicions of the French government were an obstacle in themselves. Macmillan believed that the French were afraid of British industrial competition, added to the already formidable competition of Germany; this was confirmed when French negotiators suggested that tariff arrangements between the Six and the Eleven should be negotiated on an industry-by-industry basis, and that European goods should be admitted to Commonwealth countries with preferential tariffs. Neither of these conditions were acceptable to the British, and Maudling decided that 'the French are determined to wreck it'.[7] In April Adenauer came to London, and Macmillan was able to 'counteract the poison which the French have been pouring into his ears.'[8] Unhelpfully, the last government of the French Fourth

Republic was in its final throes; it collapsed at the end of May, and Charles de Gaulle became prime minister. This entirely altered the climate in which negotiations took place. Although de Gaulle's views on Europe were not very different from the instincts of the Quai d'Orsay, his personal authority in France, even before he made himself President of the Fifth Republic in December, was such that Macmillan found himself negotiating most issues personally with the French head of state, who would then direct French policy where he wanted it to go.

On Macmillan's visit to Paris in June 1958 the European question was only third on the agenda, after nuclear deterrence and the various crises in the Middle East, but it produced headaches. Macmillan rather wanly hoped 'that this period of hesitation will now be over and that a period of decision will have begun'.[9] De Gaulle's response was to indicate a general preference for co-operation with Britain and other European countries, 'But we must find means of arriving there without destroying the equilibrium of France's economy and finances ... and without basically putting at issue the agreements existing between the six member countries of the European Common Market. You and we will have to make an effort of imagination and of will.'[10] This coincided with a renewal of French obstruction on the negotiating committee. Macmillan tried to enlist Adenauer in his support, warning him that de Gaulle 'still regards this very much as an economic problem and did not perhaps fully appreciate the political implications'.[11] The threat of a Franco-German bloc in opposition to co-operation with EFTA receded when Adenauer took offence at the first proposal to emanate from de Gaulle for a 'tripartite' defence relationship between France, Britain and the United States. Macmillan hoped to 'exploit his anger with the French ... to some account'[12] but this proved impossible since the structure of the Common Market was such that any nation had an effective veto. By October Macmillan decided that 'de Gaulle is bidding high for the hegemony of Europe',[13] and made a last attempt to get de Gaulle to see the political advantages of co-operation between EFTA and the Six. This was rudely, and finally, rejected in an official French pronouncement on 14 November that 'it is not possible to create a Free Trade Area as wished by the British'. The EFTA negotiations therefore proceeded separately, and the agreement for a Free Trade Area was signed by seven countries in November 1959.

Trade Area as wished by the British'. The EFTA negotiations therefore proceeded separately, and the agreement for a Free Trade Area was signed by seven countries in November 1959.

The lesson of EFTA was that de Gaulle had not become any easier since he had first had dealings with Macmillan in Algeria in 1942. After December 1958 the effective political leaders of the three major Western powers could trace a common association to the North African campaign of 1942–43, but these historic friendships did remarkably little to improve the harmony of the alliance. Macmillan in particular managed to gain little or no advantage from his old 'contacts' in his effort to improve Britain's standing in Europe. Shortly after the EFTA treaty was signed he reflected in a letter to Selwyn Lloyd that:

> For better or worse, the Common Market looks like being here to stay at least for the foreseeable future. Furthermore, if we try to disrupt it we should unite against us all the Europeans who have felt humiliated during the past decade by the weakness of Europe... The question is how to live with the Common Market economically and turn its political effects into channels harmless to ourselves... Since the French are fundamentally in a very strong position politically, I believe that we shall not succeed in bullying them into accepting us as a partner in Europe; we shall have to coax them... The Germans, however, are not in a strong political position, and I would have thought there was some chance of bullying them.

This rumination led to a meeting at Chequers with Lloyd, Heathcoat Amory, the Chancellor, and Maudling, the President of the Board of Trade, together with a select handful of civil servants, at which Macmillan was outspoken about 'the Jews, the Planners, and the old cosmopolitan element' among European politicians who wanted a supra-national European organisation. He declared that 'U.K. must try and preserve its position as a Great nation with world-wide responsibilities. We did not see it as part of our future policy to seek to revive a powerful Germany.' This led him to the conclusion that the Common Market increased global stability and that further efforts to disrupt it were unwise.[55]

During 1959 and 1960 British aspirations to a closer economic relationship with Europe fell into abeyance, partly, it would seem, because the British economy was temporarily strong. The political ends which Macmillan had often described for Europe were sought a different way: in particular and often cynical reactions to Macmillan's summitry were discouraging, and the effort of winning de Gaulle around afresh to every initiative was taxing. This alone suggested to Macmillan after the failure of the 1960 summit that the unity of the West needed further nurture. This led to his Grand Design document, noted above, and thus to a renewal in 1961 of the initiative which had lapsed more than two years earlier.

On this occasion the predominance of the political over the economic motive was more apparent. Knowing that he had active support from most of the Kennedy administration, Macmillan began to educate his Cabinet and his party about the political advantages of an undivided Western Europe. The problem of agriculture was recognised early and faced: the agricultural lobby in Britain was asked to state its precise needs, and in April high-level messages to Australia and Canada elicited the minimum requirements of those countries. Edward Heath was designated as a negotiator, much as Maudling had been appointed to carry through the EFTA proposal, even before the Cabinet had fully considered the decision to make an application to join, and he went to the Western European Union meeting in February to announce that Britain was prepared to consider changing its stance towards the Common Market. Then Macmillan began on his Cabinet. In April and May he wooed the doubters, among whom Butler could certainly be counted and also Duncan Sandys, who was particularly loyal to the idea of the Commonwealth. The major risk was that Cabinet doubters could lead a dissident movement within the Conservative Party, which was being stirred up enthusiastically by the Beaverbrook press. The Cabinet discussions went on alongside the answering of Parliamentary Questions, and the government was not helped to answer this attack by its lack of a formed policy. But by 22 July Macmillan was able to get a unanimous decision, and this was announced and debated in the Commons. His main concern throughout this period was with the known opponents, some of them left over from Suez (of whom the noisiest was Lord Hinchingbrooke): 'It is getting terribly like 1846. Anyway, none of these ... can be Disraeli to my Peel.'[15]

During the rather extended period in which the Cabinet was making up its mind a number of missions were sent out to Commonwealth countries, which had the incidental effect of cementing the loyalty of Sandys, who was to be 'St John the Baptist' to Australia, New Zealand and Canada. Except for Diefenbaker in Canada, most Commonwealth prime ministers were surprisingly willing to wait and see if the right terms could be achieved; and although this reserved their positions for the future it at least allowed Macmillan to argue to his own followers that the interests of the Commonwealth were being considered. As the Cabinet was getting ready to take the decision, Edward Boyle warned the prime minister that 'I don't see how the Conservative Party can avoid some sort of split on this issue. But the example of Balfour after 1903 suggests that the attempt to avoid *any* split, on some hotly contentious issue, may simply result in a far greater and more damaging one (and in electoral disaster).'[16]

In the event the Cabinet decision was unanimous and the response of the House of Commons remarkably positive; Macmillan's main critics came from the Opposition, led by Harold Wilson, and the Conservative abstentions were kept down to twenty-two. As Macmillan launched this venture for the second time, he remarked that 'I should judge the chances are "against" an agreement, unless – on political grounds – de Gaulle changes his mind.'[17] It was not a promising beginning. The formalities of application took some time, and it was not until October 1961 that the full text of the United Kingdom bid to enter the Common Market was made public in Brussels.

By that time the domestic opposition to the proposal had grown, and the attitude of the Canadian government was causing considerable satisfaction to de Gaulle, who was relying on time and Commonwealth opposition to save him from the need to veto British entry. Macmillan's problem was to balance the need for consent, both in Europe and in Britain and the Commonwealth, against the risk that delay would allow irresistible opposition to build up. In Europe he had some allies, dating back to the Council of Europe, who could keep the British informed of the possibility of progress. One of these was Jean Monnet, who had no official appointment but presided over a pressure group called the 'Comité d'Action pour les Etats-Unis d'Europe', which gave him contacts in many European governments. Monnet knew and admired Heath, whom he briefed on the French reaction, and by October was able to tell Macmillan in a personal meeting that the French view, at least, seemed to be softening. He agreed with Macmillan that it was important to 'have a quick negotiation and get it over.

If it dragged, opposition and pressure groups would grow in strength.'[18]   Monnet was convinced of Macmillan's determination to press ahead with the application because he saw a change of heart in the Cabinet: 'ils commencent à se rendre compte que les "relations privilégiées" qu'ils ont eues avec les Etats-Unis ne continueront pas....   Il y avait donc là beaucoup plus qu'une décision tactique de Macmillan, c'était le choix délibéré de changer de cap et de rejoindre le continent.'[19] In Europe, sympathy for Macmillan's position varied in proportion to the belief that he had indeed decided to 'rejoin the continent' and reconsider the Special Relationship; and also to European views of British willingness to join on exactly the same basis as other members. Monnet, in fact, had already warned von Brentano of Germany that it would be important to insist that 'il n'y ait pas d'exceptions aux règles communes qui créeraient des division d'interêts entre l'Angleterre et les autres membres de la Communauté'.[20] Since much of Macmillan's negotiation with the Commonwealth depended on implicit promises that there would be special treatment for agricultural produce, this was potentially a dangerous sticking point.

De Gaulle's active distrust of Anglo-Saxons now became the critical element in European politics. From conversations with Kennedy in November 1961 he knew first that the Americans wanted to reach a settlement with Russia over Berlin, which he did not want, and second that the Americans wanted Britain in the Common Market. This was enough to arouse his suspicions. On his visit to Macmillan at Birch Grove he was unhelpful about British entry. 'Charming, affable, mellow as the General now is', wrote Macmillan, 'his little pin-head is as small as ever. His views are inward, not outward looking. I fear he has decided to oppose us – yet, in a way, he wants us in Europe.'[21] After talking to Adenauer in December, he wrote to Macmillan that 'nous avons réaffermé notre intention de faire avancer les choses, en souhaitant tous les deux que la Grande-Bretagne puisse se joindre un jour à notre organisation dans les mêmes conditions où nous y trouvons nous-mêmes'.[22] This left the date of Britain's expected entry grandly ambiguous, and reminded Macmillan forcibly of the unpopularity of special conditions for British entry. Although de Gaulle was known to oppose a federal Europe, and in many ways to favour the sort of Europe which Macmillan himself preferred, it was painfully evident that for him the critical issue was not the structure of the new organisation but the position of France within it.

Negotiations on detail lasted just over a year. In Britain, opposition built up a head of steam just as Macmillan had predicted: the Conservative Party conferences in 1961 and 1962 were persuaded, but grass-roots Conservatism was easily swayed by appeals to Empire and xenophobia. In his memoirs Macmillan dismisses this rather too readily.[23] Although there were other reasons for the series of by-election defeats in November 1962, the Common Market issue sapped morale in a party which had been shaken by the ministerial dismissals in July. Macmillan told his senior party colleagues that Europe

> ...will come along, probably not as quickly as we think, but it will come along.... We can't say we must *definitely* go in or they will all say Yah!, so for the moment the antis can go drip, drip, drip.... If in the Common Market will have to fight; and if out, will fight hard, won't just sink back depressed.[24]

The effect of this was to raise the political stake for Macmillan, making it possible that he would suffer for success almost as much as for failure in the Common Market negotiations. But his own reasons for persisting were so strong that he remained unshaken. He told Home in April 1962 that 'there is only one issue now which dominates everything for the next few months. Shall we or shall we not be able to bring off our entry into the Common Market? On that the fortunes and probably the life of the Government depend.'[25] On a visit to de Gaulle at Champs in June 1962 he was treated to old-fashioned courtesy and traditional unhelpfulness in equal measure: de Gaulle mentioned that to include Britain in the Common Market would change its character, but linked this with a hint that a common European policy towards defence and, for example, Berlin might be achieved without economic integration. If Macmillan's motive for pursuing the European option had been strictly political this might have been appealing, but in any case it was heavily qualified by de Gaulle's demand for British help in getting an independent nuclear deterrent for France. This Macmillan was not prepared to support.[26] The final outcome of this meeting was never clear, for though Macmillan came away satisfied that the French veto would not be automatic, the nuclear issue was too important to be finessed in this way.

Macmillan's lack of effective influence over American policy and publicity now became an important handicap in his European ambitions. The American defence establishment, led by Robert McNamara, made public its own reservations about the British and French independent nuclear deterrents. Kennedy was also persuaded to criticise French ambitions for a nuclear role. Macmillan became impatient:

> ...I shall have a chance to tell Rusk ...what terrible damage the Americans are doing in every field in Europe. In NATO, all the allies are angry with the American proposal that we should buy rockets to the tune of umpteen million dollars, the warheads to be under American control. This is not a European rocket. It's a racket of the American industry. So far as the Common Market is concerned, the Americans are (with the best intentions) doing our cause great harm. The more they tell the Germans, French etc. that they (U.S.A.) want Britain to be in, the more they incline these countries to keep us out.[27]

During the negotiations for entry into the Common Market, which Edward Heath was conducting at Brussels, the fine detail of economic compromise was concerned largely with the privileged position which Britain wished to maintain for its imports of food from the Commonwealth; but the outcome was determined by French concerns about the political and strategic position of an enlarged Europe, and this in turn was influenced by de Gaulle's perception of what Macmillan was up to with the Americans.

De Gaulle's own standing was changed, for the worse as far as Britain was concerned, by his victory in October 1962 in a referendum which he called to reinforce his own position against the National Assembly by providing for the President of the Republic to be elected directly by universal suffrage. He also led his Gaullist party to a sweeping victory in a general election at the end of November. With Adenauer believed to be opposed to British entry, although the Italians were in favour, de Gaulle's perception of the French national interest assumed an overriding importance. Much would rest on the meetings which Macmillan had with de Gaulle on 15–16 December and with Kennedy at Nassau on 18–21 December. Since, as described above,[28] these discussions were dominated by the issue of the nuclear deterrent and the cancellation of Skybolt, Macmillan was acutely embarrassed in his relations both with de Gaulle and with the Conservative Party.

At his meeting with de Gaulle he had to explain that if Sky-bolt were cancelled he would ask for Polaris missiles for British submarines, and that if these were denied (but only then) he would order the building of a truly independent deterrent. Since the Americans were not expected to allow France to buy Polaris missiles, this was a sensitive issue; de Gaulle could argue that if the Americans cancelled Skybolt and allowed the British to buy Polaris, without permitting the transfer of nuclear technology to France, this would discriminate intolerably against the French independent deterrent. Even though Macmillan promised technical co-operation between France and Britain, up to the limits permitted by the Anglo-American agreements on proliferation, events had sown doubt in de Gaulle's mind. At Nassau Macmillan argued hard for the opportunity to buy Polaris, which was given, rather reluctantly, by the Americans who feared that it would upset the delicate balance of sensibilities in Europe. He was afraid of British reactions to an affair which seemed to the likes of the Beaverbrook press to demonstrate the contempt with which the American president and his advisers treated Britain, but rather neglected the impact of his limited success on the French position. In fact the Polaris agreement was financially generous to Britain, and the American expedient to mollify France by offering Polaris missiles without warheads was patently unhelpful to de Gaulle.

The other aspect of his discussion with de Gaulle had been an exploration of French attitudes to British entry to the Common Market. Macmillan's record gives the impression that he had won the arguments but already lost the debate. De Gaulle argued simply that the Common Market should remain unchanged; its extension to Britain, the Scandinavian countries, Ireland, Portugal and Spain, would change its character and present the risk that France might be outmanoeuvred at Brussels. Junior French ministers and diplomats explained privately, with varying degrees of apology, that de Gaulle was determined not to lose control of Europe, and feared that Britain would be too strong a player. Even the notorious difficulties about agricultural policy were less important than de Gaulle's political determination to retain effective control of the Community. De Gaulle's chosen moment to reveal his hand was a press conference on 14 January, in which he took the opportunity to claim that the Nassau deals about nuclear weapons, which he alleged contained secret provisions directed against French interests, were further evidence of Britain's unsuitability to join Europe. Though Macmillan was outraged at a slur on his honour, there was nothing he could do. The French Foreign Minister, Couve de Murville, demanded an end to the Brussels negotiations, and by the end of January the other Common Market nations, all of whom still seemed to want to continue negotiations on British entry, were forced to comply.

In the spring of 1963 this was a grave blow to Macmillan's own position, as well as to British policy. He was blamed by his anti-European opponents for exposing the country to an unnecessary humiliation, and those who supported him on the issue were demoralised. Opinion polls were unfavourable and getting worse, though soon enough the Common Market problem gave way to the Profumo affair. Altogether the veto was as bad for the Conservative Party as it was for Macmillan. Butler, chatting to Tony Benn on 20 February, observed that

> ...you know the Common Market breakdown was a much bigger shock for us than your chaps realised. I am very doubtful about it and I only supported it because of our exports. If we had gone through with it we might have faced a real farmers' revolt.
>
> .... Macmillan and de Gaulle had been going different ways for some time, especially with regard to the Americans in Europe. I always thought those shooting parties at Château Rambouillet were a mistake, especially getting Lady Dorothy out of mothballs for the trip. No truths were ever exchanged.
>
> .... but it may make it easier for us to win the Election.[29]

Butler, 'wildly indiscreet and of course utterly unreliable' was thinking of his own position; he was also an open opponent of the Common Market, who would not have been unhappy to see his old rival stricken by the issue. Although he was cautious about the episode's effects on his party he was in no doubt that 'the PM will carry on. He's in good shape.' He did.

. . .

NOTES AND REFERENCES

1. See above, pp. 73–7.
2. See above, pp. 96–102.
3. Harold Macmillan, *Riding the Storm* (London: Macmillan, 1971), p. 440.

4. The best basic outline of these developments remains Miriam Camps, *Britain and the European Community, 1955–1963* (Princeton and London: Princeton University Press, 1965).

5. To an unnamed correspondent, 18 April 1957, quoted in Macmillan, *Riding the Storm*, p. 435.

6. Macmillan to Thorneycroft, n.d.(July 1957), quoted ibid., p. 437.

7. Diary, 17 March 1958, quoted ibid., p. 442.

8. Diary, 19 April 1958, quoted ibid., p. 442.

9. Macmillan to de Gaulle, 30 June 1958, quoted ibid., p. 449.

10. De Gaulle to Macmillan, 5 July 1958, quoted ibid., p. 450.

11. To Adenauer (end) July 1958, quoted ibid., p. 452.

12. Diary, 9 Oct. 1958, quoted in Alistair Horne, *Macmillan 1957–1986* (London: Macmillan, 1989), p. 110. On 'tripartitism' see above. p. 159.

13. Diary, 26 Oct. 1958, quoted in Macmillan, *Riding the Storm*, p. 455.

14. Macmillan to Lloyd, 'The Organisation of Europe', 20 Nov. 1959, PREM 11/2679; 'Chronological Minute' of the Chequers week-end meeting, 29 Nov. 1959, ibid.

15. Diary, 19 May 1961, quoted in Harold Macmillan, *At the End of the Day* (London: Macmillan, 1973), p. 8.

16. To Macmillan, 20 July 1961, quoted ibid., p. 16.

17. Diary, 22 July 1961, quoted ibid., p. 17.

18. Diary, 8 Oct. 1961, quoted ibid., p. 30.

19. Jean Monnet, *Mémoires* (Paris: Fayard, 1976), pp. 677–8.

20. Ibid., p. 674.

21. Diary, 29 November 1961, quoted in Macmillan, *Pointing the Way*, p. 426.

22. De Gaulle to Macmillan, 12 Dec. 1961, quoted in Macmillan, *At the End of the Day*, p. 34.

23. Ibid., p. 333.

24. At a meeting of the Conservative Research Department's Chairman's Committee, July 1962, quoted in John Ramsden, *The Making of Conservative Party Policy* (London: Longman, 1980), pp. 219–220.

25. Macmillan to Home, 15 April 1962, PREM 11/3778.

26. Though the French later claimed that he had offered help with nuclear technology in return for help with entry to the Common Market. Horne, *Macmillan 1957–1986*, p. 328.

27. Diary, 19 June 1962, quoted in Macmillan, *At the End of the Day*, p. 335. The rocket in question was the short-range Sergeant missile, to be supplied 'on the favourable terms more commonly arranged for vacuum cleaners or washing machines'. The British Blue Water missile was cancelled to accommodate this change of policy.

28. See above, pp. 166–8.

29. Tony Benn, *Out of the Wilderness* (London: Arrow Books, 1988), pp. 6–7.

Chapter 10

'IS IT TOO GOOD TO LAST?'

POLICY AND POLITICS AT HOME
1957–63

Macmillan gave less attention to domestic policy and politics than to foreign affairs, though the imbalance was not as great as his memoirs would suggest. Like any twentieth-century administration, the Macmillan governments were preoccupied by economic problems. Macmillan himself, and one or two of his colleagues, struggled to place those problems in a large context and develop a strategy to deal with them: most of the Cabinet seems to have been buffeted by short-term disasters. At the same time the Conservative Party under Macmillan had a remarkably clear view of the social and political implications of policy. Macmillan as prime minister supported Butler, successive chairmen of the party, and the Research Department under Michael Fraser in a concerted attempt to use social and economic policy to buttress the electoral prospects of the Conservative Party, striving to create a land fit for Tories to live in. This was both a short-term effort, focused on the 1959 General Election, and a long-term strategy to outflank socialism (in any of its British forms, including but not limited to the Labour Party) by setting up a property-owning democracy in which there would always be a minimum electoral coalition supporting the Conservatives. One of the most striking features of Macmillan's premiership was the institutionalisation of that strategy by the incorporation of ministers, party officials and civil servants into a single policy-making community.

The workings of that community were far from perfect, and after the election victory in 1959 the government seemed to lose control of the economy which it had deliberately heated up for that event. At the same time, and partly for the same reasons, the Conservative Party lost some of its confidence in its leaders and began to lose direction, so that after Macmillan was forced by ill-health to resign in October 1963 the new leadership under Alec Douglas-Home was unable to focus on issues which could bring electoral victory in 1964. Even so, the 1964 election was a close-run business, and not wholly discreditable to a party which, some thought, had been dogged by presentational disasters for the previous three years. Macmillan's own reputation as politician and policy-maker has never escaped association with the 'thirteen years of Tory misrule' which was an effective slogan for the triumphant Labour Party in 1964. More recently his premiership has been assailed from the Right, on the grounds that he was persistently lax in his economic policy, permitting inflation, unruly trade unions, and uncontrolled public expenditure to sabotage Britain's recovery from the evil consequences of the Second World War and the Attlee governments.

.   .   .

FROM RETRENCHMENT TO INFLATION

So much of Macmillan's later reputation, for good or ill, rests on his apparent complacency about the British economy that his early pronouncements on the subject bear quotation. At the second Cabinet meeting of his administration Peter Thorneycroft, the new Chancellor, explained the steps he would take to protect the country from the financial effects of Suez. 'No significant increase in taxation can be contemplated – indeed, it must remain the objective to reduce taxation if possible. The necessary relief to the Budget must therefore be achieved by reductions in each of the main fields of defence, the civil estimates, and public investment.' His proposals were met with unctuous sympathy by the spending ministers, who went on to explain rather clearly why the savings requested would be difficult in their own particular cases, until they were reminded of reality by the prime minister who 'said that the defence and social services, however desirable they might be in themselves, would be of no avail if the attempt to sustain them at unrealistic levels resulted in the collapse of the economy'.[1] From this discussion flowed both the Defence White Paper and a review of public-sector investment by Percy Mills, the Minister of Power, which laid the responsibility of generating investment capital on the energy industries themselves. Similar discussions at other meetings produced a range of characteristic policies for taxation and the social services which consistently reduced public expenditure and benefited the taxpayer and saver.

This was the policy context for Macmillan's notorious 'Never had it so good' speech. He told a crowd at Bedford on 20 July 1957:

> ... most of our people have never had it so good. Go around the country, go to the industrial towns, go to the farms, and you will see a state of prosperity such as we have never had in my lifetime. What is beginning to worry some of us is 'Is it too good to be true?' or perhaps I should say 'Is it too good to last?' For, amidst all this prosperity, there is one problem that has troubled us – in one way or another – ever since the war. It's the problem of rising prices. Our constant concern today is – can prices be steadied while at the same time we maintain full employment in an expanding economy? Can we control inflation? This is the problem of our time.

The tone of this passage and the content of the whole speech both reflect the fact that Macmillan had been one of the most cautious Chancellors of the post-war period and had carried his caution with him to 10 Downing Street. His 1956 Budget, less deflationary than he had wanted because of Eden's refusal to take a political risk, had been intended to control the damage done by Butler's fat years at the Treasury. His own last months at the Treasury had been buffeted by the financial storms of Suez. In choosing Thorneycroft for the Exchequer, he was knowingly putting an austere figure in charge of the government's economic policy, who would first repair the damage to the reserves and then continue to run the economy within reasonably tight limits.

But no economic policy is socially neutral, and the effect of Thorneycroft's proposals was to challenge some of the political assumptions of his colleagues, and set a theme for debate which outlived his own chancellorship and dominated the Macmillan years at least until 1961. At the end of January 1957 Macmillan convened a small group to discuss the Budget proposals before they were seen by the full Cabinet, and Thorneycroft produced his first proposals, directed at social service expenditure. His justification was forthright:

> For many years we have had the sorry spectacle of a Government which spends too much, drifts into inflation, then seeks to cure the situation by fiscal and budgetary measures. These attempts in

turn lead to flagging production, taxes are reduced, and demand stimulated: but we shrink from the measures necessary to cut expenditure decisively, and inflation starts again. There is only one way out of this unhappy circle, and that is to cut expenditure and not to increase taxation ... but to reduce it.[2]

This was all very well, but it produced a fine crop of rebuttals. Boyd-Carpenter, the Minister of Pensions, observed that Thorneycroft's proposals on Family Allowances 'would involve a complete reversal of the policy and philosophy followed by the Government since 1951'; Macleod at the Ministry of Health protested that 'we would find it difficult to rebut the political charge that we were now beginning to dismantle the Health Service'.[3] Macleod put it better in a 'Top Secret' note to Macmillan which commented on the proposed charges for board and lodging in hospitals: '43 per cent of the beds are occupied by mental patients, many of the others by the aged and by children, and we can't tax the old and the young and the mad to help the surtax payers'.[4]

Macmillan's difficulty was that he wanted a Budget for political as well as economic effect; and surtax payers, or at least income-tax payers, were indeed the group the party most wished to help. Harold Watkinson, the Minister of Aviation urged that 'If we can make everybody anxious to belong to a broadly based and prosperous middle class, we shall also bring a great many of the more successful Trade Unionists to our side.'[5] The Cabinet agreed in principle that Thorneycroft should have £40 million in savings from the social services, and in discussion in early February of where these should be found Macmillan himself intervened to suggest cutting welfare milk and orange juice and raising money for the Health Service from a 'health stamp'. The justification for this peculiar choice of measures (the health stamp would have been a new tax) was that the other target, family allowances, would be politically controversial and 'The political difficulties indeed are all the greater if we hope to give some relief to the better-paid salaried classes in the same year.'[6] It was in the midst of this discussion that Macmillan issued his notorious question to Michael Fraser of the Conservative Research Department:

I am always hearing about the Middle Classes. What is it they really want? Can you put it down on a sheet of notepaper, and then I will see whether we can give it to them.[7]

The answer in due course came back, from Fraser and from other party figures, that Conservative voters on fixed incomes needed most help. In the event the first Budget of Macmillan's administration, in April 1957, was quite relaxed. Thorneycroft reduced taxes by a total of about £100 million, in what Macmillan cheerfully described as the 'give-away'.[8] Since he had reduced the Bank Rate from 5.5 per cent to 5 per cent in February, this appeared extremely generous to consumers and to industry. The benefits of the income tax reductions went partly to surtax-payers and partly to families with children; although Macmillan's diary record gave half to each group (£25 million each), later analysis suggested that remission of surtax was worth £35 million in a full year, extra relief to families being worth only £17 million. The rest went to reducing direct taxes. This all made an excellent impression politically, winning enthusiastic support from Conservative back-benchers and condemnation (which Macmillan accepted, enjoyed and brushed off) from the Opposition. S.C. Leslie, in charge of the Treasury's information service, declared in a note to Sir Roger Makins in the Treasury that 'the Government wants to create an opportunity state and an incentive economy', and the political message was confirmed after the Budget statement by Oliver Poole, who wrote to Macmillan that:

> I feel that this Budget gives a clear indication as to the lines that the Government will follow in its economic policy between now and the General Election, and gives us a firm base from which to start to regain the confidence of those of our supporters who have been wavering.[9]

Nevertheless, it was intended to increase the government's surplus, and in its impact on the level of demand in the economy it was among the least expansionary Budgets of the 1950s.[10]

The government's sharp response to an acceleration of price increases in the early summer and sterling crisis in the late summer of 1957 was therefore rather less of a reversal than it might appear. The attack on sterling was probably the result of speculative movements in 'hot money' and therefore not of lasting importance to the economy. The increase in domestic prices had more profound significance, and its analysis goes deeper to the heart of Macmillan's policy. Like most of his contemporaries, he was groping towards an explanation of domestic inflation. His recollections of the occasion in his memoirs and elsewhere were dominated by genuflection to Keynes, who had often said that a domestic price inflation of about 2.5 per cent per annum was an acceptable corollary of economic growth, and a preferable alternative to unemployment.[11] This was the price inflation that followed from the deliberate expansion of demand in the economy. But Macmillan and other Conservatives also believed that wage increases contributed directly to inflation by increasing costs, and were worried that organised labour was too strong for the economy, while there are hints that the Cabinet was also concerned that an increase in the money supply caused inflation. Confronted with rising prices in 1957, the government tried to address all these problems at once, with results which were somewhat haphazard and inconsistent.

An outbreak of industrial unrest in March 1957 was the first test. Negotiations in the shipbuilding industry broke down on 5 March. A threatened strike in the engineering industry had been postponed in late February, after strenuous efforts by Macleod, the Minister of Labour, but with deadlock in shipbuilding it seemed likely that it would be revived. The railway unions and the electricity supply workers were also threatening to strike. Macmillan feared a general strike, 'Yet I feel sure the men, apart from their Communist leaders, don't want anything of the kind.'[12] His own explanation was that 'we are now paying the price for the Churchill–Monckton regime – industrial appeasement, with continual inflation'.[13] Four days after making this trenchant analysis in the privacy of his diary, Macmillan left for Bermuda. Shortly before he went he met employers' representatives in the company of Macleod, and decided that it would be reasonable to settle the railway strike with an offer of 4 or 5 per cent. This, he ascertained, 'would *not* be regarded as having sold the pass by private industry'.[14] The engineering strike began the same day. Butler, as deputy prime minister, consulted Macmillan about the negotiations by telegram throughout the conference, and the prime minister was back in charge by 27 March. By 2 April the railways dispute had been settled by granting 5 per cent, and the other strikes had been called off. Macmillan described this as 'a novel and harassing experience';[15] it was also an occasion for considerable trimming, since he had simultaneously decided that the

TUC would not co-operate in moves to postpone wage-claims. Instead, he veered towards a campaign for greater productivity, 'and the better productivity is, the less objectionable the wage claims'.[16] In the absence of a real policy for greater productivity, this was not very different from the Churchill–Monckton regime, and inevitably the wage-claims came up for settlement before the productivity gains were seen.

In this uncomfortable atmosphere the exchange crisis of September 1957, in which a run on sterling appeared to threaten the gold and dollar reserves, precipitated a crisis within the Cabinet. Thorneycroft responded by treating exchange difficulties as a consequence of domestic inflation. This he sought to cure by raising the Bank Rate to 7 per cent, and restricting government expenditure.[17] Thus far, he had the support of Macmillan and his Cabinet colleagues, though Macmillan disliked the rise in the Bank Rate, arguing at first that 'So far from raising it, it should be reduced, and thereby you gain in three ways. You gain on the exchanges, you gain on the Budget, and you gain politically.'[18] He gave way to Treasury advice, which came alike from Thorneycroft, his officials, and his junior ministers Nigel Birch and Enoch Powell.[19] The government's statement was made on 19 September; Robert Hall, from the Treasury Economic Section, observed that it 'was done by Ministers and they would not listen to any suggestion that what they were saying did not make much sense as economics'.[20]

Macmillan's involvement in this early discussion was highly significant. It is clear that Macmillan and Thorneycroft shared both an economic vision and a political nightmare. Returning from his holiday in September, the prime minister circulated to colleagues a fearsome memorandum on the economic and political situation, commenting on

> ... a sense of frustration, amounting almost to despair, among certain classes of the community, who do not believe the Government have either the knowledge or the courage to handle the problem; and while the great mass of the people have never 'had it so good' there is a growing feeling that if the situation is allowed to drift, it may end in disaster. It therefore becomes not an economic but a political decision as to what we are to do.
>
> .... the Conservative Party cannot approach the next election with any confidence, for two reasons. Since the first Reform Bill it has been very rare for the same Party to win even two elections

running, and to win three is almost a miracle. Secondly, while the great mass of the working population and the majority of the entre- preneur class have gained from the inflation, those who have been injured by it are disproportionately represented in the Party organ- isation in the constituencies.

    .... the only practical thing to do is to reduce demand. This can only be done by reducing the total volume of money which comes into the system.[21]

This was quickly capped by Thorneycroft's own draft proposals for supporting sterling:

The Tory Party may lose the next election anyway. What matters is not whether it loses but why. If we are thrown out because we are thought to have been too tough in defence of what we conceived to be our national and imperial interests and have allowed a modest growth in unemployment, we shall be returned again, perhaps quite soon. If we are thrown out because we have flinched from our duty and allowed our economy to drift into disaster, I see no particular reason why we should ever be asked to resume control.... The essence of my proposal is that we take steps and be seen to take steps which will limit the level of money available in the economy.[22]

Thorneycroft's specific proposals caused some alarm in GEN 611, the Cabinet committee formed to deal with the exchange problem, partly because they might injure some parts of the economy, partly because of some risks in their presentation. Macleod warned of the dangers of over-confidence in minis- terial speeches, such that Freddie Bishop, Macmillan's private secretary, urged that ministers be told to stick to the same simple line. This was finally set out by Thorneycroft at the Mansion House on 8 October, and became a brief for min- isters by Charles Hill, the Information minister, under the theme 'We intend to keep the supply of money in line with the resources available.' Macmillan himself had put it more incisively: 'we shall not finance with new money any increase of wages that may emerge either from arbitration or from pri- vate agreement.... We must make it clear that while we will not finance inflation, we are not attacking employment. We are asking for a pause, not for a retreat.'[23] This view was crit- icised by Roy Harrod, who described it as 'pre-Keynesian.... Hardly any economists under the age of 50 would subscribe to it.' Macmillan sent his views to Thorneycroft and Hill, but did not change his position.[24]

The discussion over the September measures is important because it sets the scene for Thorneycroft's resignation early the next year, because it exemplifies the monetarist philosophy behind Macmillan's thinking at this critical point in his administration, and because it indicates the intimate relationship between economic and political strategy which was typical of Macmillan's better years in Downing Street. The exchange crisis was nearly over when consideration of expenditure plans for 1958 began; Thorneycroft argued that the estimates should be held to the 1957 figure, which amounted to a reduction of £153 million from the proposals made by the departments. Although the spending ministers reduced their estimates by about £100 million, Thorneycroft refused to contemplate anything less than capitulation to his demands, and resigned on 6 January 1958 with Birch and Powell. He was replaced by Derek Heathcoat Amory (the Minister of Agriculture), who carried out the policy on which the Cabinet had been able to agree, and very shortly afterwards began to relax the deflationary stance of the previous two years in response to improvements in the economy. It was the first major crisis of Macmillan's Cabinet, and it was appropriate and significant that this should be about economic matters.

The intensity and later notoriety of the Thorneycroft resignation crisis has tended to cast a misleading light on Macmillan's own economic attitudes. Like the resignation of Bevan from Attlee's Cabinet over prescription charges and the economics of rearmament, Thorneycroft's departure had many levels of meaning. The final occasion was a row over £50 million of expenditure, which in retrospect seems disproportionate to the outcome. Macleod at the time thought that Thorneycroft was 'obsessed and dominated by Powell', and Macmillan agreed with him; his old crony Percy Mills wrote that 'You did everything in your power to prevent a rupture – indeed much more than you could have been expected to do', and the economist R.A. Allen quoted an international financier as saying 'I would like to see the Government cutting every penny of expenditure; but if it is a matter of political judgement I would prefer to trust Macmillan rather than Thorneycroft.'[25] The Cabinet was particularly anxious that Thorneycroft should be seen as going out on ' "family allowances", "welfare milk" etc.', while Macmillan in answering the rather acerbic resignation letters was very keen to insist that the resigning ministers were not the only people to believe in resisting inflation.

Commenting later, Powell and others have discerned a fundamental difference of philosophy between Macmillan and the dissentients, whose stand on this occasion has been likened to an early commitment to monetarism which contrasted with what they saw as Macmillan's willingness to finance expansion by expanding the money supply.[26] Although this makes some sense in the 1990s, and although Heathcoat Amory's regime at the Treasury saw very much less resort to monetary measures of economic management, it does not fit so well as an interpretation of the 1950s. Macmillan himself warned the Cabinet on 8 November that:

> The most important of the general principles is simple, namely that, while we have no intention of interfering with the established processes of collective bargaining and will continue to accept the awards of arbitration tribunals, we shall refuse to create more money to finance wage awards which are not matched by increased output. This is the cardinal proposition; and on this proposition we should rest....

If this is not monetarism, it is certainly not wanton expansionism either. Moreover, if Thorneycroft took it seriously, it explains why he believed that his Cabinet colleagues had been converted to the policy of holding the money supply constant, and were now looking for a policy which would favour price stability over full employment.[27]

In retrospect Thorneycroft's desire to restrict expenditure smacks of Lord Randolph Churchill's resignation threat over the Naval Estimates in 1887: doing what Chancellors always do, but pressing the point to its limit. Churchill thought there was no one to replace him, but he famously 'forgot Goschen'. Thorneycroft's calculation was not so explicit, and both Birch and Powell were convinced that the threat of resignation would not in fact change the Cabinet's mind. Nevertheless, it was understood on both sides as a simple row about the levels of spending, and most commentators, particularly those later associated with the 'New Right' in the Conservative party, shared Macmillan's belief that Thorneycroft was driven on by Powell and Birch, scarcely understanding the principles underlying their wish to contain expenditure.[28] Macmillan's own suggestion in 1956 that Eden should 'get another Chancellor' over the subsidies on bread and milk was of the same order.

It is therefore unwise to read into the row any suggestion that dissenting Conservatives were about to divide the party over the economic theory which related inflation directly to the volume of the money supply. Thorneycroft himself had, admittedly, moved away from the Keynesian attitudes which had held the upper hand in the Treasury since the early 1950s. In August 1957, just before the September Measures, he summoned the economist Lionel Robbins from his holiday in Austria and apparently accepted from him the advice that the Treasury should be attending to the money supply and the state of the reserves rather than 'tuning' the national income aggregates to achieve a particular combination of growth and unemployment. Officials resisted, but were told that 'it was idle to protest since the policy had been settled'.[29] But Macmillan and his Cabinet colleagues could hardly be convicted, at this stage in his ministry, of buying political popularity with the taxpayers' money, since the whole thrust of his policy had been towards deflation and retrenchment. Powell is wrong to attach great significance to 1957 as the year when the proportion of government expenditure to national income began to grow again after a period of decline; in fact Thorneycroft's one and only Budget in 1957 was more expansionary than the Budget introduced by Heathcoat Amory in 1958.[30] Moreover, Thorneycroft's actions as Chancellor, even during the period of the estimates crisis, were a great deal less monetarist than his words. The money supply had in fact been falling (as a proportion of gross national product) for a long time, and began to go up after his September Measures; instead of restricting the money supply, Thorneycroft was merely reducing public expenditure like any Keynesian would do if intent on deflation.[31] The differences of approach between Macmillan and Thorneycroft were better illustrated by the argument over the Bank Rate, in which Macmillan argued for reliance upon direct controls of credit through controlling bank deposits and hire purchase agreements, while Thorneycroft preferred to rely simply on movements in the rate of interest. Nevertheless, the resulting crisis, and unfavourable press comment, laid the foundation for the criticism of Macmillan as a reckless electioneer, unwilling or unable to sustain an unpopular economic policy.

The record of the crisis gives some indication of the nature of Macmillan's attitude both to Thorneycroft and to the economy. On 22 and 23 December, Thorneycroft put his point,

first to Macmillan and then to a small group of senior ministers. Asking for what Macmillan thought was 'more, I fear,
than is feasible politically' in the way of cuts in welfare expenditure, Thorneycroft was rebuffed by his colleagues; but his
demand for £153 million in expenditure cuts was not categor-
ically rejected. A sum of £105 million of reductions had been
proposed by the spending departments in the first week in January. Thorneycroft had thus got two-thirds of what he wanted,
which compares fairly well with the 'four-fifths' which Macmillan had accepted as his price for staying on as Eden's Chancellor. He continued to ask for the full measure of cuts, and
found himself under attack not from Macmillan but from the
spending ministers. Duncan Sandys, who had actually reduced
the defence estimates below the levels of the previous year,
warned that the whole Defence team would resign if forced to
accept the abandonment of his pay and allowances proposals,
and similar grumbles emerged from the Ministers of Labour
and of Health. Thorneycroft thereupon resigned, in 'brutal
terms, calculated, if unanswered, to do the maximum injury to
sterling'.[32]

Macmillan answered his letter by pointing out that:

We have two objectives, one to restrain the supply of money, the
other to hold back pressure for more rewards, including wages and
salaries. You say that the estimates for the next year must be the
exact equivalent of the sum spent this year. The rigid application of
this formula, to be carried out immediately and without regard to
any other consideration, would do more harm than good. For, as
became clear in our discussions, to apply it literally must involve cuts
in vital services, including those especially affecting certain aspects
of family life – and this without any regard to the effect upon the
industrial front and on the task of those who have the responsibility
of working for wage-restraint.

This is not a matter of popularity. We have never shrunk from
unpopular measures. This is a matter of good judgement.

.... I feel it necessary to put on record that throughout the twelve
months in which this Government have been in office you have had
the full support of the Cabinet in the financial and economic policies
which we have worked out together.

[After being presented with higher estimates] ... the Cabinet was
able to reduce this excess to something less than one per cent of
the total of current government expenditure....

I therefore cannot accept that there is any difference of principle
between the rest of the Cabinet and yourself.... [33]

Like most resignation exchanges, this was thoroughly disingenuous and confected for publication. Thorneycroft's letter, according to Macmillan, was typed up with the month but not the day shown, for the precise day to be filled in later by hand. Macmillan was deliberately dressing up a frantic effort at compromise in the clothing of principle. Nevertheless, one is left with the impression that Macmillan and his Chancellor were not far apart either in their understanding of economic theory, or in their economic practice up to the point of resignation. If one was monetarist, so was the other. The difference between them was that Thorneycroft had Powell and Birch at his back, forcing him to dig in his heels on a very weakly expressed principle. The practice of economic management went on very much as before, at least until the middle of 1958.

Like the strike wave of the previous spring, the 1958 estimates crisis clashed inconveniently with an important foreign engagement. Macmillan, as was by now the pattern, gave priority to foreign affairs. On 6 January, after a Cabinet meeting, Derek Heathcoat Amory accepted the Exchequer, and the necessary minor changes were made in the ministry. At the end of the day Macmillan demurely 'gave a sherry party for the Commonwealth High Commissioners and their wives',[34] and departed the next day for his Commonwealth tour.

During the weekend he had spent hours of anxious effort on a press statement about the resignations which proclaimed that 'the best thing to do was to settle up these little local difficulties and then turn to the wider vision of the Commonwealth'. This magnificent gesture of unflappability was a calculated risk: it certainly set a positive tone for the Commonwealth trip, and by good fortune it left a Cabinet at home backing him to the hilt, with Butler in charge to pick up the pieces. During the Commonwealth tour he was anxious about 'great confusion and perplexity in the Party',[35] especially since the economic debate in the Commons on 24 January had seen an effective intervention by Thorneycroft. He began to believe in 'a deep plot . . . he may be calculating on another "sterling crisis" this autumn and the breakup of the Government in conditions which would allow him to seize the leadership of the party from me and Rab'.[36] Although the temper of the House after his return in February relieved his mind somewhat, the usual spring strikes and strike threats – London buses, railways, and oil-tanker drivers on this occasion, though the railwaymen accepted a 3 per cent increase and stayed at work – posed the risk that Thorneycroft, Birch and Powell would stir up the back benches. Only in July was he confident that 'the political as well as the economic tide had turned' in his favour.[37]

Although the substance was cautious, the tone of economic policy set by Macmillan and Heathcoat Amory was benignly expansionist. Macmillan was the initiator, writing to Heathcoat Amory in March that 'I am assuming... that the situation will allow of some relaxation of monetary policy. This ought really to be the prelude to tax remissions.'[38] The prime minister was soon going further, goading his Chancellor in meetings to reject the official Treasury view that there was no slump ahead.[39] He warned him against policies which tended to annoy the taxpayer: 'Those which are merely intended to annoy what remains of the possessing classes are not attractive to our Party and are better left to a Socialist Chancellor.'[40] Heathcoat Amory introduced his Budget in April with the declaration that 'as a Government, we are convinced that the long-term welfare of this country demands a steady expansion of our national economy. That is the objective of all our policies. We shall not, therefore, keep the brakes on one day longer than we must. We dislike restrictions intensely, and we are eager to resume expansion.'[41] But the need to say this shows how cautious his Budget actually was, with no change beyond small cuts in purchase tax and minor changes to investment allowances. *The Banker* described it as being 'as deflationary as anyone could wish'.[42]

Since the economy was already moving into recession, it was an unhelpful budget which stored up trouble for 1959. Between this and the next Budget, Macmillan was engaged in a constant dialogue with his Chancellor about the need for expansion. Heathcoat Amory – 'worth 20 Thorneycrofts' according to Macmillan[43] – recalled that Macmillan was 'almost a wild inflationist at that time'.[44] In practice, though, his exchanges with Heathcoat Amory were a private discussion about details in the tactical handling of a recession in the later part of 1958, not a debate about the philosophy of economic policy. The exchanges are revealing about his methods as well as his attitudes. Throughout 1957 and 1958 he kept up a regular correspondence with the economist Roy Harrod, then a Student of Christ Church. Harrod was an ebullient expansionist. Macmillan regularly sent his letters for Treasury comment, which was generally discouraging but more carefully expressed after a crisp note from Downing Street explained that 'PM did not want a draft reply [to Harrod's letter]. He wanted an informed commentary, illustrated by figures.'[45] Macmillan wanted to deal with the recession by short-term measures such as lifting credit restrictions and permitting more public investment of a sort which would not create long-term commitments.[46] His response to Treasury caution was increasingly sarcastic and impatient. The Chancellor, perhaps unwisely, sent in a disquisition on Treasury Control, which Macmillan liberally decorated with red ink:

> I would not deprecate [investment], for in the last 50 years we have been not nearly investment-minded enough. But at a time of great shortage of savings, the aggregate of Ministers' desires will always outrun the constable. We then need a system of presenting the whole picture so that Ministers can take rational choices on which is the more and which the less important. [Macmillan: 'Rot'] . . . .
>
> I am bound to say that these periodic attempts to cut or to increase short-term capital expenditure are likely to frustrate the whole objective of exercising effective control over the long-term programmes and keeping them in line with our long-term resource to carry them out. [Macmillan:'Have you ever been in a) war b) business c) active politics?']

Amory wanted to have a short term and long term programme, both of which would be published as a guide to departments, 'But if we are forced to keep on chopping and changing, our control will undoubtedly collapse altogether. [Macmillan: 'Hurrah!']'. The prime minister noted, finally: 'Chancellor of Exch. This is a *very bad paper*. Indeed, a disgraceful paper. It might have been written by Mr Neville Chamberlain's ghost.'[47]

By the end of the year demand and output were once again rising. During 1958 prices had been kept down by an international recession. Finally, in January 1959, Macmillan heeded Harrod's call for 'a thumping great above-the-line Budget deficit',[48] and decided to force expansion. With the Bank Rate already reduced to 4 per cent, and the international convertibility of sterling restored, the Budget of March 1959 gave a very significant stimulus to the economy just as the international recession was coming to an end. *The Banker* concluded that 'its aim is as reflationary as any responsible commentator had advocated, and a good deal more so than most people had advocated'. The years of deflation were over.

The combined effect of tax cuts, investment allowances and an expansion in world trade caused British industrial production to rise by 10 per cent in a single year. This was about double the figure predicted by the Treasury, and left Heathcoat Amory with an overheating economy in early 1960. The extra demand brought in imports, which jeopardised the balance of payments and the position of sterling. The 'standstill' Budget of 1960, and the resort to 'mini-Budgets' in 1961, discussed in the next section, were efforts to repair the damage caused by the policy change of 1959. In an assessment of Macmillan's economic policy, the 1959 Budget therefore looms large. There is little doubt that it was his Budget rather than Heathcoat Amory's, or that it contributed mightily to the onset of a lethal combination of inflation, balance of payments difficulties, and slow growth of industrial production in the years after the 1959 election. Nor can it be denied that the immediate effects, seen straight away in higher living standards for most of the population, were an enormous help to the Conservatives in getting re-elected in the General Election in October. But one cannot assume too much cynicism in Macmillan's thinking, nor dismiss his attitude to the expansion of the economy merely as a hangover from his reaction to poverty in pre-war Stockton. Macmillan and all his Chancellors faced the problem of dealing with the domestic economy at the same time as wrestling with the balance of payments and the condition of international trade. Movements at home did not always match movements in the wider world, yet many of the instruments then used – changes in the Bank Rate, manipulations of the level of government expenditure and thus of demand, credit controls and so on – affected both the internal and the external economy. What was appropriate for one could be very inappropriate for the other, and the fiasco of 1959–60 was caused by a particularly acute mismatch of domestic and external needs. No single line of policy, taken to an extreme, could have been right.

Macmillan's contribution to the 1959 Budget was to lean towards the expansion of domestic demand as part of a policy which also included relaxed credit controls and a low Bank Rate. As the Budget was being prepared, unemployment was rising (to a peak of 620,000). Later analysis suggests that production was also beginning to rise, and that the recession induced by the previous two Budgets was beginning to lift;

but Heathcoat Amory came under tremendous pressure to do something, and correspondingly prepared a vigorous expansionary Budget. Macmillan himself is generally credited with the major expansionary item: an increase in the size of the income tax cut from the sixpence proposed by Amory to ninepence. In retrospect it can be seen that each of the economic instruments favoured by Macmillan and his Chancellor was inappropriately applied. In all cases, they made bad guesses about the necessary changes to be made, but they were guesses about the levels to be set, not about which instruments to use. In particular, the timing of budgetary moves was inept, leaving necessary action too late so that both slumps and booms were amplified rather than damped down. Bad forecasting in the Treasury, which underestimated the likely growth in demand, contributed to their decisions.[49] Different figures would not have produced the same problems, but they might nevertheless have produced different problems which were just as bad. No prime minister or Chancellor since the war, except Thorneycroft very briefly, had actually chosen to abandon any of the instruments Macmillan used, and even Thorneycroft had used what he did use in very similar ways.

The most important question is whether Macmillan could have affected the underlying weaknesses of the British economy by anything he did or forbore to do in the 1959 Budget or the economic measures of late 1958 which preceded it, or in his handling of wage claims in these two years. The answer to this conundrum depends on the favoured interpretation of the causes of Britain's economic weakness. For those who think that excessive government expenditure was at the root of economic decline, the course of government spending since 1945 is a convenient explanation. The years 1958–59 are of pivotal importance, since they saw the reversal of a steady reduction of government expenditure as a proportion of GNP which had begun soon after the Conservatives returned to office in 1951. In contrast, for those more concerned with the inflationary pressure of wage demands, 1958 and 1959 must at least seem better years than the early 1950s. Tactical flexibility, and some good luck, held back the rate of wage increases. If, however, the explanation of decline is to be seen as the failure of British productivity to rise as fast as that of other industrial countries, the Macmillan government's acts of omission and commission before the 1959 election must be seen in a different light. From this perspective the major criticism of Macmillan's policy was that it concentrated too heavily on transient economic indicators such as the balance of payments, the rate of inflation and the growth of the money supply. The manipulation of government expenditure and credit probably did these symptoms little good, and the 1959 Budget almost certainly did them harm. However, the alternatives suggested by Macmillan's critics were no more likely to bring about radical change; in particular, those like Thorneycroft and Birch, who simply wanted a different trade-off between unemployment and inflation, had no suggestions to offer about how to improve both measures at the same time.

. . .

SELWYN LLOYD AND THE PAY PAUSE

After the 1959 election Macmillan's handling of economic policy was fitful and confusing. His expansionist instincts were always evident, but economic policy competed with the attractions of foreign affairs, especially the challenge of entering Europe. His successive Chancellors were given little credit, and relatively little support; and yet he made it clear in 1962 that he resented the degree to which the insoluble problems of the British economy were left to him to solve.

Soon after the election the macro-economic consequences of expansion became obvious. Heathcoat Amory nervously contemplated the inflation that his Budget was bound to create, and wanted to cool the economy down. Macmillan responded that a deflationary Budget would 'either be very foolish or very dishonest' after the 1959 Budget and the election victory, and urged a 'standstill' programme. The Chancellor insisted that 'a Budget which just balanced tax concessions against tax remissions would be inflationary'.[50] Macmillan set about persuading the Cabinet to deflect the Chancellor from his intentions, and largely succeeded. Politically, his problem was that Heathcoat Amory found it very difficult to look enthusiastic about a Budget which he did not like, and the effect on the House and the public was uneven. The 1960 Budget took money out of the economy at some points and put it back at others. Shortly afterwards, responding to movements on the exchanges, Heathcoat Amory imposed hire-purchase restrictions on cars and consumer durables, and increased the banks' deposit ratios in order to restrict credit. The Treasury expected that this would reduce domestic demand and release goods for export. In fact it did no such thing: employment held steady while production failed to rise (resulting in a drop in productivity) and exports remained stable partly because British prices were too high. Almost incidentally the domestic demand for cars and consumer durables dropped of its own accord, and the government was found once again to have kicked vulnerable domestic industries to the ground just as they were sinking naturally to their knees.

At the same time Heathcoat Amory made it clear that he wanted to resign, for genuine personal reasons, and Macmillan moved Selwyn Lloyd from the Foreign Office to take over the Treasury. Lloyd's appointment facilitated an apparent revolution in economic policy-making which has coloured recent interpretations of Macmillan's own policy and position. The events of 1960 persuaded many Treasury officials, who in turn persuaded Lloyd, that the sort of demand-management favoured by Chancellors since the early 1950s did not work because industry would not respond rationally and constructively to the circumstances which governments created by their budgetary decisions. The problem lay not only in macro-economic tides but in the micro-economic behaviour of British industry. Macmillan himself, with Thorneycroft, had taken rather the same view of British industry in the mid 1950s, and seen the invigorating effect of European competition as a necessary stimulant. Now Lloyd and his advisers proposed to improve industry's performance by various forms of planning, taking their cue from French models.

Early in 1961 Treasury officials and leading businessmen, with the approval of ministers, discussed French economic planning with officials of the Commissariat du Plan.[51] In July Macmillan wrote encouragingly to Selwyn Lloyd that 'I do not think we ought to be afraid of a switch over towards more direction. Our Party has always consisted of a number holding the laissez-faire tradition but of an equal number in favour of some direction.... So far as I am concerned I have no fear of it because these were policies I recommended before the war. Therefore I shall be able to claim, like Disraeli, that I have educated my party.... Besides, it is always a good thing to steal the Whigs' clothes while they are bathing, it is a very old Conservative tradition.'[52] At the 1961 party conference he urged more positive intervention in the economy. The proposal finally put forward in 1962 was that a National Economic Development Council (NEDC, soon dubbed 'Neddy'), with representation from the government and from both sides of industry, would draw up a plan which included a target for the growth rate of the British economy. A number of industrial planning groups ('Little Neddies') would work out the implications of that growth rate for their own sectors and agree the investment levels, manning and wage levels necessary to attain it. In principle, this would enable growth without inflation, through the co-operation of capital, labour and the government. This was corporatism, in a very limited and British sense, and it was the very sort of interventionist consensus-driven policy-making method against which Conservatives rebelled both under Edward Heath and, more consistently, after 1975 under Margaret Thatcher.

This large vision, later taken over and amplified by Wilson's Labour government from 1964 to 1970, but with little more effect, did not get very far at all under Macmillan, despite his personal commitment to the idea of planning. The explanation for failure lies mainly in the sequence of events after Heathcoat Amory's retirement. The new Chancellor was confronted by weaknesses in the balance of payments and the balance of trade, and the Cabinet was puzzled enough to set up an enquiry at the end of November 1960 in which Macmillan himself took a leading part as chairman of a committee on increasing exports. None of this made any measurable difference to the balance of payments. The Bank Rate, forced up in January 1960 from 4 per cent to 5 per cent, then to 6 per cent in June, had brought inflows of speculative or 'hot' money into Britain which were then withdrawn smartly in March 1961 when the German Mark was revalued. This ebb and flow was far more influential in the short term than the underlying performance of the economy. Lloyd's April 1961 Budget was launched in an atmosphere near to crisis, which did not help its reception. He made some reductions in direct taxation which Macmillan had urged, making up for the losses by miscellaneous increases in indirect taxation. He also gave himself powers to invoke 'regulators' between Budgets; these were the payroll tax, which was an addition to National Insurance contributions, and the power to vary purchase tax and some excise taxes upward or downward during the year. Macmillan later recollected how 'we thus introduced into the management of the economy the now popular concept of the stimulant and the tranquilliser'. He himself was showing signs of an addiction to external economic advice, minuting to his private secretary after reading a Treasury paper that 'I must see Roy Harrod.'[53] Unfortunately the result of his actions was anything but political tranquillity. The run on sterling caused Lloyd, under strong pressure from his officials, to invoke the purchase tax regulator in July in a 'Little Budget' which also introduced the 'Pay Pause'. At this point Macmillan himself was under extreme pressure. On 15 June he took to his bed and wrote a note of seven policy areas which were either troublesome (security matters) or insoluble (all the others: the economy, Europe, Laos, Central Africa, Berlin and recruitment to the forces).[54] Although he supported Lloyd both in his economic measures and in his refusal to go as far as Treasury officials wanted, his memoirs suggest a man almost too tired to defend the fundamentally expansionist position which he favoured. External critics, then and later, condemned the government for their preoccupation with the balance of payments and their permanent air of surprise at each succeeding crisis.

While the use of the regulators offended economic journalists, the Pay Pause upset large sections of the public. It applied only to public sector workers, and had a practical impact only on groups such as nurses and teachers who could not or would not use the strike weapon. In November 1961 the electricity workers forced the Electricity Council to breach the pause, and ministers could do nothing about it. Increasingly Macmillan came to believe that his government's handling of the economy was critical to its political survival, and that the Treasury was unable to bring about the necessary changes. In particular, there was no firm policy to follow the Pay Pause, which was due to expire in April 1962. In due course a White Paper, known afterwards as the 'guiding light' policy, appeared, an obvious compromise among a divided group of ministers and officials.[55] The guiding light was a figure of 2–2.5 per cent as a permissible range for wage increases: it did not contain any suggestion of how this was to be achieved or policed, and it bore no obvious relationship to the other elements of economic policy such as fiscal or public expenditure measures being developed by Selwyn Lloyd at the Exchequer.

Lloyd's inability to cut an effective figure was but one depressing feature of a depressing political landscape. A series of disastrous by-elections in the spring of 1962 persuaded Macmillan that his party was at great risk. The Liberal victory at Orpington, in which Eric Lubbock turned a Conservative majority of 15,000 into a Liberal majority of 8,000, was only a false dawn for the Liberals, but it scared the Conservatives; in other by-elections Liberals were forcing Conservatives into third place in Labour seats or splitting the vote in damaging ways. While Labour had nothing much to be pleased about, the Conservative leadership was convinced that the trend had to be reversed. Macleod, the chairman of the party, blamed the defeat openly on the Pay Pause. At the same time Macmillan was fulminating that his colleagues were unable to take up the challenge of reformulating economic policy, and thrusting the burden upon him. Lloyd's 1962 Budget was unhelpful, largely because it lacked any noteworthy measure except the taxation of confectionery; in retrospect it has been condemned as being one of the most pernicious of post-war budgets, in that it deflated an economy which was already on the brink of recession, but at the time its caution was rather welcomed than not.[56]

In May Macmillan found himself preparing a huge policy statement for the Cabinet, which finally discussed it at the end of the month. Its proposals were quite radical, though difficult for any government to attain. He insisted that he wanted to maintain full employment, stable prices, economic expansion and a favourable balance of payments, all at the same time; the only way to do this was an incomes policy, and he developed his reasoning in a political analysis which is discussed at more length below.[57] He won the acceptance of the Cabinet and the 1922 Committee, and set about a detailed plan. Meanwhile he had decided that Lloyd must go before long, because of his apparent inability to press on with any development of the Pay Pause. The abrupt dismissal came on 12 July, and created a political storm which lasted through the weekend and into the next year. Reginald Maudling took over; and though he took some time to get into his stride, he was clearly better fitted than Lloyd to the task which Macmillan had defined as the rôle of the Chancellor.[58]

. . .

MAUDLING AND INCOMES POLICY

Macmillan's attempt to fight his way back from the political iso-
lation brought about by the 'Night of the Long Knives' which
followed Lloyd's dismissal included an unusually full and effective speech in the confidence debate which Gaitskell introduced on 26 July. After dealing, to his own satisfaction at
least, with the accusations of political panic, he turned to economic policy with the ringing declaration that 'an incomes
policy is... necessary as a permanent feature of our economic
life'[59] and went on to launch the National Incomes Commission (NIC) as a statutory body. Of all possible routes out of
his difficulties, this was not very happily chosen. Unlike the
other innovations of the period, though, it was undoubtedly
Macmillan's own. He had overseen its development in the
Spring of 1962 by a group of civil servants, because he believed that his Cabinet colleagues had failed to find a successor
to the pay pause. The plan was logically watertight. Macmillan had determined on an expansionist economic policy and
selected Maudling as the right Chancellor to effect it, and the
principal danger in an expansionist policy was believed to be
wage-inflation. Control of incomes from employment had to
be addressed directly. The Cabinet was reluctant, and Macmillan had to write two forceful papers to get his way, urging his
colleagues that 'the feeling has grown that it is neither fair
nor possible to operate an incomes policy in the public sector
when it is not observed in the private sector'.[60] The decision
to manage an incomes policy outside the purview of the NEDC
was rather odd, though, and the NIC's terms of reference were
slow to emerge. By November 1962 it had been decided that it
would review specific wage-settlements on reference from the
government, rather than discuss general policy as NEDC was
to do. In practice it did little during the government's lifetime,
and its most significant act was to raise the 'guiding light' for
settlements from 2–2.5 per cent to 3–3.5 per cent. The trade
union movement refused to co-operate with the NIC, a sharp
contrast to its engagement with NEDC discussions. Though ostensibly a main pillar of the government's economic strategy,
the NIC was too easily portrayed as an irrelevance.

Of the rest of the economic strategy, Macmillan himself was closely identified with an expansionist policy but rather distanced from the specific activities of the NEDC. In expansion his chosen instrument was Reginald Maudling, whose intelligence and drive were undoubted. Some critics have argued that Maudling was unduly cautious in his first months,[61] but all agree that the 1963 Budget was based on an unusually clear reading of the significance of economic indicators. Even so, the Chancellor's obvious reluctance to exploit the regulators which Lloyd had bequeathed him for use between Budgets, and the rather long delay between the announcement of expansion in the 1963 Budget and the actual effect of the new tax allowances meant that the stimulus was applied long after the economy had started to expand. Conservative economic policy in the 1950s and early 1960s was cruelly described as 'either too little too late or too much too late'; Maudling erred on the side of too much, and spent the last year of his chancellorship, after Macmillan's retirement, trying to control the resulting inflation.

One reason for this was the political context in which economic policies were being made. Maudling cheerfully ignored the NEDC in the first months of his chancellorship, but suddenly took it up in early 1963 as he was preparing his Budget. The Budget itself, the main political purpose of which was 'to obtain union support for an incomes policy',[62] was deliberately generous and closely followed the terms of the NEDC's ambitious plan for a 4 per cent growth rate. None of this was informed by a profound belief in the effectiveness of tripartite arrangements for policy discussion or planning. Instead the government was driven by recurrent crises, not just on the foreign exchanges and in the balance of payments figures, but also in industrial relations. Over the winter of 1962–63 the most egregious case was that of the electricity industry, in which the winter's pay dispute was only settled in March 1963 with a 6 per cent award which the government promptly referred to the NIC. The combination of an incomes policy which obviously did not work with a policy for economic growth which did little to reduce unemployment was a daunting prospect. Maudling's flirtation with the NEDC had much to do with a political effort to induce the trade unions, who were represented on it, to cooperate in controlling wage increases; planning, in the sense that the NEDC itself understood the activity, was less important either to Macmillan or his Chancellor.

Towards the end of his premiership, in November 1962, Macmillan wrote a memorandum on 'The Modernisation of Britain'.[63] Its two main points were that 'in order to enhance our competitive power and to ensure a level of exports commensurate with full employment at home, we have to increase our productivity by bringing our productive capacity into full use, by eliminating restrictive practices and by developing to the utmost the new methods which technology is bringing within our reach'; and that 'we have to re-organise the structure of the island in such a way as to rectify the imbalance between south and north – between the "rich" areas and the "poor" regions, the under-employed regions – and redress the grave social anomalies which are created by this imbalance'. Although this note now resonates with cliché, like the 'never had it so good' speech quoted at the beginning of this chapter, both are good illustrations of his personal response to economic problems, and there is a genuine and marked difference between them. When he first reached 10 Downing Street Macmillan still had a Treasury pallor: he was determined to manage public expenditure and national income aggregates, as a Keynesian, to permit growth without inflation, and in his first two years he was more anxious about inflation than about growth. Moreover, he had to be aware of the need to recover from the financial consequences of the Suez crisis, for which he himself was largely responsible. His personal interventions in questions of taxation, interest rates and the money supply were sometimes eccentric, but in essence he left it to his Chancellors to manage the economy as best they could, subject to the political guidelines about which he was never reluctant to remind them. His economic views were indeed so inchoate that it is difficult to say whether he was or was not an early monetarist: his views on the importance of containing the money supply were clear, but like Macleod's at the same period they did not prevent him from disagreeing profoundly with Thorneycroft about the political expediency of particular measures.

Macmillan's personal commitment to growth left him uneasy when the 1959 Budget was followed by inflation without sustainable growth. This did not produce a U-turn, such as two subsequent Conservative prime ministers have attempted at least once,[64] but rather shifted his attention away from the perennial crises of the rate of unemployment, the gold and dollar

reserves and the balance of payments and towards the medium-
and long-term concerns which appear in his 'Modernisation'
memorandum. While he continued to interest himself in economic affairs by chairing Cabinet committees, his direct interventions with his Chancellors were even more infrequent than
in the previous premiership. It is scarcely surprising that he
found this frustrating, especially in 1962 when Selwyn Lloyd
seemed unable to manage short-term macro-economic problems, long-term structural planning, or the nuances of political
presentation.

Some of Macmillan's disengagement from economic questions in the last years can be explained as the weariness of a dis-
illusioned man; but that disillusion took the very specific form
of a search for structural cures for what he regarded as a structural problem. Critics of British economic policy in the 1950s
and early 1960s have taken up Samuel Brittan's metaphor of a
'Macmillan Cycle' in economic management.[65] This, allegedly,
was a four-year sequence in which governments would fear to
intervene during a boom, when they should have been cooling demand, and then would panic just after the boom broke,
so that their deflationary measures sent the economy into a
dive. Some time after the inevitable recovery had begun, the
same governments would begin to inflate the economy, starting the cycle all over again. Brittan, at least, acknowledged that
Macmillan had only been one of many who indulged in this
behaviour. In recent mythology Macmillan has also been condemned for financial incontinence, weakness in the face of the
trade unions, over-confidence in the techniques of demand-
management and an excessive liking for government expenditure. There was no period in his premiership or his chancellorship about which all of these charges could be sustained; there
were long periods, especially at the beginning, for which none
of them could. It should not be surprising that even in terms
of the economic indicators which he and his contemporaries
tended to favour to excess, such as the balance of payments,
the unemployment rate, the gold and dollar reserves and inflation, the 'Macmillan years' were markedly better than the
1970s and the 1980s. This is perhaps faint praise, since the
economies of industrialised Europe were forging ahead, but it
is a proper corrective to the myth.

. . .

MANAGING THE PARTY

Macmillan's achievement in restoring Conservative political fortunes in time for the 1959 General Election has been described by one historian as 'bringing his party back from the dead'.[66] This is hardly an exaggeration. Suez was a major blow to the party, the worst accident to befall the Conservatives as a governing party in peacetime in the twentieth century. The impact upon the back bench was at first numbing, with many MPs unable to decide whether the operation or the withdrawal was the greater mistake, and uncertain of their political future under their new leader. *The Economist* remarked soon after his appointment that it was 'presumably intended to bind up the wounds of Suez, but what it has really enswathed beneath the bandages is not, at first sight, the harm to the nation but the hurt feelings of the Conservative party itself'.[67] In the country the popular perception of the Conservatives as a party of prosperity and competence gave way to distrust; in June 1957 a Gallup poll showed Labour 7 per cent ahead, with fewer than a third of the electorate approving of Macmillan's performance as leader of the party and prime minister. The measure of his achievement is that in August 1959 67 per cent of voters polled by Gallup approved of his performance. By the time of the election, timed for October 1959 to take advantage of the favourable consequences of the 1959 Budget, the Conservatives, under a competent and apparently confident leader, would have found it extremely difficult to lose office.

This reversal of fortunes was achieved by a strengthening of the party organisation and an improved presentation of its policies and of its leader. Without taking a direct part in organisational renewal, Macmillan enthusiastically supported Oliver Poole (who was not an exciting figure) and Lord Hailsham (who was), in their efforts as chairmen of the party to make the structure set up by Lord Woolton as efficient as possible. Macmillan himself counted the first year of his premiership as an unmitigated electoral failure. The Conservatives suffered adverse swings in every by-election, and although this was to be expected by a party in office the average swing was much larger than in 1955 or 1956. In Warwick and Leamington, in March 1957, a comfortable majority of nearly 30 per cent of the vote was reduced to less than 5 per cent, a swing of 12.2 per cent; lesser but still unpleasant swings were sustained at Edinburgh South (10.2 per cent) and East Ham North (8 per cent) in May and at Gloucester (10.5 per cent) in September. In Gloucester, which had been a Labour marginal, Liberal intervention cut the Conservative share of the vote by two-fifths, without affecting the Labour vote at all. This was doubly worrying because popular support for the government did not seem to be recovering at the same rate as back-bench Conservative support in the Commons.

Macmillan's solution was to demote Oliver Poole, who had been chairman of the party since Woolton retired in 1955, and replace him by Hailsham. Poole retained the deputy chairmanship, and continued to run Central Office, while Hailsham set out to inspire the party. The 1957 Conference, in Brighton, was marked by the regular early morning appearance of Hailsham in a bathing suit on the beach (in October) and his energetic ringing of a handbell. Though distasteful to some, particularly the more refined spirits on the Labour front bench, this appears to have had an important effect on the rank and file of the party. This change of tone was followed by a major recruiting drive, 'Roll Call for Victory', in 1958, which concentrated on recruiting a broader spectrum of social groups into the party. Concern for the party's image as the party of privilege had earlier inspired an advertising campaign, launched by Central Office in June 1957, with themes chosen to appeal to women and to the more prosperous elements of the working classes. Thus began an effort, more enthusiastic and more successful than anything undertaken by Labour, to come to terms with social change and to present the Conservative Party as a party of the whole nation. The theme of prosperity for all classes – the attitude captured by the apocryphal claim that 'You've never had it so good' – was the basis of the party's highly effective appeal in 1959. Although it resonates down the years, this phrase did not in fact sum up the whole of the party's appeal, which was also directed more conservatively to the narrow self-interest of the middle classes.

There is no doubt that Macmillan approved of this development and in large part inspired it. He cheerfully used language about economic policy – the 'give-away' in Budgets was a favoured phrase – which makes him appear a cynical and showy manipulator of public greed and an exploiter of any social trend which tended to weaken the loyalty of Labour voters to their party. However the campaign was not at first based on his own personality. His name and photograph were deliberately excluded from the first advertising campaign,[68] and it was not until 'Roll Call for Victory' that he became a central image. By this time his public *persona* had been successfully cultivated. Indefatigable international travel, especially the Commonwealth tour in early 1958 which had been carefully managed for the Press, helped to make him a statesman. So did television: in May 1958 his personal approval rating in the Gallup poll was 37 per cent, but two months after a televised interview with the American journalist Ed Murrow this had risen to 50 per cent, with some indication that television viewers were more likely than non-viewers to have changed their minds about him.[69] Although the Murrow interview in retrospect appears stilted, it was considerably better than anything achieved by any previous prime minister, and it capitalised on his carefully crafted reputation for 'unflappability'.

Meanwhile Macmillan was engaged in an exercise much closer to his heart, the reconstruction of Conservative policy in preparation for 1959. As a prime minister he was not noted for interfering in his colleagues' departmental affairs, and in home policy his efforts can even seem sporadic and unhelpful when compared with his steady application to grave foreign problems. But his commitment to forward thinking and to the development of a modern form of Conservatism had been a consistent theme of his career since he entered Parliament, and he expected the party to reflect this enthusiasm. By his ministerial appointments he enhanced the stature of the Conservative Research Department in the policy-making process. Macleod, Maudling and Powell, all former members of the department's staff, became ministers and ultimately Cabinet ministers; Macmillan's secretary, John Wyndham, was also a former member of the department. Other structural changes helped to co-ordinate the presentation of policy in the country. A 'Liaison Committee' of representatives from the government, Central Office, the Whips and the Party Chairman met to co-ordinate the presentation of policy, and even to advise on the timing of policy initiatives which might seem controversial.

More important, Macmillan set up a 'Steering Committee' consisting of himself, Butler, Hailsham, Macleod and Heath (the Chief Whip), together with party officers, which tried

to develop coherent policies for a Conservative Party in government. This committee apparently originated in an acute
memorandum by Michael Fraser, deputy director of the Research Department.[70] Fraser remarked that 'our political aim
in this period of office should have been to achieve some
rehabilitation of the middle-class in the widest sense of that
word, while not in the process alienating that wider measure
of manual-working support which we had gained by 1955 and
upon which we depend for a reasonable majority'. Conservative strategy could either be a gradualist policy like that of 1951
to 1955, or a two-stage process 'concentrating on wooing our
hard middle-class core in the early years of the Parliament and
on wooing the margins later'. Because of Suez and its impact
on the economy neither course had been followed consistently.
Fraser suggested an early concentration on anti-inflation measures, leading to 'the re-establishment of a pattern in the public
mind', and this was undoubtedly the policy implied by Macmillan's own attitudes in 1957 and the economic policies described
above.[71] Organisationally he wanted a means to feed the policy
ideas of Conservative Party groups 'within the limits of constitutional propriety' into the government machine 'for more
detailed analysis and criticism'.

With a formidable membership, the Steering Committee was
intended to oversee this process. Its method of work in its first
two years was simple and effective. Issues were brought up, by
members or officers, and delegated as appropriate to the Conservative Research Department or to mixed groups of MPs and
officials, or even to ministers. The results of their efforts were
reviewed by the Steering Committee, and the ministerial members, with Macmillan in the lead, could if they wished push
policy forward in government. To a remarkable extent this
had the support of senior civil servants. The Cabinet Secretary, Norman Brook, offered that his official colleagues would
'take more responsibility for day-to-day administration ... and
thus give senior Ministers a little more time to think at large
and to join with you, as required, in political planning'.[72] The
more important function of the Steering Committee was to
guide the preparation of the next election manifesto, a task
which began in earnest in April 1958. In this part of the work
Macmillan's instincts predominated: he identified the problem of 'how to present what is in fact "Safety First" into a policy
which looks as if it is moving forward', and influenced the tone

of the campaign towards 'On the basis of what has been done, move on.'[73] Although most of the work of drafting the manifesto was undertaken by party officers, calling particularly on the Research Department, the manifesto went through many drafts and was frequently reviewed by senior ministers under the chairmanship of the prime minister. This was one of a number of ways in which Macmillan successfully fused party and government.

After the highly successful 1959 campaign, the Steering Committee met less frequently – about twice a year – and the conduct of policy research was left more to the initiative of the Conservative Research Department, under Fraser. Though no bad thing in itself, this development reflected the relative lack of inspiration from Macmillan and from his ministerial colleagues. The successive policy failures of the early 1960s, from the abrupt reversal of budgetary policy in 1960 through the failures of summitry to the Night of the Long Knives, won Macmillan little public credit and began to erode his support within the Conservative Party, both in Parliament and outside it. He was constantly aware of the risk to the party's position, reminding his Cabinet colleagues before the 1960 Party Conference that 'since Parties depend for their continuing strength upon the new voters coming in, we must not allow the thought to develop over the next year or two that we have done well but that we have completed our task'.[74] It was an uphill struggle. In February 1961 he warned Selwyn Lloyd that 'the youth and energy of President Kennedy are in danger of creating a kind of image that he and his country are young and full of ideas and that we are out of date, governed by ageing politicians'.[75] The cure on that occasion was to remind the House of Commons that Britain did not have American rates of unemployment, but every twist in economic policy seemed to make the party's situation worse.

From the middle of 1961 Macmillan grew more preoccupied with a listlessness in Cabinet which seemed to reflect his own exhaustion. Although Lloyd pressed ahead woodenly with economic measures which were broadly to Macmillan's liking, he produced few new ideas. The burden of innovation fell instead on the prime minister's shoulders, as by-election disaster followed by-election disaster. His major policy statement to Cabinet on 28 May 1962, which launched the idea of an incomes policy to succeed the pay pauses, constituted a political analysis as well as an economic prescription. He returned to the risk of staleness in government, urging his colleagues that 'we must leap forward in the same kind of way and in the same kind of spirit that we should have done had we been now in Opposition instead of in power for eleven years'. Besides the incomes policy itself, he was seriously attempting to re-launch Conservatism as a party of national appeal:

> First the working classes as we are apt in this room to call them, but I suppose there's some new name for them now. If they are to accept an incomes policy however promulgated by whatever Government or by a wider body, in my view the time has come now to state definitely we can no longer accept the difference of status between the wage earner and the salary earner. We must work toward the ending of the sharp division between the manual worker and the staff. I think we should state that clearly as our purpose...If the working classes are to play in this hand they must feel that they play as full members of the team and not fighting for their strength and therefore tending to abuse their strength. Secondly the middle classes – the Orpingtonians. At present they feel the victims of both sides, pushed about between large industry and the Trade Unions to whom they see us what they call surrender. They have immensely to gain from an incomes policy and it shouldn't be difficult to persuade them...They suffer in a free for all unless of course we were to throw the full employment ball away and go for a violently deflationary policy somewhat like that between the wars, when undoubtedly the standard of living of the middle classes was high...But I am sure that no one anymore seriously proposes the creation of large scale unemployment; nor do I think any Government is likely to survive it, so that that really cannot be a hope for the middle classes.

To this idiosyncratic version of the traditional Conservative appeal to inter-class unity he was determined to add 'a new attitude towards the unity of the nation as a whole and their different claim upon each other, to try and create a kind of moral position on which it is almost anarchical and indecent to oppose this line of thought'.[76] This rather unexpected moral tone was carried through in his first incomes policy paper, which included 'the idea that in the long run Britain's contribution to the present dramatic changes in human society and in world relations demands not only a sound economic basis, but a realisation of the spiritual and moral issues at stake. The new approach would be presented as the first step, but only as the first step, in a new total phase of our national development and our national influence for good.'[77]

The Conservative Party's experience in the early 1960s does not suggest that this lunge for the high moral ground was ever likely to be successful as a strategy for party unity. While the economic failures probably had the greater effect on public opinion, and thus posed the more serious threat to the re-election of the party, it was the challenges of external policy which undermined the relationship between Macmillan and his back-benchers. Quite simply, Macmillan and his ministers were capable of deciding on policies towards Europe and the colonies which many of their parliamentary supporters would not stomach. Local party associations were also divided, especially when MPs were prepared to voice their suspicions. As a result the party organisation was positively relieved when the Common Market negotiations failed, and a Research Department committee noted in 1961 that 'the party is divided over Colonial policy into (a) the progressives (mainly the younger members) who endorse it, (b) the great majority, who accept it, with regret, as inevitable, as, of course, it is and (c) the right wing (mainly the older members ...) who are frankly critical.'[78] The Macmillan Cabinets, especially after 1959, were preoccupied with what they saw as the inevitable decline in Britain's power to influence world events unaided. In this, and in home affairs, they were reconciled to change, and made it their business to control it and influence its direction. This was a difficult position to explain to some of their followers, who were impatient when told that policy, for example towards the colonies, 'raises difficult problems of timing: if we go too fast, we risk having a Congo on our hands; if we go too slow, we risk having an Algeria on our hands'.[79] Plenty of Conservatives did not want to go anywhere at all, fast or slow, and were prepared to blame the prime minister for making them do so. Ministers had to make decisions, and some later regretted that they had moved so fast to decolonise,[80] but the passions of their followers did not make it easy to plan coolly.

Back-bench suspicion of Macmillan's foreign policy, stretching back to Suez and the resignation of Lord Salisbury, made opportunities for a small number of MPs whom he identified as personal enemies. Not all of them were significant actors, and many were in fact more critical of his domestic policies, but they thrived on his vulnerability to criticism from traditionally-minded sections of the party, such as the agricultural lobby (over the Common Market) and the local associations where loyalty to the former Empire was important. Macmillan was perhaps unduly sensitive to parliamentary criticism from 'the usual malcontents': back-benchers such as Robin Turton, Lord Hinchingbrooke and Nigel Birch. Birch in particular, who never forgave the prime minister for the 1958 estimates crisis, was capable of wounding interventions, of which the 'Never glad confident morning again' rebuke to Macmillan's leadership over the Profumo affair was merely the most memorable.

Macmillan had other enemies within the party who were too significant to ignore, and these he made into colleagues. Thorneycroft and Powell, unlike Birch, returned to office and were treated with distant respect. Butler formed a constructive working relationship with his rival, though his leaks and ambiguous asides to journalists left no doubt that he would have preferred to be leader himself. The result, as in most governments, was that back-bench loyalties were sometimes directed to particular leading ministers rather than exclusively to the prime minister himself. Until 1963 this gave the government safe majorities, and in practice reassured Macmillan about his political future.

. . .

LLOYD, PROFUMO AND ENCIRCLING GLOOM

The dismissal of Selwyn Lloyd in 1962 and the resulting reshuffle known as the Night of the Long Knives, was to be a breakpoint in the life of Macmillan's last government. In early July 1962 Macmillan discussed his intention of removing Lloyd with R.A. Butler, who soon leaked the news to the *Daily Mail*. At that stage the prime minister was only thinking of a general Cabinet reshuffle in the autumn, which could be the occasion for a number of useful moves. The *Mail* printed the story on Thursday 12 July, which was the morning of a Cabinet meeting at which Macmillan's latest paper on incomes policy was discussed.[81] The Chancellor, who took little part in the discussion according to Macmillan's recollection but contributed fully according to his own,[82] had an appointment to see Macmillan at 6.00 p.m. to discuss repayment of Britain's IMF loan. Shortly beforehand, Macmillan's private secretary, Tim Bligh, warned Lloyd that he was going to be dismissed. The interview was difficult for both men, and in the tension of the moment Macmillan apparently opened up a new perspective in which Lloyd's departure was to be part of a general reshuffle including Lord Mills and Lord Kilmuir, the Lord Chancellor.

Overnight Macmillan concluded that matters could not rest there, and when he heard the next morning that Lloyd's junior minister, John Hare, was proposing to go too he decided to outflank further trouble by carrying out the whole autumn reshuffle in a single summer's day. On 13 July, in addition to Kilmuir and Mills, Harold Watkinson left Defence, David Eccles left Education, John Maclay left the Scottish Office and Charles Hill lost his position as Minister of Housing. Maudling went to the Treasury from the Colonial Office, which was amalgamated with the Commonwealth Office under Duncan Sandys. Butler left the Home Office to become a sort of deputy prime minister with responsibility for Central Africa, and was replaced by Henry Brooke. Thorneycroft, now rehabilitated, was promoted to be Secretary of State for Defence, and Macmillan's son-in-law, Julian Amery, went to Aviation. William Deedes became Minister without Portfolio, Sir Edward Boyle went to Education and Sir Keith Joseph to Housing. Sir Reginald Manningham-Buller became Lord Chancellor. Although some of the new men were more pliable than those they replaced, and Boyle and Joseph were markedly clever, the new team did not look so very much better than the old that the Press and the public were convinced.

By the Saturday it was clear that the reshuffle had been a political disaster, and Macmillan went to Birch Grove to rest. A Liberal MP remarked that 'Greater love hath no man than this, that he lay down his friends for his life', and the mud stuck. For almost a week the Press criticism and parliamentary suspicion continued, dying away only after a reasonably good meeting of the 1922 committee on 19 July. But no one could easily forget such an act of mass disloyalty, and Macmillan's reputation never recovered. Gaitskell made the best of his opportunity in Parliament by observing in the economic debate on 26 July that 'there is really no doubt that this was the act of a desperate man in a desperate situation, and the desperate situation was the steady, remorseless and steep decline of the Conservative Party's fortunes in by-election after by-election'.[83]

With hindsight it must be observed that the decision to dismiss Lloyd was not a bad one, and that Macmillan's only mistake was to panic and hold his reshuffle all at once. There was an urgent need for new blood at the Treasury, and the inadequacies of the previous year must be attributed in part to Lloyd's lack of imagination, as well as the unusually incompetent Treasury forecasts which informed his Budgets. The practice of delegation, which normally allowed Macmillan to concentrate on tricky external problems, had clearly broken down, and put on to the prime minister's shoulders a burden which it was not reasonable for him to bear. Butler's leak was unfortunate, and the consequent panic reflected badly on Macmillan himself.

The next political disaster, the Profumo affair, was a watershed, and one of the few parliamentary episodes to merit singling out as a turning point in Macmillan's political career. The outlines of the story are clearly imprinted on British political memory, though some of the details remain tantalisingly unclear. John (Jack) Profumo, was appointed Secretary of State for War in 1960. In 1961, at Lord Astor's house at Cliveden, he began an affair with Christine Keeler, a semi-professional prostitute. This came to an end by December 1961. It is likely, but not certain, that Keeler was at the same time conducting an affair with the Soviet Naval Attaché, Captain Ivanov. In March 1963 two of Keeler's other lovers were charged, separately, with assaults on her, and the Press became aware of rumours linking her with Profumo. The matter was raised in the Commons, as a security issue, by George Wigg, Labour's self-appointed expert on security matters.[84]

On 22 March 1963 Profumo made a personal statement to the House, denying 'impropriety'. Macmillan evidently believed him, but the Opposition were not tempted to share his confidence in Profumo's honesty, and produced on 9 April a memorandum by Wigg which described not only Profumo's affair but also the mediating rôle of Stephen Ward, an osteopath and acquaintance of Lord Astor, who ostensibly acted as pimp for Keeler. In May, after Harold Wilson had sent in a second letter and included a long note from Ward accusing Profumo of lying to the House, Macmillan began to take the matter seriously and referred it to MI5. On 4 June Profumo confessed that he had had an affair with Keeler and that he had lied to the Commons. Within a week the *News of the World* was serialising Keeler's life story which, though brief (she was only twenty years old), was well stocked with matters of interest to readers. Macmillan, who had realised only at the end of May that this was a major political problem, was obliged to defend his government in the Commons, and finally did so in a debate on 17 June.

It is significant that even with the hindsight of autobiography Macmillan did not see how much damage this incident did to his own standing. His case was good in parts. He had not moved in Profumo's circle, and he had not been told until very late by the Security Services that Keeler might have been asked to obtain nuclear secrets from Profumo. He was aware that the implicit charge against him was that he had not pressed Profumo when the first statement was made, and that he had allowed himself and the House to be deceived. His answer was open: he had thought it better to let the Chief Whip ask the questions, and for his own part he preferred to be loyal to his friends and colleagues until any accusation against them was proven. He found it impossible to conceive that a man would behave as Profumo behaved, so he did not jump to unpalatable conclusions. He was deeply unwilling to talk or even think about sexual impropriety, and, so it would appear, had preferred to ignore the few hints that came to him. Aware that the party might have asked more from its leader, the Whips made it clear to the back bench that Macmillan would resign if his majority were cut. He survived, but only just, with a majority of fifty-seven and the sound of Nigel Birch's denunciation ringing in his ears: 'I myself feel that the time will come very soon when my Right Hon. Friend ought to make way for a much younger colleague.... [he quoted Browning's 'Lost Leader'] "Never glad confident morning again!" – so I hope that the change will not be too long delayed.'

Things duly got worse rather than better. The chairman of the 1922 Committee was known to have talked about a new leader; a Gallup poll was damning; Cabinet colleagues were thought, by Butler, to have muttered in corners; the quality Press was condescendingly critical and outraged by turns. The appointment of Lord Denning as a one-man commission of inquiry into the security aspects of the case deflected some public curiosity, but the trial of Stephen Ward for living off immoral earnings, and Ward's suicide on 3 August, excited it once more. The publication of Denning's report in September gave little foothold to the critics, though: despite some censorious subheadings, Denning concluded that there was less in the Keeler–Profumo–Ward–Ivanov story than met the eye. Gallup polls, and the evidence of the Downing Street and party postbags, suggest that sympathy for Macmillan began to increase after July, and was still increasing when his sudden illness plucked him from office. This in turn suggests that the Profumo affair only confirmed the impression of Macmillan's loss of grip upon the leadership of the party, rather than creating a doubt which had not been there before. Macmillan's political touch had been in question since the Night of the Long Knives, and he had never truly regained it.

· · ·

DUSK

Hindsight lends an inevitability to Macmillan's departure from office in October 1963, but in the summer of that year there was no such clear expectation. The impact of the Test-Ban Treaty, announced to the House on 11 July, burnished his reputation as an international statesman. Though Macmillan himself was overcome with emotion, and the Commons' reaction was favourable, it did not restore public enthusiasm for the government. With the certainty of an election before October 1964, the question of the Tory leadership could not be shirked indefinitely. Macmillan's age was beginning to tell against him: the sudden death of Hugh Gaitskell and the election of Harold Wilson as Labour leader had pointed an unfavourable contrast between youth and experience. Although the Profumo affair was dying away, it had added permanently to the minority of Conservative MPs who wanted a new leader, and reports of 'scheming' in June were a straw in the wind.[85] Macmillan continued to play on the party's reflex loyalties with a successful appearance before the 1922 Committee in July and consoled himself that his government was gaining in the opinion polls, though it was still trailing the opposition. In private, however, he was already beginning to brood about resignation and it seems clear that the metabolic effects of the early stages of prostate disease were contributing to an indecisive moodiness. Throughout August and September he travailed, getting conflicting advice from senior colleagues and Conservative Party officers. By mid-September he had apparently made up his mind sufficiently to inform the Queen that he would not lead the party in the next election.

A symptom of his state of mind was that this 'decision' was almost immediately reversed, and in the very last days before the Party Conference, which was to begin on 8 October, Macmillan was thrashing the matter over with colleagues, especially Lord Home, with his family, especially his son Maurice, and with the party hierarchy. Oliver Poole for the party officers was convinced that he should go. Maurice Macmillan agreed, but Macmillan's brother-in-law, James Stuart, thought that there was support for his staying on. Senior Cabinet colleagues, when asked on 7 October, indicated a majority in support of his staying on to fight the election. He decided that day to go on, and to announce to the full Cabinet on 8 October that he would continue.

It was in the middle of the night of 7–8 October that Macmillan was seized by the 'excruciating pain' of his prostate illness. Despite this, he announced to the Cabinet on 8 October that he intended to carry on to fight the election, and his colleagues, apparently discounting his pallor as the usual hypochondria, accepted his decision.[86] Then, in an extraordinary collapse of mood, he succumbed to despair in a series of interviews with doctors. The doctors persuaded him that he had to have an immediate operation; Macmillan persuaded himself that this meant that he could not carry on. Much controversy has since surrounded the events of 8 October, with some arguing that the late arrival of his usual physician, Sir John Richardson (who was in the Lake District when called), allowed Macmillan to be influenced unduly by the advice of the surgeons who warned that he would be unfit for some months. However the rapid play of feeling is to be interpreted, the consequence was that in the evening of 8 October Macmillan told Butler explicitly that he could not fight the election and that the party must be told. On 9 October he wrote to the Queen warning her that he must resign, and on 10 October he underwent an operation which removed his prostate gland and, as it transpired, gave him twenty more years of remarkably active life.

Macmillan's message to the party was read out by Alec Home to the Party Conference in Blackpool on the afternoon of 10 October. There ensued the most extraordinary and undignified display of naked ambition and mutual backstabbing, which finally undermined the credibility of the Conservative Party's historic methods of choosing its leaders. With two peers, Hailsham and Home, in the ring because recent legislation had allowed them to resign their peerages, the long-serving heir-apparent Butler waiting perpetually for his just recompense, and the late entry of Reginald Maudling as a representative of the post-war generation, both party and country were treated to a spectacle of indecision and mistrust. Hailsham quickly disqualified himself in the eyes of most senior Conservatives by thrusting himself forward as a candidate within hours of the announcement. Macmillan, extraordinarily, took the view that he could not formally resign until he knew how to advise the monarch about his successor. He thus took control from his sickbed of a process of decision in which ultimately only the Cabinet was involved, though MPs and constituency parties were consulted hurriedly. One important result of the haste was that the name of Home emerged late in the proceedings as the only man who could unite the Cabinet, even though he was hardly considered during the consultation of MPs and the constituencies. He was also Macmillan's own clear choice, by the end, and he therefore became prime minister on 18 October, although he would have been thought a rank outsider if the fateful Cabinet meeting of the 8th had decided to look for a successor. Butler, Maudling and Hailsham, abetted by Macleod and Powell, raised their voices in protest and for twenty-four hours it seemed possible that Home would have to form his Cabinet without them; but like most such protests it rapidly collapsed and all but Powell and Macleod, both passionate supporters of Butler, eventually joined. Macmillan's life at the top was suddenly ended.

. . .

NOTES AND REFERENCES

1. CAB 128/31, C[abinet] C[onclusions] (57)4, 21 Jan.
2. CAB 129/85 'Social Services: Possible Economies', C(57)16, 30 Jan. 1957.
3. CAB 129/85 C(57)20 of 30 Jan. 1957; C(57)19 n.d.
4. Macleod, 'Social Service Expenditures', 31 Jan. 1957, PREM 11/1805.
5. Watkinson to Prime Minister, n.d., PREM 11/1816.
6. Harold Macmillan, 'Economies vs. Expenditure', 5 Feb. 1957, PREM 11/1805.
7. Macmillan to Fraser, 17 Feb. 1957, PREM 11/1816.

8. Diary for 9 April 1957, quoted in Harold Macmillan, *Riding the Storm* (London: Macmillan, 1971), p. 348.
9. Leslie to Makins, 11 March 1957; Poole to Macmillan 11 April 1957, PREM 11/1815.
10. It added 0.3 per cent to consumers' purchasing power as a fraction of GNP. Butler's 'October Measures' of 1955, Macmillan's Budget, and the 1958 Budget were more restrictive; all others far more generous. See J.C.R. Dow, *The Management of the British Economy* (Cambridge: Cambridge University Press, 1964), p. 200.
11. Alistair Horne, *Macmillan 1957–1968* (London: Macmillan, 1989), p. 70, quoting a taped interview.
12. Diary, 15 March. 1957, quoted ibid., p. 66.
13. Ibid., quoted in Macmillan, *Riding the Storm*, p. 346.
14. Diary, 19 March 1957, quoted ibid., p. 346.
15. Ibid., p. 347.
16. Macmillan to Macleod, n.d., cited ibid., p. 347.
17. It had been 2.5 per cent when the Conservatives came into office in 1951, drifting steadily up to 5.5 per cent in February 1956. The origin of the September Measures is described in the *Manchester School*, XXXVII (1959).
18. Diary, 17 Sept. 1956, quoted in Macmillan, *Riding the Storm*, p. 356.
19. Birch was Economic Secretary, Powell Financial Secretary.
20. Robert Hall Diaries, 22 Oct. 1957, p. 126.
21. Macmillan, 'Some thoughts which have occurred to me during my short holiday', C(57)194, 1 Sept. 1957, PREM 11/1824.
22. Peter Thorneycroft, 'The Pound Sterling', 4 Sept. 1957, PREM 11/1824, finally circulated as C(57)195.
23. 'Explaining the Economic Situation. Note by the Prime Minister', 4 Oct. 1957, C (57) 225.
24. Harrod to Macmillan, 8 Oct. 1957, PREM 11/1823.
25. Macmillan, *Riding the Storm*, p. 368; Percy Mills to Macmillan, 6 January 1958, PREM 11/2421; R.A. Allen to F. Bishop, 8 Jan. 1958, ibid.
26. Powell in the *Spectator*, 24 April 1971.
27. See the discussion in Andrew Shonfield, *British Economic Policy since the War* (Harmondsworth: Penguin Books, 1958), pp. 248–9.
28. Personal communication.
29. Alec Cairncross and Nina Watts, *The Economic Section 1939–1961* (London: Routledge, 1989), p. 229.
30. A point well made by Dow, *The Management of the British Economy*, p. 200.
31. Samuel Brittan, *Steering the Economy* (Harmondsworth: Penguin Books, 1969), p. 212.
32. Diary, 6 Jan. 1958, quoted in Horne, *Macmillan 1957–1986*, p. 73.
33. Quoted in Macmillan, *Riding the Storm*, p. 371.
34. Ibid., p. 373.
35. Diary, 19 January, quoted ibid., p. 374.
36. Diary, 31 January 1958, quoted in Horne, *Macmillan 1957–1986*, p. 78.
37. Ibid., p. 90, quoting an unspecified diary entry.
38. Macmillan to Heathcoat Amory, 4 March. 1958, PREM 11/2305.
39. Macmillan to F. Bishop, 16 March 1958, ibid.

40. Macmillan to Heathcoat Amory, 2 April 1958, ibid.
41. *H.C. Debs*, 1957–58, Vol. 586, 15 April 1958, col. 55.
42. *The Banker*, CVIII (1958), 283.
43. Diary, 31 July 1958, quoted in Horne, *Macmillan 1957–1968*, p. 141.
44. Ibid., p. 140, quoting an interview.
45. The Harrod–Macmillan correspondence is in PREM 11/2973; it tails off after 1961.
46. 'Employment – Directive by the Prime Minister', 27 Oct. 1958, PREM 11/2311.
47. Heathcoat Amory to Macmillan, with annotations, 23 Oct. 1958, PREM 11/2311. Heathcoat Amory, after a 'good war', had in fact been involved both in business and in active politics.
48. Harrod to Macmillan, 3 Jan. 1959, PREM 11/2973.
49. Dow, *Management of the British Economy*, p. 142.
50. Macmillan to Heathcoat Amory, 27 Feb. 1960, quoted in Macmillan, *Pointing the Way*, p. 221; Heathcoat Amory to Macmillan, 29 Feb. 1960, PREM 11/2962.
51. See Jacques Leruez, *Economic Planning and Politics in Britain* (Oxford: Martin Robertson, 1975).
52. Macmillan to Lloyd, 'Planning', 15 July 1961, PREM 11/3883.
53. Macmillan to Tim Bligh, 23 Feb. 1961, PREM 11/3762.
54. Macmillan, *Pointing the Way*, p. 374.
55. *Incomes Policy: the next step*, Cmnd 1626.
56. C.D. Cohen, *British Economic Policy 1960–1969* (London: Butterworth, 1971), pp. 71–2.
57. 'Transcript of Prime Minister's remarks to the Cabinet on May 28th, 1962', PREM 11/3930. I am grateful to Professor Peter Hennessy for bringing this to my attention soon after it was released under the 30 Year Rule. There is a reasonable précis in Macmillan, *At the End of the Day*, pp. 69–71.
58. See below pp. 259–60.
59. Harold Macmillan, *At the End of the Day* (London: Macmillan, 1973), p. 105; the full text is in *H.C. Debs.*, 1961–2, Vol. 663, 26 July 1962, cols 1751–68.
60. 'Incomes Policy. Memorandum by the Prime Minister', 19 June 1962, CAB 129, C(62)99.
61. Samuel Brittan, *The Treasury under the Tories, 1951–1964* (Harmondsworth: Penguin, 1964), pp. 256–8; Cohen, *British Economic Policy*, p. 71.
62. Brittan, *The Treasury under the Tories*, p. 263.
63. Cited by Horne, *Macmillan 1957–1986*, p. 469 from the Macmillan Archive; it was circulated as Cabinet Paper C(62)201 of 30 Nov. 1962.
64. Douglas-Home had too little time to change his mind; but Heath and Thatcher were both persuaded to reverse themselves on one or other key issue of their economic strategies.
65. Brittan, *The Treasury under the Tories*, p. 289.
66. John Ramsden, *The Making of Conservative Party Policy* (London: Longman, 1980), p. 190.
67. *The Economist*, 12 Jan. 1957, p. 90.

68. David Butler and Richard Rose, *The General Election of 1959* (London: Frank Cass, 1960), p. 24. Butler and Rose based their analysis of tactics on conversations with senior Central Office figures.

69. Butler and Rose, *The General Election of 1959*, p. 31.

70. Michael Fraser, 'Some Thoughts on the Present Situation' 20 Sept. 1957, PREM 11/2248

71. See pp. 228–36 above.

72. Norman Brook to Prime Minister, 14 March 1958, PREM 11/2248.

73. Ramsden, *The Making of Conservative Party Policy*, p. 203.

74. Prime Minister to Chancellor of the Exchequer [a circular to all colleagues], 26 Sep. 1960, PREM 11/3883.

75. Macmillan to Selwyn Lloyd, 1 Feb. 1961, ibid.

76. 'Transcript of Prime Minister's remarks to the Cabinet on May 28th, 1962', PREM 11/3930.

77. 'Incomes Policy. Memorandum by the Prime Minister', 19 June 1962, C(62)99.

78. Ramsden, *Making of Conservative Party Policy*, pp. 212–14.

79. Letter drafted by the CRD for Macmillan to send to a constituent, April 1962, cited ibid., p. 214.

80. Personal communication from Lord Home of the Hirsel.

81. See above, pp. 247–8.

82. Macmillan, *At the End of the Day*, p. 94; D.R. Thorpe, *Selwyn Lloyd* (London: Cape, 1989), p. 340.

83. *H.C. Debs* 1961–2, Vol. 663, 26 July 1962, col. 1735.

84. Wigg's opportunity came with the discussion of the Vassall case. W.J. Vassall, a cipher clerk in the Moscow embassy, was convicted of spying in October 1962. The press found and published material linking Vassall, who was demonstratively homosexual, with Thomas Galbraith, a former junior minister at the Admiralty; and a special tribunal was set up under Lord Radcliffe. Two journalists who had refused to give evidence to the Radcliffe committee were sent to prison in March 1963. The Commons' excitement was ostensibly about freedom of the Press, not about sex.

85. Reported by Lord Home, cited by Horne, *Macmillan 1957–1986*, p. 528.

86. Enoch Powell dissented.

Chapter 11

MACMILLAN IN PERSPECTIVE

Macmillan's rapid recovery from the physical illness which precipitated his resignation left him in an unusual and uncomfortable position, especially after his party went down to defeat under his chosen successor ('an Edward Grey, not an Asquith') in 1964. Though many observers blamed Macmillan's legacy for the débâcle, he himself did not and his belief in his own political skills did not diminish. His massive exercise in autobiography, completed in 1973, helped to convince him that he had been right most of the time. He was therefore a frustrated and sometimes a dangerous elder statesman. Although he expressed private impatience at the difficulties of the Heath government in the early 1970s, he waited a long time before making his public criticisms of the Thatcher administration, finally delivering a notorious speech regretting the 'sale of the family silver' to the Tory Reform Group in November 1985, little more than a year before he died. By then he was remarkable not just for his longevity but for the trenchant intellect and sense of mischief which he preserved almost to the end.

The legend of Supermac was largely Macmillan's own invention, with some retrospective assistance from his official biographer. Alistair Horne's biography, more usefully, has elaborated the fragility and complexity of Macmillan's character, in which anxiety, introversion and a tendency to debilitating depression were represented as strongly as moral courage and caustic wit. But perhaps because Macmillan remained in the public eye as a particularly showy elder statesman, his political position has been subject to the misunderstandings of modern polemic. Especially after the 'family silver' speech, critics from the Conservative Right emphasised his contribution to inflation, through the 1959 Budget, and to the growth of 'collectivism' through

269

the habit of dealing with trade unions and eventually the establishment of the NEDC. The other wing of the party seized on
his 'Middle Way' period but also on his commitment while in
office to the 'One Nation' imagery which left-wing and centrist
Conservatives commonly use to celebrate the politics of consensus. Neither of these is easy to reconcile with the historical
record.

Macmillan can easily be represented as a monetarist and
proto-Thatcherite, both in economic and in social policy. As
Chancellor of the Exchequer and then for a time as prime minister he enthusiastically limited public expenditure, and relied
openly on monetarist tactics (if not a full-blown monetarist
policy) to control inflation. This suited the *rentiers* in his party
very well, and what he used cheerfully to call the 'giveaway'
in his Chancellors' Budgets was as often as not given to the
reasonably well off rather than to the poor. Like most Conservative prime ministers since the war (including Mrs Thatcher),
he enjoyed trimming the defence budget, except for nuclear
weapons, and he was sceptical about government measures
which had the effect of transferring resources from what he
called 'the possessing classes' to others. He inveighed against
restrictions on economic activity, and without ever abandoning
an ironic detachment presided over a Cabinet with leanings towards social libertarianism, for example towards betting shops
and the legalisation of some forms of homosexual activity.

There was an obvious discontinuity between the Macmillan
of 1955–58 and the Macmillan of 1959–63. During 1958 he embraced the idea of expansion and encouraged his Chancellors
to a series of measures which had the effect of overheating the
economy without providing the means to supply the demand
which fiscal largesse had created. After that point Macmillan's
governments were committed to demand-management as their
main weapon of economic policy. It was used with ever increasing enthusiasm to protect the balance of payments and the
value of the pound. From this period grew the legend of the
'Macmillan Cycle', much criticised by economists such as Sam
Brittan and taken into the folk-memory of the Conservative
Party as a reason for not trying to intervene counter-cyclically
as Keynes and his followers might have suggested.

But it is difficult to argue that this justifies modern criticisms of Macmillan's fundamental policy. Many of the errors
of Heathcoat Amory, Lloyd and Maudling can be attributed to

the lack of sound information and forecasting ability, so that the Treasury's intervention amplified the business cycle rather than smoothing it down; they were comparable in that sense with the 'Barber boom' of 1972 or the 'Lawson boom' of 1987. Macmillan's ministries were further hampered by their commitment to a strong pound. This might have been mistaken, but it is not the mistake for which he is usually castigated.

Another important dimension of Macmillan's politics was the ease with which he used social and economic policy to reinforce the electoral position of the Conservative Party. Although the loyal Michael Fraser found reason to criticise his ministerial colleagues for lack of focus in their use of policy weapons before the 1959 election, Macmillan himself had a consistent record of building up the 'possessing classes', both by increasing their numbers by such means as a private housing programme and by rewarding with fiscal generosity the *rentiers* who existed already. Without much sentiment for the 'proletarian hides' of the organised and unionised working classes who wanted a socialist order, he was content to encourage social mobility (so long as it did not reach the aristocracy) and individual prosperity for working-class families. The one instrument of policy from which he tended to shrink was unemployment, but this again supported the effort to consolidate an electoral coalition behind the Conservative Party.

Macmillan would have wished to be remembered as an international statesman. The essence of his policy was to maintain British influence in the world by finesse rather than force. He consistently overestimated what could be achieved by attaching Britain to the policy of the United States and bending American policy to British interests. The potent metaphor of the British as Greeks to the American Romans blinded him to the inconsistencies between British and American interests, and allowed him to believe, even after Suez, that the United States would be prepared to favour British interests over those of other Western states. In return he was anxious to give the Americans as little reason as possible to withhold assistance. This exaggerated concern for the 'special relationship', among other misapprehensions, fatally crippled his approach to the Common Market in 1962.

In contrast he suffered from rather fewer illusions in his dealing with the end of empire. Macmillan could see, from the beginning of his premiership, that the colonies would cost too much to keep. His objective was to get rid of them with the minimum damage to British political and strategic interests. The policy questions, which he generally left to his colonial secretaries and, for the Central African Federation, to Butler were often intractable but rarely as tricky as the difficulties they caused for the Conservative Party. While apparently sharing his party's discomfort at the contemplation of majority rule in the countries of the former African empire, he managed to deflect the attacks of his Conservative opponents by ignoring them and appealing wearily to historic inevitability. The Winds of Change speech, above all, reflected a realism which was beyond the grasp of many of his back-benchers; nevertheless, like so many of Macmillan's insights, it did not lead to decisive action to solve the problems which it analysed.

But above all he was an *aficionado* of the Cold War. Without the consistent hostility and mutual suspicion between the West and the Soviet bloc which characterised the 1950s and early 1960s, none of Macmillan's foreign policies would have made sense. Though a self-proclaimed economiser in defence expenditure, he assumed without agonising reflection that Britain's defence should consume a higher proportion of the national wealth than in any other European country, with all the consequences that fact had for other aspects of policy. He told the Commons in 1958 that 'never has the threat of Russian and Soviet Communism been so great, or the need for countries to organise themselves against it so urgent'.[1] He assumed a world rôle, where other European nations saw a continental rôle for themselves. He assumed that sterling would exist as a reserve currency for the West and for allies of the West throughout the world. He assumed that Britain had a unique rôle to play in Europe but not of it, because of a divine mission to cement the alliance between Western Europe and the United States against the Soviet threat. Each of these propositions now seems contestable, but without them his policies would have led nowhere.

Macmillan made much of his past. His play-acting as a faded Edwardian in the 1950s was an agreeable joke. More seriously, he used his own experience in the Great War, as a Northern MP between the wars, and particularly his opposition to Chamberlain's foreign policy, as reference points in his presentation of himself and his policies when he was prime minister. There was a cynicism, but also a nervousness in his self-regard. In

1961 he composed a classic cameo:

> Mr Gaitskell accuses me of what he calls Edwardian nonchalance –
> what others have called unflappability. I think if he had a little more
> experience of life he would know that sometimes in dangerous mo-
> ments it is advisable, even if one feels alarm, to cultivate an outward
> show of confidence. I learned that in early youth under fire on the
> battlefield. Unfortunately, for reasons which I wholly understand,
> this experience was not vouchsafed to Mr Gaitskell, Mr Wilson, Mr
> Brown, Mr Jay, and the other leading members of the Labour front
> bench.

This gem was entrusted to George Christ, who was in charge
of wounding observations at Conservative Central Office, 'for
some suitable Garden Party or possibly even Party Conference'.
Even the normally brazen Christ found it difficult to stomach,
and replied firmly that it really ought to come from some other
minister, not Macmillan himself. Macmillan, on reflection,
agreed.[2] He was also inclined to overdo his private joke about
his age and infirmity. During the Suez crisis, even before he
became prime minister, he told the Commons that 'I could also
look forward ... if these unlikely events had not taken place
and when I had reached what is the end of, normally, the last
decade of one's life, political life at any rate, to retirement from
many of these troubles'. At this, some impatient Honourable
Members interjected 'Cheer up.'[3] In later years he was more
vulnerable than he liked to pretend to the charge that he had
lost his touch. Although he told colleagues who protested at
the satires of the television programme 'That Was The Week
That Was' that 'It is a good thing to be laughed at. It is better
than to be ignored',[5] but he was often worried that he was
genuinely suffering the effects of age and tiredness.

The record suggests, though, that these references to the
past were largely oratorical tricks, and even the constant Munich references were symbolic utterances as much as guiding
principles of action. If he could kindle his audience's memories and its prejudices, especially against the men of Munich
or the experience of the dole-queues, he could move them
towards the objective of the moment, whatever that objective
might be. When Macmillan began to believe his own rhetoric
of the past, as he clearly did over the Anglo-American relationship, he fast began to make mistakes. The more successful
Macmillan was the relentless innovator: building houses, in-

venting Premium Bonds, wrenching like an economist's Mr Toad at the controls of the stop–go economy, pulling together a hasty pastiche of French economic planning machinery into NEDC, negotiating a Test-Ban Treaty, or marching the Conservative Party towards a politically and economically united Europe by reminding them of their historic hatred for the French. So fearless was he of innovation that he could rarely resist the comparison with two fiercely innovative Conservatives of the 19th century, Peel and Disraeli. On more than one occasion he reminded colleagues that 'it is always a good thing to seize the Whigs' clothes while they are bathing, it is a very old Conservative tradition.'[6]

He also developed, towards the end of his premiership, a refreshing impatience with the conservatism of the party in power, even though it was his own party under his own leadership. This was evident in his teasing of Selwyn Lloyd: 'I suppose you read the *Daily Worker*. It is much the best paper for us to study.'[7] It could also be heard in his private remarks to Cabinet as he introduced his incomes policy in May 1962 with the advice that 'we must leap forward in the same kind of way and in the same kind of spirit that we should have done had we been now in Opposition instead of in power for eleven years. We must appear full of life and vigour with some new plans to put before the people.'[8] Not long before that meeting, complaining about a Treasury ruling on racing cars because 'my grandsons tell me that we have lost the sympathy of youth and enterprise', he delivered a broadside against the hapless Selwyn Lloyd which could have been aimed at the whole party:

Whenever Britain seems to excel or have the chance to excel in anything, H.M.G. clamps down. We have the drivers; not in future the cars. Drab; second-rate; without zest or pride. That's what we risk Britain and British people becoming.[9]

By the end of his premiership, Macmillan's attitude to the Conservative Party had nearly come full circle: the rebel of the 1930s was a rebel still.

It is a stern test of statesmanship that a prime minister should leave Britain stronger, diplomatically or economically, than he or she found it. None have passed it this century, and Macmillan certainly did not. But he had a broader vision than most leaders of the 1950s and 1960s, and greater courage in facing change. In his time he avoided many of the obvious pitfalls and rescued a little dignity from the wreckage. One man alone can do little more.

.   .   .

NOTES AND REFERENCES

1. *H.C. Debs*, 1957–58, vol. 577, 5 Nov. 1957, col. 40.
2. Macmillan to Christ, 30 July 1961 and Christ to Macmillan, 1 Aug. 1961, PREM 11/3479.
3. 4, 1956–57, vol. 560, 12 Nov. 1956, col. 688.
5. Macmillan to William Deedes, 10 Dec. 1962, PREM 11/3479.
6. See e.g. Macmillan to Selwyn Lloyd, 15 July 1961, PREM 11/3883.
7. Macmillan to Lloyd, 3 October 1961, Ibid.
8. 'Transcript of Prime Minister's remarks to Cabinet on May 28th, 1962', PREM 11/3930.
9. Macmillan to Lloyd, 28 Feb. 1961, PREM 11/3883.

CHRONOLOGY

1894	*February 10*	Born, 52 Cadogan Place, London SW
1906		Scholar of Eton
1912		Classical Exhibitioner, Balliol College, Oxford
1914	*March*	Elected Junior Treasurer, Oxford Union
	October	Commissioned King's Royal Rifle Corps
1915	*August*	To France with 4th Bn, Grenadier Guards
	28 September	Wounded at Loos
1916	*20 July*	Wounded on the Somme
	15 September	Wounded near Ginchy and evacuated to England
1919	*March*	Appointed ADC to the Duke of Devonshire, Governor-General of Canada
1920	*21 April*	Married to Lady Dorothy Cavendish
		Enters Macmillan publishers
1923	*December*	Stands unsuccessfully as Conservative candidate for Stockton-on-Tees at the general election
1924	*October*	Elected for Stockton
1927		Joint author of *Industry and the State*

1928		Helps Winston Churchill with Industrial De-rating Bill
1929	*May*	Loses Stockton in general election
		Dorothy Macmillan commences lifelong affair with Robert Boothby
1930		Expresses qualified support for Mosley Memorandum
		Supports Beaverbrook's campaign against Baldwin's leadership of the Conservative Party
1931		Nervous breakdown
	October	Re-elected for Stockton in general election
1932	*March*	*The State and Industry*
	May	*The Next Step*
1933	*December*	*Reconstruction*
1935		Helps to form *Next Five Years'* group
1936	*June*	Resigns Tory Whip over Abyssinia
1937	*June*	Reapplies for the Whip, June
1938	*December*	*The Middle Way*
1940	*February*	Mission to Finland
	May	Appointed Parliamentary Secretary, Ministry of Supply
1942	*February*	Parliamentary Under-Secretary for the Colonies
	December	Minister-Resident in North Africa
1943	*21 February*	Injured in air-crash, 21 February
	May	Axis surrender in North Africa
	June	Becomes Minister-Resident for Mediterranean theatre
	July	Negotiates Italian Armistice
1944	*October*	Liberation of Greece, from October liberation of Yugoslavia

277

1945	*May*	Klagenfurt Cossack episode
	May	Appointed Secretary of State for Air
	July	Defeated at Stockton in general election
	November	Elected in by-election for Bromley
		Joins Opposition front bench
1947	*May*	Contributes to *The Industrial Charter*
1949	*August*	Delegate to Council of Europe
1951		Minister of Housing
1952		Presses for active European policy
1953	*December*	300,000 houses target reached
1954	*October*	Appointed Minister of Defence
1955	*April*	Appointed Foreign Secretary in new government by Eden
	December	Appointed Chancellor of the Exchequer
1956	*April*	Premium Bond budget
		Advocates 'Plan G' for European Free Trade Area
	November	Suez crisis
1957	*January*	Appointed Prime Minister
		At Home:
	January	Imposes financial stringency on Government departments with help of Thorneycroft
		Initiates Defence White Paper
	March	Industrial unrest
	September	Balance of payments crisis in September leads to further spending cuts and the Estimates Crisis
	September	'Steering Committee' for Party set up
		Abroad:
	March	Bermuda Conference with Eisenhower

1957	*March*	Archbishop Makarios released
	April	'Plan G' negotiations commenced
	June	Commonwealth Conference in London
	July	Intervention in Oman, July
	July	Macmillan begins negotiations towards Test- Ban treaty
	October	'Declaration of Common Purpose' with United States
1958		*At Home:*
	January	Thorneycroft resigns
	February	Industrial unrest
	April	Heathcoat Amory's first Budget
		Abroad
	January	Macmillan's Commonwealth tour
	May	Charles de Gaulle becomes French prime minister
	July	Iraqi monarchy overthrown
	August	Qemoy and Matsu bombardment begins
	July	Macmillan begins to negotiate Cyprus settlement
	November	Berlin crisis
	December	French reject Common Market–EFTA deal
1959		*At Home:*
	March	Expansionist Budget
	October	General election victory
		Abroad:
	February	Macmillan visits Russia
		Proposes summit conference
	February	Cyprus agreement signed
	February	Riots in Central African Federation
	November	EFTA agreement signed

1960   *At Home:*

January	Bank rate forced up
March	'Standstill Budget'
July	Lloyd succeeds Amory as Chancellor
November	Macmillan chairs unemployment enquiry

Abroad:

January	African tour
February	'Winds of Change' speech, Cape Town
February	Monckton Commission goes to Central African Federation
March	Sharpeville massacre
March	Macmillan visits Washington to procure Skybolt missile
May	Paris summit conference
July	War in Congo begins
December	Macmillan prepares 'Grand Design' document, December–January
December	London Conference on Central African federation

1961   *At Home:*

April	Lloyd's 'regulators' Budget
July	'Little Budget' introduces Pay Pause
September	National Economic Development Commission launched

Abroad:

March	Macmillan meets Kennedy at Key West
March	Commonwealth Conference on South Africa
May	Macmillan begins negotiations on 'tripartitism' with France
August	Common Market application renewed
August	Berlin Wall erected
December	'Congo bombs' crisis
December	Bermuda meeting

1962   *At Home:*

March	Orpington by-election
12 July	'Night of the Long Knives'
July	National Incomes Commission launched
September	Vassall case

Abroad:

March	Disarmament talks recommence, Geneva
March	Butler put in charge of Central African Federation business
October	Cuban Missile Crisis
December	Dean Acheson's West Point speech declares Britain's global rôle 'about played out'
December	Skybolt cancelled, Polaris bought

1963   *At Home:*

March	Profumo affair breaks
June	Profumo resigns
September	Denning Report
9 October	Macmillan resigns because of ill-health

Abroad:

January	French veto on Common Market entry
June	Kenyan self-government
July	Test-Ban Treaty

FURTHER READING

SOURCES

Macmillan's own correspondence and papers, evidently volu-
minous, were used by Alistair Horne in the official biography
but remain closed to historians. Macmillan also kept an extensive diary for much of his life. Extracts from his period
as Minister-Resident are published in his *War Diaries* (London:
Macmillan, 1984), and his memoirs, especially of the premiership, obviously depend on the diaries and reprint copious extracts from them. Like most prime ministers, Macmillan made
extensive and arguably improper use of government papers in
his memoirs, in which he often paraphrases Cabinet papers
when he does not reproduce them verbatim.

Primary sources for his early political life are thinner, but
there is useful material in the Lloyd George and Beaverbrook
collections (in the House of Lords Record Office) about his
political tergiversations in the 1930s. Among printed primary
sources for that period, Stuart Ball (ed.), *Parliament and Politics
in the Age of Baldwin and MacDonald: the diaries of Sir Cuthbert
Headlam, 1924-1935* (London: Historians' Press, 1992), are
the recollections of a County Durham MP who was as close
to Macmillan as any politician; but he made little impact on
other published diarists, such as Harold Nicolson, Hugh Dalton, Lord Crawford, or Chips Channon (except for references
to the Boothby affair deleted by Robert Rhodes James when he
edited *The Diaries of Chips Channon* for Weidenfeld and Nicolson in 1967).

For the war period his own diaries, mentioned above, can be supplemented by skimpy references to his work preserved in the Public Record Office in the records of the Ministry of Supply and the Colonial Office, and more fully by his direct correspondence with Churchill when he was Minister-Resident, in PREM 3, and his telegrams which are in FO 660. As an ambitious Conservative in opposition he left some mark on the papers of the Conservative Research Department in the Bodleian Library (much of it critical commentary on his views or pretensions by Research Department staff); and inevitably he also made an impact on R.A. Butler's papers, now at Trinity College, Cambridge, in which Butler's own memoranda, especially in boxes G18 to G33, provide intermittent commentaries on the rest of Macmillan's career.

As Minister of Housing and Minister of Defence his office correspondence is of course preserved in the Public Record Office, but other sources for that part of his career include his comments on Europe which are more conveniently found in *Documents on British Policy Overseas*, series 2, I, (1950–52) than in the Foreign Office papers; and his participation in Cabinet discussions and in dialogue with the prime minister are found respectively in Cabinet minutes and papers, CAB 128 and 129, and in PREM 11. For his service as Foreign Secretary the principal source is FO 371, usefully supplemented by the diaries of Sir Evelyn Shuckburgh printed in *Descent to Suez: diaries 1951-56* (London: Weidenfeld and Nicolson, 1986); there is also correspondence with Eden in the Avon papers in the University of Birmingham which in addition covers the next phase in his career, the Chancellorship of the Exchequer. As Chancellor his office papers are in T 172, with a useful special set on the Suez crisis in T 236; the diaries of Sir Robert Hall, printed in Alec Cairncross (ed.), *The Robert Hall Diaries, Vol. II 1954-1961* (London: Unwin Hyman, 1991) contain some acute comment.

The volume of government paper on his premiership is immense, and at the time of writing it is 'open' for the period until 1962. A great deal of sensitive, and therefore interesting, material has been withheld from the Public Record Office, especially on nuclear policy and on Anglo-American and Anglo-Soviet relations. It must be said, though, that this leaves plenty to be going on with, and the best place to start is undoubtedly PREM 11, the prime minister's Private Office papers. Most of the material by Macmillan which is eventually found in Cabinet papers in CAB 129 can also be located here, along with a great deal else. Because of Macmillan's consistent interest in the party-political consequences of government policy, there is much to be gained by following issues through from PREM 11 to the papers of the Conservative Party and the Conservative Research Department. Conservative Party papers also offer insights into Macmillan's electoral performance. Lord Woolton's 'diary', in the Bodleian Library, contains a few gems from this period, as do the papers of Walter Monckton in the same archive. Of the published sources for the period, few are truly primary, except for Harold Evans, *Downing Street Diary: the Macmillan years 1957–63* (London: Hodder and Stoughton, 1981), the recollections of the Downing Street press officer.

. . .

BIOGRAPHY AND AUTOBIOGRAPHY

Macmillan's own six volumes (*Winds of Change 1914–1939* (London: Macmillan, 1966); *The Blast of War 1939–1945* (1967); *Tides of Fortune 1945–1955* (1969); *Riding the Storm 1956–1959* (1971); *Pointing the Way 1959–1961* (1972); *At the End of the Day 1961–1963* (1973)) constitute a *tour de force* of historical self-justification, overwhelming subsequent historians with detail and a plausible, sometimes witty and self-deprecating account of the predicament of an ambitious politician. They are valuable principally for the quantity of primary material which they reprint, especially from the private diaries.

The first, slightly premature attempt at a retrospective biography was Emrys Hughes, *Macmillan: portrait of a politician* (London: Allen and Unwin, 1962), which in keeping with the time in which it was written portrayed its subject as a profound cynic. A more balanced account appeared in Anthony Sampson, *Macmillan: a study in ambiguity* (Harmondsworth: Penguin, 1967), raising an interest in the intricacies of Macmillan's political *persona* which was developed in Larry Siedentop's essay, 'Mr Macmillan and the Edwardian Style', in Vernon Bogdanor and Robert Skidelsky (eds), *The Age of Affluence* (London: Macmillan, 1970). By contrast Nigel Fisher's *Harold Macmillan: a biography* (London: Weidenfeld and Nicolson, 1982) seems slight and superfluous.

The official biography by Alistair Horne is in two volumes, *Macmillan, 1894–1956* (London: Macmillan, 1988) and *Macmillan 1957–1986* (1989). Its strengths are the rich mine of personal recollection tapped by a biographer who enjoyed his subject's confidence, and its exclusive use of Macmillan's own diary and archive; some material is printed which does not appear in the autobiography. Its weakness is its majestic indifference to almost every other primary source which might bear on Macmillan's life, except for some material from American presidential papers. In particular it neglects British government records and the available private collections of British politicians. It is therefore in some respects an extension of Macmillan's own projection of himself, though it is helpful and candid about aspects of Macmillan's private life which were entirely omitted from the autobiography.

MACMILLAN'S WRITINGS

Macmillan tried to make his political career by writing extensively for the press when he was being ignored in Parliament. His output of books and pamphlets, all helpfully published by Macmillan, began with *Industry and the State* (1927), written with John Loder, Oliver Stanley and Robert Boothby. Two pamphlets, *The State and Industry* (1932), and *The Next Step* (1932), were followed by *Reconstruction: a plea for National Unity*, a substantial volume published in 1933. He can safely be accounted author of at least part of *The Next Five Years: an essay in political agreement* (1935), and, with the help of Allan Young, of *The Middle Way* (1938). *The Price of Peace*, a pamphlet published in October 1938, was his last pre-war work. Between the end of the war and his return to office his output was confined to the press and a number of pamphlets drafted and redrafted within the Conservative Party machine. He did not return to authorship until his resignation; besides the autobiography he produced *The Middle Way: Twenty Years After* in 1966, which reprinted the original work with a lecture, first delivered in 1956, explaining to his own satisfaction how the Conservative Party was the natural party of reforming government, and *The Past Masters: politics and politicians* in 1975.

SPECIAL TOPICS AND PERIODS

Party politics in the 1920s is unevenly covered in the literature. John Ramsden, *The Age of Balfour and Baldwin* (Harlow: Longman, 1978) is an authoritative account, concentrating on the party organisation but covering the problems of minorities such as the YMCA. There is also much material and valuable insight in Stuart Ball, *Baldwin and the Conservative Party: the crisis of 1929–1931* (London: Yale, 1988); in Philip Williamson, *National Crisis and National Government* (Cambridge: Cambridge University Press, 1992); and in Robert Self, *Tories and Tariffs: the Conservative Party and the politics of tariff reform, 1922–1932* (New York: Garland, 1986).

A longer tradition of writing about the 1930s bears more directly on Macmillan, starting with Arthur Marwick, 'Middle Opinion in the 1930s: planning, progress and political agreement', *English Historical Review*, 79 (1964). Arthur Marwick, *Clifford Allen: the open conspirator* (Edinburgh: Oliver and Boyd, 1964), is complemented by Martin Gilbert (ed.), *Plough my own Furrow* (London: Longman, 1965) on the relationship between Macmillan and Allen; other aspects of Macmillan's 'reconstruction' politics are covered in John Campbell, *The Goat in the Wilderness: Lloyd George's Political Career, 1922-1945* (London: Jonathan Cape, 1977), Max Nicholson, 'The 1930s: Organisation, Structure, People', in John Pinder (ed.), *Fifty Years of Political and Economic Planning* (London: Heinemann Educational Books, 1981), and L.P. Carpenter, 'Corporatism in Britain, 1930–1945', *Journal of Contemporary History*, XI (1976), 3–25. Simon Haxey (pseudonym), *Tory M.P.* (London: Gollancz, 1937) was fairly tolerant of Macmillan in the midst of a wholesale condemnation of the Tory Party. See also Robert Rhodes James, *Bob Boothby: a portrait* (London: Hodder and Stoughton, 1991).

Appeasement and anti-appeasement is the stuff of which historical myths are made. Macmillan was rather more circumspect in his opposition to Chamberlain's policies than he allowed to appear in his memoirs, but so were most of those who later wrote about it. One must therefore turn to Neville Thompson, *The Anti-appeasers: Conservative opposition to appeasement in the 1930s* (Oxford: Clarendon Press, 1971), Anthony

Eden, *Facing the Dictators* (London: Cassell, 1962), Martin Gilbert, *Winston Churchill Vol. V* (London: William Heinemann, 1976), and Maurice Cowling, *The Impact of Hitler: British politics and British policy 1933–1940* (Cambridge: Cambridge University Press, 1975), which say much about anti-appeasement but less about Macmillan. Adrian Smith, 'Macmillan and Munich: the open conspirator', *Dalhousie Review*, 68 (1988), 235–47, tackles the question head on, and Jorgen Rasmussen, 'Government and intraparty opposition: dissent within the Conservative Party in the 1930s', *Political Studies*, 19 (1971), 172–83 is also useful.

For Macmillan's early war J.A. Bayer, 'British policy towards the Russian–Finnish Winter War', *Canadian Journal of History*, 16 (1981), 27–65 provides a useful background, and for his stint at the Colonial Office M. Cowen and N. Westcott, 'British imperial economic policy during the war' in D. Killingray and R. Rathbone (eds.), *Africa and the Second World War* (Basingstoke: Macmillan, 1987). For his service in the Mediterranean the essential background is Michael Howard, *Grand Strategy, Volume 4* (London: HMSO, 1972) and the same author's *The Mediterranean Strategy in the Second World War* (London: Weidenfeld and Nicolson, 1968). See also John Charmley, 'Harold Macmillan and the making of the French Committee of Liberation', *International History Review*, 4 (1982), 553–67. The Greek episode has been particularly well covered, notably in E.D. Smith, *Victory of a Sort: the British in Greece 1941–1946* (London: Hale, 1988). On the Balkans, see P. Auty and R. Clogg, eds., *British Policy towards Wartime Resistance in Yugoslavia and Greece* (London: Macmillan, 1975). The 'Klagenfurt conspiracy' first appeared in Nicholas Bethell, *The Last Secret* (London: Deutsch, 1977), then in Nikolai Tolstoy, *Stalin's Secret War* (London: Cape, 1981), Nikolai Tolstoy, 'The Klagenfurt Conspiracy', *Encounter*, 60 (May 1983), 24–37, and finally Nikolai Tolstoy, *The Minister and the Massacres* (London: Hutchinson, 1986). It was deflated by Robert Knight, 'Harold Macmillan and the Cossacks: Was there a Klagenfurt Conspiracy?', *Intelligence and National Security*, 1 (1986), 234–54, and finally destroyed by a libel judgement. Relations with Eden are well covered in Robert Rhodes James, *Anthony Eden* (London: Weidenfeld and Nicolson, 1986), which continues to be a useful source.

On his return from Europe Macmillan became enmeshed

in a political system which was not entirely ready to accept him. Besides the Eden biography, Anthony Howard has much to say in *R.A.B: the life of R.A. Butler* (London: Cape, 1987). On the party in general J.D. Hoffman, *The Conservative Party in Opposition 1945–1951* (London: Macgibbon and Kee, 1964), though dated, remains useful, together with John Ramsden, *The Making of Conservative Party Policy: the Conservative Research Department since 1929* (London: Longman, 1980), which discusses the Industrial Charter and is also illuminating on government–party relationships throughout Macmillan's premiership. Macmillan's ministerial contributions under Churchill are discussed rather blandly in Anthony Seldon, *Churchill's Indian Summer: the Conservative government 1951–1955* (London: Hodder and Stoughton, 1981), and more sharply, as to Housing, in Harriet Jones's unpublished London Ph.D. thesis 'The Social Policy of the Conservative Party, 1951–1955' (1992).

Richard Lamb, *The Failure of the Eden Government* (London: Sidgwick and Jackson, 1987), though somewhat breathless and inordinately critical of Macmillan's part in the Messina affair, is useful for many aspects of his ministerial rôle in these years. For Macmillan's short stint as foreign secretary it is necessary to go to treatments of particular themes over longer periods, which therefore tend to be useful also for his premiership. Notable among these is J. Baylis, *Anglo-American Defence Relations 1939–1980: the special relationship* (London: Macmillan, 1981). At the Exchequer his work becomes part of the general problem of British economic policy-making, and must therefore be studied in J.C.R. Dow, *The Management of the British Economy 1945–1960* (Cambridge: Cambridge University Press, 1965) and in Sam Brittan, *Steering the Economy* (Harmondsworth: Penguin, 1972). The Suez affair was a problem by itself, which has produced a huge volume of historical writing since the records were partially released in 1987. David Carlton in *The Suez Crisis* (Oxford: Basil Blackwell, 1989) is characteristically hard-hitting, as befits the author of *Anthony Eden* (London: Allen Lane, 1981). W.R. Louis and Roger Owen (eds), *Suez 1956: the crisis and its consequences* (Oxford: Oxford University Press, 1989) contains a number of extremely authoritative chapters, as does S.I. Troen and M. Shemesh (eds), *The Suez-Sinai Crisis, 1956: retrospective and reappraisal* (London: Cass, 1989); some of these, such as Julian Amery's chapter in Troen and Shemesh and Max Beloff's in Louis and Owen, cover the political consequences during Macmillan's premiership. W. Scott Lucas, *Divided We Stand: Britain, the U.S. and the Suez crisis* (London: Hodder and Stoughton, 1991) gives a blow-by-blow account at policy-making level, including the discussions with the United States in which Macmillan was most involved and arguably most at fault. The financial side is discussed by Diane Kunz in her contribution to the Louis and Owen collection, 'The Importance of Having Money: the economic diplomacy of the Suez crisis', pp. 215–32, and by Lewis Johnman in 'Defending the pound: the economics of the Suez crisis, 1956' in T. Gorst, L. Johnman and W.S. Lucas (eds), *Postwar Britain 1945–64* (London: Pinter, 1989), pp. 166–81. In the same volume W. Scott Lucas discusses 'Neustadt revisited: a new look at Suez and the Anglo-American "alliance"', pp. 182–202. Amid all this exact and exacting modern scholarship it is refreshing to return to the great self-justifying simplicities of Selwyn Lloyd, *Suez, 1956* (London: Cape, 1978) or Anthony Nutting, *No End of a Lesson* (London: Constable, 1967).

Once the premiership is reached it is all the more difficult to focus on Macmillan as an individual; so much of the ebb and flow of historical interpretation is about the Macmillan government as a whole, rather than about Macmillan himself. Moreover the Macmillan governments have thus far attracted rather less scholarly attention than the Churchill and Eden governments which preceded them and whose documentary spoor has been longer in the public eye, or even than the Wilson governments, whose history can be written without time-consuming recourse to the public records. This is partly because his governments contained no expert diarists, besides himself. One must therefore rely on the usual crop of memoirs, such as R.A. Butler's *Art of the Possible* (London: Hamilton, 1971); Lord Kilmuir, *Political Adventure: Memoirs* (London: Weidenfeld and Nicolson, 1962); John Boyd-Carpenter, *Way of Life* (London: Sidgwick and Jackson, 1988); Reginald Maudling, *Memoirs* (London: Sidgwick and Jackson, 1978); Lord Home, *The Way the Wind Blows* (London: Collins, 1975); and, perhaps most usefully, John Wyndham, *Wyndham and Children First* (1968), written by Macmillan's unpaid secretary and longstanding friend. More memorable than most of these are Clive Irving, Ron Hall and Jeremy Wallington, *Scandal '63* (London: Heinemann, 1963) and Wayland Young, *The Profumo Affair: As-*

pects of Conservatism (Harmondsworth: Penguin, 1964). Interest in the Profumo affair, or rather the fate of Stephen Ward, has recently been revived by Anthony Summers and Stephen Dorril, *Honeytrap: the secret worlds of Stephen Ward* (London: Weidenfeld and Nicolson, 1987) and in Phillip Knightley and Caroline Kennedy, *An Affair of State: the Profumo case and the framing of Stephen Ward* (London: Cape, 1987); and in Ben Pimlott, *Harold Wilson* (London: Harper Collins, 1992) there is an interesting account of the Labour party's use of the affair to rattle the government.

On domestic policy the big issue was the economy. In addition to J.C.R. Dow's magisterial work cited above, it is necessary to consult the rather technical C.D. Cohen, *British Economic Policy 1960–1969* (London: Butterworth, 1971), which sadly lacks any narrative account and must therefore be supplemented by Samuel Brittan's tendentious analysis in *Steering the Economy* (Harmondsworth: Penguin Books, 1971). Andrew Shonfield, *British Economic Policy since the War* (2nd edn, Harmondsworth: Penguin, 1959) was a remarkable contemporary study, as was Michael Shanks, *The Stagnant Society* (Harmondsworth: Penguin, 1961). The tradition of criticism is carried on in F. Blackaby, *British Economic Policy 1960–1974* (Cambridge: Cambridge University Press, 1978) and in S. Pollard, *The Wasting of the British Economy* (London: Croom Helm, 1982). Sir Leo Pliatzky, in *Getting and Spending* (Oxford: Basil Blackwell, 1982) offers an unusually sharp Treasury memoir, complemented by Alec Cairncross and Nina Watts, *The Economic Section* (London: Routledge, 1989). Discussion of the administration's late conversion to planning can be found in Keith Middlemas, *Power, Competition and the State, Vol I: Britain in Search of Balance 1940–1961* (Basingstoke: Macmillan, 1986) and *Vol II: Threats to the Postwar Settlement 1961–1974* (Basingstoke: Macmillan, 1990).

On external affairs the menu is richer, not least because of the salience of Anglo-American relations and the enormous literary productivity of retired American politicians. The general background is given by F.S. Northedge, *Descent from power: British foreign policy, 1945–1973* (London: Allen and Unwin, 1974). W.R. Louis and Hedley Bull (eds), *The 'Special' Relationship: Anglo-American relations since 1945* (Oxford: Oxford University Press, 1986) collects a large expert team; some special Anglo-American issues are covered in W.R. Louis, *Imperialism at Bay: the United States and the de-colonization of the British*

Empire (Oxford: Oxford University Press, 1977); Alan Dobson, *The Politics of the Anglo-American Economic Special Relationship 1940–1987* (Brighton: Harvester Press, 1987); David Nunnerly, *President Kennedy and Britain* (London: Bodley Head, 1972); Timothy J. Botti, *The Long Wait: the forging of the Anglo-American nuclear alliance, 1945–1958* (New York: Greenwood, 1987); Margaret Gowing, 'Britain, America and the bomb', in David Dilks, ed., *Retreat from Power, Vol II* (London: Macmillan, 1981), pp. 120–37; Richard D. Mahoney, *JFK: Ordeal in Africa* (New York: Oxford University Press, 1983), Richard Neustadt, *Alliance Politics* (New York: Columbia University Press, 1970). General works on American foreign policy which bear especially on Macmillan's premiership include George Ball, *The Past has Another Pattern* (New York: Norton, 1982); Dwight D. Eisenhower, *The White House Years: waging peace, 1956–1961* (London: Heinemann, 1966); William Kaufmann, *The McNamara Strategy* (New York: Harper and Row, 1964); Robert McNamara, *The Essence of Security: reflections in office* (London: Hodder and Stoughton, 1968). Graham Allison, *Essence of Decision* (Boston: Little, Brown, 1972) examines the Cuban Missile Crisis, which is also laboriously covered, along with much else, in Arthur Schlesinger, *A Thousand Days: John F. Kennedy in the White House* (London: Deutsch, 1965).

Besides the pleasures and pains of the special relationship, Macmillan's contribution to decolonisation can best be understood against the background of John Darwin, *Britain and Decolonisation: the retreat from Empire in the postwar world* (Basingstoke: Macmillan, 1987). See also R.F. Holland, 'The Imperial Factor in British Strategies from Attlee to Macmillan', *Journal of Imperial and Commonwealth History*, 12 (1983), 165–86. On the unlamented Central African Federation, see Roy Welensky, *Welensky's 4000 Days* (London: Collins, 1964).

Last, the question of Europe. Miriam Camps, *Britain and the European Community* (Oxford: Oxford University Press, 1964) is the first, and still the most useful, account of the evolution of policy and the negotiations leading up to the first rejection, but see Jeremy Moon, *European Integration in British Politics 1950–1963: a study of issue change* (Aldershot: Gower, 1985) and Robert J. Lieber, *British Politics and European Unity* (Berkeley: University of California Press, 1971).

INDEX

Department of Defense, (U.S.),
166–7
Devlin, Mr Justice, 182
Devlin report, 188
Devonshire, Duchess of (Evie),
11
Devonshire, Duke of, 10, 13, 38
Diefenbaker, John, 191
Die-Hards, 16
Disarmament, 133–4, 137–8,
142, 156, 162, 168
Disarmament Conference
(Geneva), 135
Dixon, Pierson, 58
Dominion Party, 182
Domino theory, 208
Donald, P.G., 28
Douglas, George, 28
Dulles, John Foster, 103–4,
110–1, 113–4, 130–6, 139,
141–3, 145, 203–4, 206–207
Duncan, Sir Andrew, 47–8

EAM (Greek National Liberation
Front), 58, 60–61
Eccles, David, 123, 260
Economic Advisory Council, 35
Economic Aspects of Defence, 45
Economic policy, 2, 83, 84, 163,
227–51
Economist, The, 252
Eden, Anthony, 37–8, 44–6,
53–4, 56–8, 60, 66, 70, 74–9,
84–5, 88–91, 95–8, 101–2,
104–8, 110–2, 114–7, 120–1,
123, 127–8, 130, 176–7, 199
Eden group, 44, 46
Education Act (1944), 78
Egypt, 102–5, 110, 132, 202,
204–6
Egypt Committee, 111–7
Egyptian Treaty (1936), 103
Eighth Army, 63
Eisenhower, General, 51, 54–5,
110–1, 114, 117–8, 122, 130–6,
139, 142–3, 145–7, 149–50,
153, 156–8, 203, 207–8
Eisenhower Doctrine, 132, 203
ELAS, (Greek National
Liberation Movement) 58,

60–1
electricity industry, 249
Elliott, Walter, 2,
Empire, 130, 176, 221, 258, 272
Empire Free trade, 21
Empire Industries Association,
16
Enabling Bill, 26–7, 34
EOKA, 100, 102, 179, 180
Enosis, 100
Eton, 8
Europe, 4, 74, 79, 133, 212–24,
258, 273
Europe, British entry into, 167
European Assembly, 74, 76, 89
European Coal and Steel
Community, 88, 213
European Defence Community,
87–90, 97–9, 213
European Economic Community,
53, 83, 155
European Free Trade Area, 127,
137, 212–7
European integration, 88–90,
96–99, 129, 212–24
European Movement, 70, 74–5
Evans, Harold, 130
Excess Profits Levy, 84
Fascism, 21, 24
Farouk, King of Egypt, 103
Fawzi, Mohammed, 115
Federal Reserve Bank, 117
Federation of British Industries,
22, 24–5, 35
Feisal, King of Iraq, 206
Finnish war, 143
First World War, 5, 272
Firth, Sir William, 28
Foot, Sir Hugh, 179
Force X, 52, 53
Foreign Office, 52, 54, 56–7, 59,
65, 67, 78–9, 88, 90–1, 95–8,
100, 102, 104- -5, 199, 206
Forster, W.Arnold, 30
France, 56, 112, 115, 141, 143,
159, 196, 215
independent nuclear deterrent
221–3,
Fraser, Michael, 226, 229, 255,
256, 271